JESUS
AND HIS
FATHER
BY HIS FAMILY AND FRIENDS

Jesus
and his
Father
by his family and friends

"Jesus did many other things as well. If every one of them were written down, I suppose that even the whole world would not have room for the books that would be written."

John 21:25

Trevor Galpin

Published by TLG Mins

First Published in Great Britain in 2014.

Unless otherwise stated Scriptures are taken from the Holy Bible, New International Version.
Copyright © 1973, 1978, 1984 by International Bible Society.
Used by permission of Hodder & Stoughton.
All rights reserved.

Copyright © Trevor Galpin

The right of Trevor Galpin to be identified as the author of this work has been asserted by him in accordance with the Copyright, Designs and Patents Act 1988.

All rights reserved. No part of this publication may be reproduced, stored in a retrieval system, or transmitted in any form or by any means, without the prior written permission of the author, nor be otherwise circulated in any form of binding or cover other than that in which it is published and without a similar condition being imposed on a subsequent purchaser.

Cover design by Tom Carroll

British Library Cataloguing in Publication Data

ISBN: 978-0-9575318-3-3

CONTENTS

Acknowledgements	9
Introduction	13

The Story Tellers

Mary, the Mother of Jesus	23
John, the Baptist	45
James, the Brother of Jesus	63
Andrew, the First Disciple	85
The Woman Jesus Met at the Well	103
Simon, the Terrorist	115
Simon, the Pharisee	131
Nicodemus, the Council Member	155
Thomas, the Twin	173
Simon, the Fisherman	191
John Mark, the Gospel Writer	221
Salome, Jesus' Aunt	235
Mary, from Magdala	257
John, the One Jesus Loved	279

ACKNOWLEDGEMENTS

The first book I wrote just happened because it was my story but this one was different. It came about as something grew in my heart that excited me and challenged me. I have always been fascinated by the stories behind the stories. In that sense the Gospels have been of particular interest to me all my life. One of the first books I read was called 'The Robe', by Lloyd C Douglas. I devoured it and then found 'The Big Fisherman' by the same author. These two novels were set against the backdrop of the New Testament Gospels. I loved the idea of the novels and that the characters were real people who had met Jesus. My enthusiasm gave birth to a play set in the early chapters of Acts, which I wrote and produced in my home church when I was 17! It is extraordinary that people took it seriously and wanted to act in it. It was about people like John Mark and his mother Mary, Stephen, Rhoda, and Barsabbas Justus. These are all people on the periphery of the biblical stories.

Later, I studied Theology and Church History and grew up! But my interest in the people has not lessened. Now forty-four year later I find myself going back to these people and wondering what they were like. What they thought when they met Jesus. I have been particularly drawn to the whole idea of how Jesus talked with people and what they understood from what he was saying and doing.

Also since then I have had the immense privilege of meeting people who have walked with me on my spiritual journey and have introduced me to God as my Father. I always knew he was a Father and all my life served him but it is only in the last few years that I have encountered him as my Father who loves me unconditionally. I am very grateful to James and Denise Jordan of Fatherheart Ministries who have encouraged me on my journey. Their teaching and support have been immense and it is because of this that I began to look at the Gospels again and especially how Jesus revealed his Father in the conversations he had with people. I know no one who has a revelation of the Father like they do.

In addition, I have enjoyed being part of a growing conversation with a number of writers and theologians who have influenced my thinking and helped reshape some of my theology. Most noticeably, C Baxter Kruger has given my much to think about and his writings have stirred me and brought me great joy. Wm Paul Young encouraged me to write a couple of years ago too and I am thankful for his inspirational style of writing and speaking.

Then there are those who have helped this book become a reality. Thanks Mark Gyde and Ellie Carman for your wise and sensible advice, ruthless handling of my grammar, spelling and style. Thanks Tom Carroll for your design and artistic skill.

Finally there is my wife Linda, who has helped me persevere and believed I could do it, who made me get up and walk as well as sit and write. I couldn't have done it without you.

INTRODUCTION

Jesus never wrote a book. However, he could read and write. He was not an illiterate first century Galilean peasant. He could write but the only record we have of him writing is when he squatted on the ground and wrote in the sand when the Jewish religious elite in Jerusalem tried to trap him into condoning the stoning of a woman. We don't know what he wrote but his friend John included it in his gospel.

Jesus could read Hebrew. He read from the scroll in the synagogue in Nazareth in Galilee according to Luke's account of his life. That would have been written in Hebrew, the language of all the Jewish scriptures.

He spoke Aramaic, the language of first century Galilee and Judea. This language or dialect is still spoken by some people in Turkey. We have only a few short sentences of these words recorded. "Talitha koum" were the words he said over Jairus' dead daughter. Mark tells us this in his account of the life of Jesus. We hear these words from Jesus' lips because someone in the room was so deeply impacted that they later told Mark. It may have been Jairus or his wife who were there to see their daughter come back to life. Perhaps it may have been Peter or the Bar Zebedee brothers, James and John, who Jesus took into the house with him. I suspect it was Peter because from the very earliest days of the Christian Church, Mark's Gospel was believed to be based on the teaching and reminiscences of Peter.

What we know about Jesus, or what we know of the things he said or taught does not come from anything he personally wrote down as far as we know. Instead it is passed on to us in the language of the first century Roman world which is known as Koine Greek. This is not the complicated and deeply philosophical classical Greek of Homer or of

Plato but the rough and ordinary street language of everyday people who went about their daily lives two thousand years ago. It is the language of Roman Governors sending reports to the Emperor in Rome; the words of merchants and shop keepers ordering their goods; the language of the grief stricken who carved their laments and messages on tomb stones; the thoughts of clients scratched on the walls of brothels in Pompeii; the shopping lists thrown into rubbish dumps in first century Alexandria that have survived to this day in the dry desert sands; the rude remarks made about politicians painted on the walls at election time; the love letters of soldiers on the Roman frontiers to their girlfriends back home. It is the language that Mark and Luke, Matthew and John used to write down what they had heard and knew and remembered about the things that Jesus said and did.

In themselves these are translations from the original words that Jesus spoke in Aramaic into Koine Greek which were then given to us through the translations of the Gospels into our own languages. Lost in translation is a well know idiom, but is this true in what we read of Jesus? Even translations rely on the skill and accuracy and to some degree the interpretations of difficult terms made by the translators. Can we know for sure what he said, what Jesus really did? Added to that the earliest complete copies for the New Testament come from around the middle to late third century. Codex Siniaticus is probably one of the most famous and most important. It was found by the nineteenth Century Russian scholar and manuscript expert, Constantin Tischendorf, at the very ancient monastery of St Catherine at the foot of Mount Sinai in Egypt. He was a nineteenth century version of Indiana Jones who made several visits to the monastery and found a large number of pages from this ancient codex or papyrus book. It is reported that he found a monk throwing old manuscripts into the fire to warm himself. The discovery of this book was of immense significance for the study of these ancient manuscripts.

The best we can hope is that these ancient manuscripts are copies of copies of the originals. The oldest fragment of all was found in the Roman rubbish dumps of Alexandria. This small fragment of John's Gospel, measuring less than nine centimetres high, is one of a collection of Greek papyri in the John Rylands Library, Manchester in the UK. On one side it contains parts of verses 31-33, on the other side parts of verses 37-38 of the eighteenth chapter of John's Gospel. The importance of this fragment is quite out of proportion to its size, since it may with some confidence be dated in the first half of the second century AD, and thus ranks as the earliest known fragment of the New Testament in any language.

Many scholars and theologians in the past have questioned the validity and reliability of the Gospels. It has been fashionable to try to seek what was called "the Historical Jesus" or the Jesus of history. This is based on the premise that we cannot really know what Jesus said and did from the accounts we have in the Gospels. It is thought that it all happened just too long ago and what we have in the Gospels is filtered through church tradition and teaching and is not considered authentic. This view does not generally come from those who believe the records they are studying. They so typify the 'wise and learned' that Jesus once said could not receive the revelation that he brings.

One of the basic premises of these literary critics is that the Gospels were not written by the historical Matthew, or John, the beloved disciple. Critics say that Mark and Luke were documents of the late first century or early second century, written long after the events described, not by contemporaries of Jesus, but by Christian apologists, maybe two or three generations removed from the actual events. They have all been filtered through a theological lens of the early church so therefore have to be questioned as not accurate. This is all based on an unwillingness to face the truth that these Gospels contain the revelation about the God who comes to us in Jesus and that Jesus came to reveal who God is, our Father.

However, how do we know what Jesus said and did other than through these four gospels? Even though so-called literary critics might dispute this, it is my belief that it is completely conceivable that the Gospels were written within living memory of the events they recount. The early church maintained that Mark recorded the teaching and memories of Peter. So it is extremely likely that Mark's Gospel was written well within the lifetime of many of the people who witnessed the events he described.

In reading through the Gospels, I cannot ignore the authentic detailed content of many of the stories. They have such a ring of truth and eyewitness quality about them. There are a growing number of Christian writers and theologians who are revisiting these documents through the eye not only of faith but critical analysis. One such writer, Richard Bauckham, has written a book called *'Jesus and the Eyewitnesses.'* He says that Mark was the earliest and "that the other three canonical Gospels - Matthew, Luke and John, were written in the period when living eyewitnesses were becoming scarce, exactly at the point in time when their testimony would perish with them were it not put in writing. Throughout the lifetime of eyewitnesses, Christians remained interested in and aware of the ways the eyewitnesses themselves told their stories. So, in imagining how the traditions reached the Gospel writers, not oral tradition but eyewitness testimony should be our principal model."

Bauckham explores the whole nature of this eyewitness testimony that is found in the Gospels. He says, "An irreducible feature of testimony as a form of human utterance is that it asks to be trusted. Trusting testimony is not an irrational act of faith that leaves critical rationality aside; it is, on the contrary, the rationally appropriate way of responding to authentic testimony. The Gospels understood as testimony are the entirely appropriate means of access to the historical reality of Jesus."

He continues, "Theologically speaking, the category of testimony enables us to read the gospels as precisely the kind of text we need in order to recognise the disclosure of God in the history of Jesus. Testimony enables us to read the Gospels in a properly historical way and a properly theological way, it is where history and theology meet." Bauckham, *"Jesus and the eyewitnesses"*, Eerdmans Publishing Co. 2006.

I am absolutely convinced that we have in the Gospels a treasury of eye witness accounts of the life of Jesus. The Gospel writers drew from a rich pool of testimony. Mark drew heavily from Peter. John was present for many of the events he describes and seemed also to record the testimony of a number of people who had meetings or encounters with Jesus when they were the only person present. An example is the Samaritan woman who Jesus talked with at the well in Sychar. Matthew was thought to have collected a large number of the sayings of Jesus that he had heard personally including those that were circulating around the early Christian communities. It has been suggested that Matthew wrote these down in Hebrew. Luke undoubtedly set out to collect information about Jesus. He intentionally used the word 'eyewitnesses' to describe what others had recorded. He says in the opening paragraph of his gospel,

> *"Many have undertaken to draw up an account of the things that have been fulfilled among us, just as they were passed down to us by those who from the first were eyewitnesses and servants of the word. With this in mind, since I myself have carefully investigated everything from the beginning, I too decided to write an orderly account for you, most excellent Theophilus, so that you may know the certainty of the things you have been taught."* Luke 1:1-4

Luke says he himself had carefully traced everything from the beginning so that his readers, initially his patron Theophilus, would have a clear, orderly account of the life of Jesus and that there would be no doubt about the authenticity of their faith.

In the Gospels we have the collected and written memories of Jesus' family and friends as reminded and inspired by the Holy Spirit. Through these memories and testimonies Jesus consistently spoke what he heard his Father saying and did the things he saw his Father doing. The theme of this book is to explore how Jesus revealed the nature and heart of his relationship with God his Father, through his life, his teaching and his interactions with people.

I have selected a number of people who figure in the Gospel stories and in each chapter I have imagined them talking to someone about their memories and experiences. This is presented as a person telling their story.

All these stories I have based primarily on several different characters who appear in the Gospels and linked these accounts together to produce a narrative. I have used dramatic license here and there as I have sought to construct conversations with these people. I have tried to imagine how they might have reacted and thought about the events they witnessed and experienced. The originals, of course, can be found in the four Gospels at the beginning of the New Testament.

One issue that kept coming up was what some have called the discrepancies in the Gospels, the differences between them or the apparent lack of consistent data. As I looked at these stories what impressed me was that sometimes there were different accounts of the same events. This to me added to the authenticity and the feel of eyewitness accounts generally. We are all aware how three people can see the same event and all bring versions and detail unique to them. This does not devalue their accounts, rather in my mind it enriches it and adds to its life and vitality. In the same way each Gospel is unique and remarkable in its own way and handles these people according to the style and intention of the writer. Along with this, hovering over the whole process, was the beautiful superintending of the Holy Spirit who brings these stories to life and applies the truth to our hearts.

In the second century AD around 170, Tatian, a former pupil of the early church Father Justin Martyr (c110 - 165AD), decided to help people get a clear chronological view of the life of Jesus. He took the four gospels and wove them into one continuous narrative. He called this the Diatesseron, which means 'one through four'. He did this by removing any repetitions, harmonising apparent discrepancies, and even correcting what he considered omissions. Sadly, he was not always very accurate and even slipped a few bits from the Gnostic Gospel of the Hebrews into the story. To be fair to him, in his day, not everyone was sure which Gospels were authentic and originating from an eyewitness in the first century.

Effectively, it was the first ever translation of the Gospels as it was translated from Greek into Syriac and for about three hundred years was the official Syriac version of the Gospels. It was hugely popular and as a synopsis many felt it was easier to use. Its use and influence was extensive in the eastern Roman Empire and spread into India, China and even Mongolia. In 423 AD, the then Bishop of Cyrrhus in Syria, Theodoret, 'sniffed out the dodgy bits' relating to the spurious Gospel to the Hebrews and it was declared heretical and he took steps to destroy all available copies.

My account here is not intended to be a harmony of all the Gospel stories. I have not included everything. Instead, I have selected only those stories relating to specific people mentioned in the Gospels. I have pieced together their stories. I have tied together isolated incidents and tried to give some suggestion of how events may have unfolded. I have also attempted to imagine what they would have thought about what they were hearing and seeing. Obviously I cannot be objective about this which may annoy some people. I have also had some fun here and there in the stories. So if a twenty-first century Theodoret doesn't like it and declares it heresy, so be it. As long as he pays for any books he burns I won't mind.

Where possible I have put some background into these stories to help the reader see the context. Otherwise, I have included some of this at the end of each story as explanatory notes and added some additional thoughts about them.

I have endeavoured to describe and explore the nature of the revelation of the Father that Jesus brings through these people. It was the work of the Holy Spirit to bring all this revelation together into the Gospels that we have in the New Testament.

This is what I most wanted to trace in this book. For years as a Christian, I had really missed the point that Jesus came to reveal the Father to us. I am a "Johnny come lately" to this revelation. However, now I can hardly turn a page of the Bible without being surprised how the Father is there in almost every chapter. So my desire is to explore some aspects of this within the confines and contexts of this book. It has been an interesting and rewarding journey as step by step, conversation by conversation, Jesus revealed the Father afresh to me.

So enough of an explanation and on to the first person to tell their story.

THE FIRST STORY TELLER

MARY
THE MOTHER OF JESUS

"Every mother has a treasury. It's where we keep our most precious things. No one can take it away from us. It goes with me wherever I go and it is my most valuable possession. Mine is full indeed. My treasury is in my heart and hardly a day goes by that I do not go there and look at some of those precious, treasured memories.

I am old now, even I have to admit that, though inside I feel like a young woman still. I can remember, oh so clearly those events that happened long ago, when I was just a young girl before I was married. I have talked about them a lot lately. I imagine it is like that for most of us when we get old. We like to talk about the past.

I have been spending quite a bit of time talking to the young doctor recently. Not that I am ill or anything like that. Just talking about the past to him. The doctor, as we call him, is a lovely young man. His name is Lucas or Luke for short. He came through here recently with his friend Paul. Paul told us all and the elders of the church here in Ephesus that this would be his last visit. He was going back to Jerusalem. Everyone knew this would be very dangerous for him and they tried to dissuade him from going. You know what Paul is like don't you? You do know Paul don't you? Yes, I thought you would. Once Paul believes that the Father has spoken to him no one can tell him otherwise. He has such a wonderful way with words. He is really helping us see what it all really means, what it is to be a follower of the Way. The Greeks especially like him. They say he has such a sharp mind but more than that they like his heart. Some of the Jewish believers struggle with what he says though. They say he has become too lax these days. That is partly why he is going to Jerusalem to meet with them and try to help them see that we are living in a new day. He calls it a new covenant. That really upsets some of them. He told me that ever since my son Jesus rose from the dead we are living in this day of the new covenant. I could listen to him for hours.

Well now, where was I? Oh yes, Paul had gone off back to Jerusalem. Jerusalem is very dangerous for most of us these days, so indeed is Galilee. Ever since my sister's poor boy, James bar Zebedee was killed by that tyrant Herod Agrippa it has been difficult for us there. His poor mother Salome, she was my sister, you know, I don't think she ever got over that, losing her son like that. That dreadful Herod, he was a nasty bit of work, just like the rest of his clan before him. His grandfather was the one who sent his soldiers into Bethlehem looking for us just after my boy was born. Those poor mothers. It was so terrible, killing all those babies. Another of Herod the Great's sons, was Herod Antipas. He was the same one who killed my cousin Elizabeth's boy, John and tried my boy before sending him off to Pilate the Roman procurator. Herod Agrippa died too, not long after he had poor James beheaded. The foolish man, claimed to be God! No wonder he was taken.

Oh dear I have digressed again, it's what we old people do. James' brother, my nephew, John bar Zebedee, has been looking after me ever since that day when….when they crucified my dear son. That was so terrible a day for us all, even though he had said he would rise from the dead. Until it actually happened we didn't really believe it. Anyway, not long ago John suggested that it would be better for me to move away from Galilee to go somewhere safer. The locals in Nazareth all knew me and who my son was and I was often harassed by some of them. The local leaders in our assembly of followers and my son James in Jerusalem, thought it would be best if I moved away right out of the country in order to give me some peace and where I would be safe. So anyway John, my adopted son as I like to call him, told me about a new community of my son's followers that was in Ephesus. He thought it would be safer there for me. He said there were already a number of Jewish believers in the city, even some who had been followers originally of Elizabeth's boy. So that is how I came to leave Galilee after all those years. John brought me here and stays here often himself when he can. He is a good boy that John. He calls himself, 'the one Jesus loved!' I think that is very funny. My son loved them all! Even that Judas!

Where was I? Oh yes that lovely young doctor, Lucas. He has been with Paul quite some time now. He came here with Paul and I was introduced to him. We spent such a long time talking. Like so many, who are new followers of the Way, they all want to know about my son and what he said and did. Lucas was so easy to talk to, he had such a way about him. He asked all sorts of questions. I suppose being a doctor it was not surprising he wanted to know about my first pregnancy. It was rather unusual after all. Well, I told him all about it and he asked if I would mind if he wrote it down. He said he was writing an orderly account of the life of my son for a new believer called Theophilus. I got the impression it was someone he used to work for. So I told Lucas many things, things I have kept for years in my treasury, mostly about my early life. That was what interested him most.

Lucas told me that John Mark had also recently written an account of the life of Jesus but he had written it after having spent a lot of time with Simon Peter and it was mostly from Simon's perspective. Simon has always been a bit like that. Well, anyway, Lucas wanted to know all about those early days. He had a copy of this new scroll that Mark had written and I asked him if he would leave us a copy here in Ephesus so we could all read it. He was slightly embarrassed because he said there was a rip in the last section of the scroll and the end was missing. He said he hoped he could find Mark and get him to add it back. He said reading it without the last page leaves out the best bit, that Jesus rose from the dead. Well, we all know that so I said it didn't really matter. Bless him, he had a copy made while he was here and we keep it and read from it when our little community of believers meet together to pray and eat.

I told him all about those early days when I first heard that I was specially chosen to carry in my womb 'The One'.

He was particularly interested in how I found out about the pregnancy, the visitation I had from that angel. I will never forget that day. I was so young and naive. I had only just been betrothed to Joseph and we were not intimate or anything like that. You can read it in Lucas' scroll so I won't repeat it all again for you. I told him about John's birth too. As I said there are a number of people here in Ephesus who knew John so he talked to them also. He was very good at collecting these stories, very thorough. He had an eye for detail. I suppose that is on account of him being a doctor. He even wanted to know about my delivery in that stable. Oh my goodness! What a night that was. Not quite what I had planned. My mother was very upset when she found out about it and said I should never have gone with Joseph all that way down to Bethlehem. We didn't really have much of a choice with the census taking place, especially as Joseph's family originated from there, being a descendant of King David. I gave him a few suggestions of other people he should talk to as well especially up in Galilee. They might be able to help him with his book. I asked Lucas to make sure we had a copy of his account of the life of my son when he has finished it.

Many years ago Matthew told me all about the prophecies about the Messiah's birth. I could see it all made sense and I have always felt that God our Father was overseeing the process right from the beginning. If I hadn't believed that I don't know how I would have managed. Even that sudden departure to Egypt turned out to be part of the Father's plan according to Matthew. Who would have thought a tax collector like him would have such a grasp of prophecy and how it all was fulfilled by the coming of Jesus.

I would not be surprised if we don't hear that Matthew is writing an account of Jesus' life too sometime soon. If he does I imagine it would be more from his perspective as a Jew and his interest in fulfilled prophecy. He has a very good memory and remembers some of the words and teaching of my son so well. When he speaks them I close my eyes and it is as if Jesus was there in the room saying them himself. Matthew just laughed when I said that to him. He says he gets help when he speaks. He says it's the Spirit reminding him. I think it may also have to do with him being an accountant. He has a good memory for figures. He used to be a tax collector you know. They never forget a thing, who owes what and how much.

Quite some time later after Lucas went off with Paul to Jerusalem I found out that dear John was writing an account too. They all seem to be doing it these days! I know it makes sense as those of us who knew him are getting fewer. And there are so many new people who follow the Way who never met Jesus in person. It is very good for them to read what happened. John told me he wouldn't include all the information about Jesus' birth as Lucas had written it so well in his version. He did ask me a few things but mostly he was there himself with Jesus.

Did I mention that wedding we all went to in Cana all those years ago and how the wine ran out? As soon as I heard that they had no more wine I had an idea that maybe Jesus could help. My son seemed a bit surprised when I suggested that the servants of the bride's father ask Jesus what to do! I was as shocked as anyone at what happened. John told me he would put it in his story as he thinks it was the first time that Jesus did anything miraculous like that. He felt it was significant.

John and I often talked about my son, especially how he used to refer to the Lord God as his Father. I had known since I was first pregnant that God would be his Father in a unique way. I did not understand those things as I was just a young girl. I trusted what I had been told by that angel. I don't know why, I just did. When he was born all those scruffy shepherds came to see him. They told me they had been sent by angels. Then there were those very exotic foreigners who turned up later saying they had followed a star all the way from Persia or somewhere. I forgot to tell Lucas that part of the story but I will make sure Matthew knows. All these visits were very surprising but extremely reassuring to Joseph and me.

I will never forget the day I first heard Jesus refer to God as his Father. I told Lucas all about it and he felt it was so important that he would put it in his account. It was that time we went as a family to celebrate the Passover in Jerusalem when Jesus would have been about twelve.

We went to Jerusalem every year at the Feast of the Passover. That year when the feast was ended, as we were returning, Jesus stayed behind in Jerusalem but we didn't know he had. We supposed him to be in the group with some of the other youngsters. We went a day's journey, and as we made camp for the night we began to search for him among our relatives and acquaintances. Joseph hadn't seen him all day. I am still surprised that he hadn't got his eye on him. When we couldn't find him we became very concerned and decided somehow he must have stayed behind in the city so we returned to Jerusalem, searching for him. We got there late in the night and had no idea where to begin looking. We went to all the people we knew in the city and no one had seen him. I was beside myself with anxiety. You see, Joseph and I were the only ones who knew who he really was and how special he was. The angel had said he was God's own son and we had been entrusted to care for him and bring him up. Now we had lost him!

After three days of searching everywhere I was distraught. We decided to go to the temple. Joseph said we had better go and talk directly with the Lord God and tell him what had happened. Then to our absolute amazement we found Jesus in the temple, sitting among the teachers, listening to them and asking them questions! All who were listening to him were amazed at his understanding and his answers. He was right in the middle of them. I wondered where on earth he had been sleeping and what had he had to eat.

When we saw him, we were astonished too. I was so relieved but we were exhausted emotionally and physically. It was the best part of five days he had been missing. He was only twelve after all. So I just blurted it out and asked him why he had treated us like this. I told him his father and I had been searching for him in great distress for days.

Then do you know what he said? I will never forget it! He asked us why we had been you looking for him. Why had we been searching for him? I ask you! He was a twelve year old boy! He had been missing for five days. He could have been kidnapped, sold as a slave, murdered, anything! I was so distressed. This was a typical response from a young boy. Then he said it.

"Didn't you know that I must be in my Father's house?" There was a stunned silence. I did not understand initially what he was saying. I think some of those wise and learned men in the temple did though. They looked shocked and some just stared at him because it was blasphemous to describe God as his Father. They looked at him and they looked at Joseph and me and we just took our son by the hand and suggested we leave and go home. So he came with us and we went back to Nazareth. He was such a good boy and he stayed at home with us from then on. He grew into a fine young man. He was such a help to us and when Joseph died he was such a support to me and the other children. He never mentioned it again, God being his Father, but I knew and he knew. But to everyone else he was content to be known as the carpenter's son. It was only when he began his public ministry that he started talking about God being his Father. It was one of the things that got him into so much trouble with the Pharisees and the temple crowd. But that is another story.

As for me I added these memories to my treasure trove and put them safely away in my heart."

JESUS' MOTHER MARY IN THE GOSPELS

We obviously know a large amount of personal detail about Mary from the birth stories of Matthew and Luke. We first meet her in Nazareth in Galilee and Luke places her there in the late first century BC. A late second century writing, the Gospel of James, is the first source to name her parents as Joachim and Anne but like many of these later, non canonical gospels, it is not very reliable.

Luke records the Roman Emperor Augustus issuing a decree to conduct a census at a time when Quirinius was governor of Syria. Matthew, whilst not mentioning the census, does place the birth of Jesus in Bethlehem in Judea during the reign of King Herod the Great. This would have dated the birth of Jesus as sometime before 4BC when Herod died. There has been a large amount of debate about the census. This is mainly because of Josephus the main extra biblical Jewish authority who wrote in the first century AD. He does not mention the census. Josephus also places Quirinius as governor of Syria around 6/7 AD. The assumption is made that Josephus is correct and Luke wrong. That of course is a matter of opinion and perspective. Those who fundamentally wish to doubt the historicity of the Gospels are very likely to come to that conclusion. Generally, Luke's historical references are very accurate, especially those in Acts where he was often a participant in the events he describes. The fact that he is referring to a governorship perhaps fifty years before the time of writing may give him some freedom to be less than 100% accurate. That is assuming it is him that is wrong rather than Josephus!

Matthew specifically names Mary as Jesus' mother and Joseph as the presumed father. Both Gospel writers state that their betrothal had taken place before the announcement of the conception of Jesus by the Holy Spirit. Both also state that the official marriage was not enacted or consummated until after the birth of Jesus. These details affirm the virgin state of Mary at the time of Jesus' birth.

The cultural world of first century Judaism would suggest that Mary may have been as young as twelve at the time of her betrothal and her marriage would have been some time after that. It has always been believed that Mary was a young teenage girl at the time of the annunciation by the angel Gabriel. Whilst to modern minds this would be somewhat shocking it was the normal practice then.

Both Gospel writers, Luke and Matthew, trace Jesus' lineage according to the custom in contemporary writing. Matthew is believed to follow the line through Joseph. Luke however, may have been following the line through Mary. Some of those who consider that the relationship with Elizabeth was on the maternal side, consider that Mary, like Joseph, to whom she was betrothed, was of the House of David and so of the tribe of Judah, and that the genealogy of Jesus presented in Luke 3 from Nathan, the third son of David and Bathsheba, is in fact the genealogy of Mary. This would make the genealogy from Solomon given in Matthew 1 that of Joseph. Lists such as these were a feature of the culture of the day and the Gospel writers may have sourced such lists.

Luke's narrative of the birth of Jesus places the delivery possibly in a stable in Bethlehem because there was no room in the inn. The stable is assumed because the new born child is placed in an animal's eating trough, the manger.

After eight days, he was circumcised according to Jewish law, and named Jesus, as instructed by the angel. Joseph had also been told to call him Jesus in a dream. After Mary continued in her purification rites of another thirty-three days, she and Joseph brought her burnt offering and sin offering to the temple so the priest could make atonement for her sins and she would then be cleansed from her blood. All this is in accordance with Jewish custom as described in Leviticus. They also presented Jesus to the Lord. Luke quotes this passage from Exodus,

> *"As it is written in the law of the Lord, every firstborn male is to be consecrated to the Lord."* Luke 2:23

After the prophecies of Simeon and the prophetess Anna, Joseph and Mary took Jesus and returned into Galilee, to their own town Nazareth.

At this point there is some difficulty in harmonising the sequence of events as it appears in Matthew's Gospel. They may have either remained in Bethlehem much longer or returned at some point to Bethlehem. Either way, it is while there, perhaps as much as two years later, that Matthew records the "Magi" or "wise men" showed up at the "house" where Jesus and his family were staying. They received the gifts and again warned in a dream, they fled by night and stayed in Egypt for a while to avoid King Herod's paranoiac slaughter of all the boys under the age of two in Bethlehem. The family returned after Herod died in 4 BC and set up permanent home again in Nazareth.

We know little about Mary's immediate family other than a relative or cousin, Elizabeth who is the mother of John the Baptist and her sister Salome, who was also at the cross. Matthew's Gospel records a reference to Jesus having brothers and sisters.

> *"Isn't this the carpenter's son? Isn't his mother's name Mary, and aren't his brothers James, Joseph, Simon and Judas? Aren't all his sisters with us?"* Matthew 13:55-56

In the parallel passage in Mark, Jesus is called just the carpenter rather than the carpenter's son.

It was Jerome, the fourth century AD translator of the Vulgate, an extreme ascetic and strongly opposed to marriage, who first suggested a different translation for these brothers and sisters. He translates them as cousins. The Vulgate was the first translation of the Bible into Latin and completed around 400AD by Jerome. Theologians before Jerome had started to describe Mary as a 'perpetual virgin' and Jerome obligingly doctored his translation accordingly. Roman Catholic writers and theologians since then have interpreted these relatives to be cousins rather than children of Mary thus maintaining their belief in the perpetual virginity of Mary. This was used to undergird the doctrine that she was sinless. The implication behind this is the erroneous belief that the sexual act of procreation between a married couple is less than holy and is an indication of sin. Non Catholics find this an unnecessary presumption.

Mary appears a number of times in the Gospel narratives. Luke records the incident in the temple when Jesus is twelve years old. John's first mention of her is at the marriage of Cana but he does not mention her by name. This is the only text in the canonical gospels in which Mary speaks to the adult Jesus. She appears occasionally during the time of Jesus' ministry. Mark refers to Jesus' mother in Mark 3:31.

The second reference in John, also exclusively listed in his gospel, has the mother of Jesus standing near the cross of her son together with the also unnamed "disciple whom Jesus loved" along with Mary the wife of Cleopas and Mary Magdalene. Matthew adds "the mother of the sons of Zebedee", this is also the Salome mentioned in Mark 15:40. Mary's presence at the cross gave rise to a very powerful picture depicted in much religious art and sculpture in which Mary cradles the dead body of her Son. This is not recorded in the Gospel accounts, but it is a common motif in art, the classic being Michelangelo's "Pieta" which stands just inside the door of St Peter's Basilica in the Vatican.

MARY AFTER THE DAY OF PENTECOST

We do not know much about Mary the mother of Jesus after the resurrection though she alone of all the women who figure in the gospel narratives is mentioned by name as being in the group of one hundred and twenty who met together after the ascension. This group were described as being the ones in Acts 2 who were all together when the Holy Spirit was poured out on the day of the feast of Pentecost. So we can assume she received that outpouring along with all the others.

Mary the mother, passes from the pages of recorded history at this point and has become the focus of legend and myth and then became a figure of great importance in the development of theology. The fact that she was a virgin when Jesus was born and that her womb carried the eternally incarnate, fully divine and fully human Son of God, raised her status considerably in the thoughts and expressions of theologians in the early centuries of the church. Today she is venerated and adored by millions in the Roman Catholic and Orthodox churches. All manner of traditions that are not found in the Scriptures but have been believed for many centuries by great swathes of the church have elevated her to a position that I am sure she would have been totally surprised by. I have wondered what she would have made of all this.

It is not my intention to enter that debate in this book. Others have more than adequately discussed this adding much heat to the argument.

There are a few hints that may give us some idea about her after those verses in Acts chapter 1. I have drawn heavily on the widespread belief that she was a major source of the material at the beginning of Luke's Gospel for the birth narratives of Jesus. Very few biblical scholars would dispute that Luke's detailed account could only have come from Mary herself. The nature of the detail and the intimacy of the narrative dramatically reflects a firsthand eyewitness account. Luke's particular interest in the role of women, the work of the Holy Spirit and his medical background are all interwoven in the stories themselves.

In the 19th century, a house near Ephesus in Turkey was found, based on the visions of an Augustinian nun in Germany. It was believed to have been the house of Mary and has since been visited by numerous Roman Catholic pilgrims who consider it the place where Mary lived until her 'assumption'. The Assumption is the Catholic belief that Mary was taken up bodily into heaven rather than dying because it was believed that she was sinless, thus having no need to die. The Gospel of John states that Mary went to live with the disciple whom Jesus loved in. This disciple is identified as John the author of the fourth Gospel. Irenaeus writing in the late second century around 177 AD and Eusebius of Caesarea, the church historian who wrote in the early fourth century, both record in their histories that John later went to Ephesus which may provide the basis for the early belief that Mary also lived in Ephesus with John.

Christian devotion and attachment to Mary goes back to the late 2nd century and predates the emergence of specific doctrinal statements about Mary, following the first council of Ephesus in 431. The Council itself was held at a church in Ephesus which had been dedicated to Mary about a hundred years before. This may indicate some connection with Mary and Ephesus from an early date.

ALMIGHTY GOD, YAHWEH, HAS A SON

The fact remains that Mary was a source of information about Jesus that no others had. We would not have these precious insights of major significance if she had not shared them with Luke. Indeed she was the first to hear that Jesus would be the Son of God. Also from her lips, we hear Jesus' first words. They are astonishing words, he called the Lord God Almighty, "my Father."

When Jesus came into our world he came with the clear and expressed intention of revealing to us his Father and to bring us back into relationship with the Father. It had always been the triune God's intention to have sons and daughters to share in their love and joy. Paul had a revelation of this and wrote about it.

> *"For he chose us in him before the creation of the world to be holy and blameless in his sight. In love he predestined us to be placed into sonship through Jesus Christ, in accordance with his pleasure and will."* Ephesians 1:4-5

Peter also understood why Jesus came. He wrote in his first letter that Jesus was chosen before the creation of the world but was revealed in these last times for our sake. 1 Peter 1:20.

The coming of Jesus and his revealing of the Father come in the context of a Jewish world at the eastern end of the Mediterranean Sea, in Israel. He revealed the Father through his interactions and his conversations with ordinary people in an ordinary world.

To this young Jewish girl, barely into her teens, it was revealed that she would be the one in whose womb would be conceived the eternal Son of God. This initial revelation announced to her by the angel Gabriel was astonishing. The angel Gabriel says to Mary,

> *"You will conceive and give birth to a son, and you are to call him Jesus. He will be great and will be called the Son*

of the Most High. The Lord God will give him the throne of his father David, and he will reign over Jacob's descendants forever; his kingdom will never end." Luke 1:31-33

The announcement to Mary was startling. She who was still a virgin would conceive. She would give birth to a son and he would be called Jesus. Each of those three facts alone are incredible. The conception without the activity of a father was amazing in itself. She was told what sex the child would be. In those days no one knew the sex of a child prior to its birth. Then she was told what his name would be.

The next sentence spoken by the angel would change the course of history. He will be great and will be called the Son of the Most High. This was no poetic description, it was rather the bald and astounding fact that Jesus was none other than God's Son. Never before had anyone ever heard so explicitly that God, the Most High had a Son! Mary is the first to know. This is a revelation of incredible proportions and significance. God the Father has chosen to reveal something of his very nature not to a wise or learned scholar or prophet but to a young girl, barely out of childhood. He has chosen the weak things of the world to shame the wise and learned.

The angel then declares to the young girl that her child will be gifted with the throne of his ancestor, Israel's greatest King, David, not as a temporal monarch but an eternal one.

The overwhelming nature of this revelation impacted Mary so deeply that she remembered these words for the rest of her life and was able to report them many years later to Luke. To her however, in that moment, the overriding concern was a highly practical one.

"How will this be since I am a virgin?" Luke 1:34

What follows is the most beautiful description of the activity of the triune God in bringing to birth the most amazing miracle of all time, the incarnation of Jesus. The angel says,

> *"The Holy Spirit will come on you, and the power of the Most High will overshadow you. So the holy one to be born will be called the Son of God."* Luke 1:35

All three persons of the trinity participate in the miracle that is about to take place. It is beautiful and magnificent, tender and powerfully dynamic, majestic and gentle all at the same time.

Equally astonishing was the humble and willing response of the young girl. Mary's willing and heartfelt response displays a trust and openness that makes her truly worthy of admiration and honour.

> *"I am the Lord's servant. May your word to me be fulfilled."* Luke 1:38

The King James Version words it so beautifully.

> *"Behold the handmaid of the Lord; be it unto me according to thy word."*

JESUS KNOWS GOD IS HIS FATHER

It is through the eyes and ears of Mary, reported to Luke, that we read of the only single incident in the life of Jesus between the birth stories and his baptism at the age of thirty.

It is the story of the time when Jesus was left behind in the temple at the age of twelve. This is recorded in Luke 2: 41 - 52. What is remarkable about this story are the words that Jesus spoke on that occasion. These are the first words we read coming from the lips of Jesus. Indeed they are the only words we hear from him in the first thirty years of his life. This adds to the weight and significance of them. This story came straight out of Mary's treasury.

When questioned by his parents he says quite simply,

"Didn't you know I had to be in my Father's house?"
Luke 2:49 (NIV)

Or in the beautifully archaic King James, "Wist ye not that I must be about my Father's business?" I once heard it reported that this was the scriptural injunction used to prohibit card games! What did Jesus say? Was it "Father's house" or "Father's business". There is a difference. Most translators agree that while the word house is not in the Greek, the context of the sentence is that Jesus is saying he must be 'in' my Father's therefore by context in my Father's house. Even if the older translation was accepted the great truth here is that Jesus is calling God his Father.

No one called God Father at this time. In the Old Testament there are a few references where God is called Father not least being the poignant longing of the Father expressed through Jeremiah the prophet,

"I thought you would call me Father!" Jeremiah 3:19

The idea of God having a Son is found embryonically and prophetically in Psalm 2:7 where the king in the Psalm is described as God's Son and Yahweh has become his Father.

However, at the time of Jesus there was no mention of God as Father. No one referred to God in this way. Instead Yahweh, the unspoken holy name of God was expressed as Adonai. The name was too holy to be uttered by mere humans. The temple of Yahweh in Jerusalem was seen as the abode of God Almighty who was unapproachable and fearsome. The great temple in Jerusalem, that took forty six years to build by the tyrant King Herod the Great, was the holy temple of Yahweh. The construction included an outer court where Jesus would have been found by his parents. This was known as the Court of the Women, Mary would have been permitted only this far into this inner courtyard. Beyond that was the Court of the Men where only adult Jewish men could enter. Beyond that was the place where only the priests could go. Finally within this inner holy sanctum was the Holy of Holies where the Ark of the Covenant was kept. To this place, just once a year, the High Priest would enter on the Day of Atonement, to offer sacrifice for the sins of the people. This was the most fearsome place of all. If the priest died in that place or was struck down by God for some infringement of the law, a rope which had been attached to the priest leg, would be used to pull him from the Holy place behind the great curtain of separation.

This was no friendly God who anyone knew as Father. Then came this twelve year old boy with wisdom and knowledge beyond his years into the outer court of the great Temple of Almighty God. This boy, who astounds the wise men and teachers of the law with his questions and answers; this boy, the son of a Jewish woman from Nazareth and her husband Joseph who have been searching for him for three days or more; this boy, who says that this is my Father's house, this is my Father's place and I must be about my Father's business. Whichever way you read this, the astounding, earth shattering, world changing statement from this boy is that God Almighty, that Yahweh, that El Shaddai, that the Lord of Hosts, that the Creator of the universe, that Adonai, the LORD, is his Father!

Jesus may have had the body and mental development of a twelve year old but he was also the eternal pre-existent, uncreated Son of God, fully human and fully divine, and he knows exactly who he is and who his true Father is. What an incredible opening statement of the revelation of the Father through the lips of his son. It is not through the lips of the wise and the learned, rather these things are being revealed by a little child. The twelve year old Jesus.

It is no wonder that they did not understand what he was saying to them.

Mary heard these things. She may not have understood them at the time but she treasured them in her heart. After the resurrection she began to understand the fuller implications of the sonship of Jesus as did others. Paul, in the first letter he wrote, perhaps the first piece of Christian literature written, even before Mark or Luke had begun to write their accounts, said to the Galatians Christians,

> *"But when the set time had fully come, God sent his Son, born of a woman, born under the law, to redeem those under the law, that we might receive our position of sonship. Because you are his sons, God sent the Spirit of his Son into our hearts, the Spirit who calls out, "Abba, Father."* Galatians 4:4-6

Like Jesus, we too can now call God, my Father. It would be another eighteen years before we receive the next piece of the story.

THE SECOND STORY TELLER

JOHN
THE BAPTIST

"People had always thought I was a little eccentric. Now, here I am sitting in prison because that snake, King Herod Antipas, has not had the moral courage to keep his house in order. I have upset his wife because I have been speaking the truth. Prison gives you time to reflect. That is what I am doing, I am reflecting on my life and what the Lord God has been doing in me and through me.

I have always felt different. I suppose it was something to do with my birth and upbringing. My parents had been quite old when I was born. In fact it was amazing that I was born at all. They were childless because my mother Elizabeth was not able to conceive. People thought this was the judgment of God on them for some sin or other. But both of them were righteous in the sight of God, observing all the Lord's commands and decrees blamelessly. They were both very old. My father Zechariah belonged to the priestly division of Abijah.

Once when his division was on duty he was chosen to go into the temple of the Lord and burn incense. He told me that when the time for the burning of incense came, an angel of the Lord appeared to him, standing at the right side of the altar of incense. My father was terrified. My father told me the exact words many times and he had me commit them to memory. The angel said to him: "Do not be afraid, Zechariah; your prayer has been heard. Your wife Elizabeth will bear you a son, and you are to call him John. He will be a joy and delight to you, and many will rejoice because of his birth, for he will be great in the sight of the Lord. He is never to take wine or other fermented drink, and he will be filled with the Holy Spirit even before he is born. He will bring back many of the people of Israel to the Lord their God. And he will go on before the Lord, in the spirit and power of Elijah, to turn the hearts of the parents to their children and the disobedient to the wisdom of the righteous—to make ready a people prepared for the Lord." My father would often recount those words to me. My father then asked the angel, how could he be sure of this as he was an old man and my mother was getting old. The angel then told him that he was Gabriel who stood in the presence of God, and he had been sent to speak to him and to tell him this good news. Gabriel then told him because he did not believe these words he would be unable to speak until the day it happened.

Meanwhile, the people outside were wondering why he stayed so long in the temple. When he came out, he could not speak to them. They realised he had seen a vision in the temple, for he kept making signs to them but remained unable to speak. He was dumb until the day I was born.

Sometime later my mother became pregnant! A few months after that my mother had a visit from her young cousin from Nazareth, Mary, who was engaged to Joseph bar Jacob who was a carpenter in their town. It turned out that she was already pregnant too. She also had been visited by an angel and her pregnancy was as supernatural as my mother's. Mother told me when Mary entered their home I leapt in her womb, and my mother was filled with the Holy Spirit. She blessed Mary for believing that the Lord would fulfil his promises to her. My mother had a great understanding of what the Lord God was doing in our family.

There was great joy when I was born because the neighbours and all the relatives heard that the Lord had shown great favour to my mother. On the eighth day they came to circumcise me, and they were going to name me after my father Zechariah, but my mother spoke up and said that I was to be called John. There is no one among our relatives who has that name, so they made signs to my father to find out what he would like to name me. He asked for a writing tablet, and to everyone's astonishment he wrote that my name was to be John. Immediately he began to speak again. All the neighbours were filled with awe, and throughout the hill country of Judea people were talking about all these things. Everyone who heard this wondered about it, and talked about what I was going to be when I grew up. They recognised the Lord's hand was with me. So it is not surprising that people have always looked at me somewhat oddly. My parents were deeply affected by these encounters with the Holy Spirit and they taught me to be sensitive to him and to learn to recognise his voice.

When I was a young child we had some contact with my mother's relative. Her baby was born not far from us in Bethlehem and as a family we met them from time to time. There was a real bond between the two women. My relative was called Yeshua bar Joseph, Jesus as he is known by everyone. I really liked him. He was only a few months younger than me. We got to know each other well and over the years we kept in touch as best we could. As we grew up I sensed that we were joined in some great destiny together.

I loved my parents and was very sad that they died when I was still young. They had arranged for me to be cared for by friends and eventually I went to live with a community of people near the Dead Sea who my father trusted and had great respect for. They had an openness to the

Spirit and a depth of insight into what they believed the Lord was doing. He felt that they would continue to nurture me and train me in the ways of the Lord.

I loved the deserts around the Dead Sea. I spent much time on my own and I began to experience an amazing sense of the Lord's presence. I think the people in the community thought I was different right from the start. I spent so much time out in the wilderness. I knew the best places to find wild honey and was always welcomed back when I had found some. I know I was eccentric. I had met tent dwelling Beduins in the desert and spent many months with them. When my clothes wore out I started wearing the clothing made from camel's hair that the Beduins made. It really was very comfortable and ideal for the desert but it looked odd to the respectable Jews in Judea. I also developed a taste for a real desert delicacy, fried locust. I loved them. I still do, but they are not considered clean by the Jews. They are delicious dipped in wild honey. They are my favourite snack.

The older I became I increasingly had a sense of a calling on my life, a destiny given me by the Lord God. I spent many years working this through in my heart. I looked at all the scrolls and teachings of the desert community and began to feel that the Lord God was talking directly to my heart. The desert community certainly influenced me but I was hearing directly from God. I began to see that he was calling me to preach but I had a deep sense that this preaching would clear the way for something so much greater.

When I was about 30 years old I came out of the wilderness, and started preaching about being baptised as a sign of repentance for the forgiveness of sins. It seemed like the whole of the Judaean countryside and all the people of Jerusalem came out to hear the message. They began confessing their sins, and I started baptising them in the Jordan River.

I began to see there would be one who comes after me more powerful than I, the straps of whose sandals I am not worthy to stoop down and untie. I had began to preach and to baptise people with water, but I saw that the one coming would baptise with the Holy Spirit. It would be like fire. I had a growing sense that he would come very soon.

One day I had a delegation from Jerusalem come and question me. They sent priests and Levites to ask me who I was. I did not hold back I just told them how I saw things. I told them very clearly that I was not the Messiah. They asked me if I was Elijah or the Prophet. Of course I am none of these. Finally they said they needed an answer to take back to those who sent them.

I replied in the words of Isaiah the prophet that I was the voice of one calling in the wilderness to make straight the way for the Lord. That seemed to satisfy them.

One night I had a strong sense of the Lord speaking to me. He told me that his chosen one was about to be revealed; that he would be the sacrificial Lamb who would take away the sins of the world. I would see him and recognise him. The sign would be that I would see the Spirit come down and remain on him. He told me that the man on whom I see the Spirit come down and remain on would be the one who will baptise with the Holy Spirit.

The next day I went out to baptise again. There were crowds of people from all over, they even came from Galilee. Then I saw my cousin, Jesus, who had come from Galilee coming down to the Jordan to be baptised. I tried to deter him and told him that I needed to be baptised by him, and not him by me. Jesus was not one of the people I had in mind who needed to repent. Yet Jesus insisted and said it was right for him to do this to fulfil all righteousness. So I consented.

As soon as Jesus was baptised, he went up out of the water. At that very moment heaven was opened, and I saw the Spirit of God coming down on him like a dove and alighting on him. Then I heard a voice from heaven that said, "This is my Son, whom I love; with him I am well pleased."

Suddenly it all made sense! I knew who he was and what he had come to do. The next day I saw Jesus coming toward me and I told those around me that this was the Lamb of God, who would take away the sin of the world. This is the one I meant when I said before that a man who comes after me has surpassed me because he was before me. I did not know him at first, but the reason I came baptising with water was that he might be revealed to Israel. I told the people who were with me that I had seen the Spirit come down from heaven as a dove and remain on him. I knew this because the one who sent me to baptise with water told me to look out for this sign. I saw it and I testified that he is God's Chosen One."

The next day I was there again with two of my disciples. It was a young man, Andrew from Galilee and a friend of his, Philip. When I saw Jesus passing by, I said to them, "Look, the Lamb of God!" Soon after that they went to join Jesus who was also starting to teach.

Now I was still baptising at that time and an argument developed between some of my disciples and a man over ceremonial washing. They came to me and asked me about Jesus because many people were now going to hear him teach. I told them that a person can receive only what is given them from heaven. I reminded them that I had said I was not the Messiah but was sent ahead of him. I told them that the bride belongs to the bridegroom. The friend who attends the bridegroom waits and listens for him, and is full of joy when he hears the bridegroom's voice. That joy was now mine, and it was now complete. I wanted to make sure that Jesus become greater and I become less.

I realised that the one who comes from heaven, that is Jesus, is above all; the one who is from the earth belongs to the earth, that's me, speaks as one from the earth. He testifies to what he has seen and heard, but no one accepted his testimony. For the one whom God has sent speaks the words of God, because God gives the Spirit without limit. I realised that the Father loves his Son and has placed everything in his hands. Whoever believed in the Son would have eternal life, but whoever rejects the Son will not see this life, for God's wrath would still be on them. I knew that Jesus was God's Son.

Not long after this I was arrested and put in this prison."

THE END OF JOHN'S STORY
AS RECORDED BY JOHN MARK

Herod himself had given orders to have John arrested, and he had him bound and put in prison. He did this because of Herodias, his brother Philip's wife, whom he had married. For John had been saying to Herod, 'It is not lawful for you to have your brother's wife.'

So Herodias nursed a grudge against John and wanted to kill him. However, she was not able to, because Herod feared John and protected him, knowing him to be a righteous and holy man. When Herod heard John, he was greatly puzzled; yet he liked to listen to him. Finally the opportune time came. On his birthday Herod gave a banquet for his high officials and military commanders and the leading men of Galilee. When the daughter of Herodias came in and danced, she pleased Herod and his dinner guests. The king said to the girl, "Ask me for anything you want, and I'll give it to you". And he promised her with an oath, "Whatever you ask I will give you, up to half my kingdom".

She went out and said to her mother, "What shall I ask for?" "The head of John the Baptist", her mother answered. At once the girl hurried in to the king with the request. "I want you to give me right now, the head of John the Baptist, on a platter." The king was greatly distressed, but because of his oaths and his dinner guests, he did not want to refuse her. So he immediately sent an executioner with orders to bring John's head. The man went, beheaded John in the prison, and brought back his head on a platter. He presented it to the girl, and she gave it to her mother.

On hearing of this, John's disciples came and took his body and laid it in a tomb. Mark 6:14-29.

JOHN THE BAPTIST, A MAJOR HISTORICAL WITNESS

I know it stretches the point to include the story of John the Baptist who was executed soon after Jesus began his ministry. It is an example of my use of dramatic license! John the Baptist was a pivotal character in preparing the ground for Jesus to begin his ministry. All four gospel writers mention him and describe his role in preparing the way for the coming of Jesus. He was known as the baptist or baptiser by his contemporaries. He is referred to specifically in the writings of the Jewish historian Josephus who wrote in the latter half of the first century.

Josephus mentions him in his Antiquities;

> *"John, that was called the Baptist; (117) for Herod slew him, who was a good man, and commanded the Jews to exercise virtue, both as to righteousness towards one another, and piety towards God, and so to come to baptism; for that*

the washing would be acceptable to him, if they made use of it, not in order to the putting away of some sins, but for the purification of the body; supposing still that the soul was thoroughly purified beforehand by righteousness."
Antiquities 18.5.2

Jesus declared John the Baptist to be the greatest man to have ever lived and that no one was greater than he was. Luke 7:28. John's influence continued long after his death. There were followers of John the Baptist who continued for several decades. A group of his followers were encountered by the Apostle Paul in Ephesus according to the gospel writer and author of the Acts of the Apostles, Luke, in Acts 19.

The angelic messenger says that John's mother, Elizabeth, was a relative of Mary the mother of Jesus in Luke 1:36. The two women were pregnant at the same time. The Bible says in Luke 1:41, when the two expectant mothers met, the baby leaped within Elizabeth's womb as she was filled with the Holy Spirit. The angel Gabriel had already foretold the miraculous birth and prophetic ministry of John the Baptist to his father Zechariah. The news was a joyous answer to prayer for the previously barren Elizabeth. John was to become the God-ordained messenger proclaiming the arrival of the Messiah.

After the death of his parents it seems John spent most of his time growing up in the desert hill country to the east of Jerusalem that drops down to the Dead Sea. There are those who believe that John grew up in one of the communities known as the Essenes that were located in that area.

The Essenes have become known in recent years as a result of the discovery of an extensive group of religious documents referred to as the Dead Sea Scrolls, which are commonly believed to be the Essenes' library, although there is no proof that the Essenes wrote them. These scrolls include well preserved, multiple copies of the Old Testament, untouched from as early as 300 BC until their discovery in 1946. Also numerous other manuscripts that add a great deal of understanding to the life and times of Jesus.

The first reference to the Essenes is by the Roman writer Pliny the Elder (died 79 AD). Pliny relates in a few lines that the Essenes do not marry, possess no money, and had existed for thousands of generations. Pliny places them in Ein Gedi on the shores of the Dead Sea.

A little later Josephus gave a detailed account of the Essenes in The Jewish War (c. 75 AD), with a shorter description in Antiquities of the Jews (c. 94 AD) He claimed first hand knowledge, he lists the Essenoi as one of the three sects of Jews alongside the Pharisees and the Sadducees. He describes them as practicing piety and celibacy, the absence of personal property and of money, the belief in communality and commitment to a strict observance of Sabbath. He further adds that the Essenes ritually immersed themselves in water every morning, ate together after prayer, devoted themselves to charity and benevolence, forbade the expression of anger, studied the books of the elders, preserved secrets, and were very mindful of the names of the angels kept in their sacred writings.

All of this has led many scholars to conclude that John spent some extended time with the Essenes or indeed may have been part of that community. This is speculation but may provide some insight into his background and some of the emphases of his ministry, especially concerning baptism and knowledge of the angelic visit of Gabriel.

The remarkable ministry of John the Baptist included the recognition of the character and nature of Jesus and his baptism in the River Jordan. John did not lack boldness as he challenged even Herod to repent of his sins. In approximately 29 AD, Herod Antipas, the son of Herod the Great, had John the Baptist arrested and put in prison. Later John was beheaded through a plot devised by Herodias, the illegal wife of Herod and ex-wife of his brother, Philip.

Josephus records his end in his Antiquities of the Jews 18.5.2

> *"Now, when many others came in crowds about him, for they were greatly moved [by hearing his words (John the Baptist), Herod, who feared lest the great influence John had over the people might put it into his power and inclination to raise a rebellion (for they seemed ready to do anything he should advise), thought it best, by putting him to death, to prevent any mischief he might cause, and not bring himself into difficulties, by sparing a man who might make him repent of it when it should be too late. (119) Accordingly he was sent a prisoner, out of Herod's suspicious temper, to Macherus, the castle I before mentioned, and was there put to death. Now the Jews had an opinion that the destruction of this army was sent as a punishment upon Herod, and a mark of God's displeasure against him."* Jews 18.5.2

John the Baptist challenged the people to prepare for the coming of the Messiah by turning away from sin and being baptised as a symbol of repentance. Although he held no power or influence in the Jewish political system, he delivered his message with the force of authority. People could not resist the overpowering truth of his words, as they flocked by the hundreds to hear him and be baptised. And even as he attracted the attention of the crowds, he never lost sight of his mission to point people to Christ.

JOHN AND HIS REVELATION OF THE FATHER

Did John have a revelation of God being a Father? Did he recognise in Jesus his relationship as the Son of God? These are questions difficult to answer. Jesus undoubtedly recognised that John was a key person in opening up people's hearts and preparing a way for his own ministry and the revelation that he would bring. Jesus described him as among those born of women to be the greatest. Jesus says this after he was visited by some of John's disciples bringing a message from their imprisoned leader. John had sent them to Jesus to ask if he was the one to come or should they expect someone else.

Jesus had been healing many who had diseases, sicknesses and evil spirits, and gave sight to many who were blind. So he replied to the messengers,

> *"Go back and report to John what you have seen and heard: The blind receive sight, the lame walk, those who have leprosy are cleansed, the deaf hear, the dead are raised, and the good news is proclaimed to the poor. Blessed is anyone who does not stumble on account of me."* Luke 7:18-23

After John's messengers left, Jesus began to speak to the crowd about John. He said,

> *"What did you go out into the wilderness to see? A reed*

swayed by the wind? If not, what did you go out to see? A man dressed in fine clothes? No, those who wear expensive clothes and indulge in luxury are in palaces. What did you go out to see? A prophet? Yes, I tell you, and more than a prophet. This is the one about whom it is written: 'I will send my messenger ahead of you, who will prepare your way before you." Luke 7:24-27.

Jesus not only recognises John as the forerunner, but as the Elijah prophesied by Malachi,

"See, I will send the prophet Elijah to you before that great and dreadful day of the Lord comes. He will turn the hearts of the parents to their children, and the hearts of the children to their parents; or else I will come and strike the land with total destruction." Malachi 4:5-6

This is in accord with the prophetic revelation John's father Zechariah had at the time of the announcement of John's birth,

"And he will go on before the Lord, in the spirit and power of Elijah, to turn the hearts of the parents to their children and the disobedient to the wisdom of the righteous—to make ready a people prepared for the Lord" Luke 1:17

The answer to whether John had a revelation of God as Father cannot be separated from the revelation that Jesus is the Son of God. Two important clues are found in these stories. The first is the description of Jesus as the lamb of God and the second is in what John heard when Jesus was baptised.

THE FATHER SENDS HIS SON AS THE SACRIFICIAL LAMB

One of the unique things about John is that he receives special revelation himself from God about the exact nature and destiny of Jesus. One such revelation that he receives is that Jesus is none other than the sacrificial Lamb of God who will take away the sins of the world. This description of Jesus as the Lamb of God appears twice in John's Gospel, both times on the lips of John the Baptist. It is taken up again by John the Apostle in Revelation as a common motif that describes Jesus. In much of Christian teaching the view is that the "Lamb of God" refers to Jesus in his role of the perfect sacrificial offering. However he is not identified with the term from the Old Testament concept of a "scapegoat" which is a person or animal subject to punishment for the sins of others without knowing it or willing it. Notably Anselm in the 11th Century taught that Jesus chose to suffer on the cross as a sign of his full obedience to the will of his Father, as an obedient son and servant of God. The Lamb of God is thus related to the Passover lamb which is viewed as foundational and integral to the message of Christianity.

The Lamb of God title is widely used in Christian prayers of a liturgical nature, and the Agnus Dei, the Latin for The Lamb of God, is used as central part of the Catholic Mass. This also forms a part of the musical setting for the Mass. As a visual symbol the lamb has been most often represented since the Middle Ages as a standing haloed lamb with its foreleg cocked. It is "holding" a pennant with a red cross on a white background. The Moravians in the eighteenth century adopted this as their particular symbol.

John Calvin, the 16th Century reformer, presented the same view of "The Lamb as the agent of God" by arguing that in his trial before Pilate and while at Herod's Court Jesus could have argued for his innocence, but instead remained mostly quiet and submitted to the cross in obedience to the Father, for he knew his role as the Lamb of God. The writer to the Hebrews describes Jesus going to the cross willingly,

> *"for the joy set before him endured the cross.."* Hebrews 12:2

The fact that God Himself has provided the offering that atones for our sin is part of the glorious good news of the gospel that is so clearly declared in 1 Peter who writes,

> *"For you know that it was not with perishable things such as silver or gold that you were redeemed from the empty way of life handed down to you from your forefathers, but with the precious blood of Christ, a lamb without blemish or defect. He was chosen before the creation of the world, but was revealed in these last times for your sake. Through him you believe in God, who raised him from the dead and glorified him, and so your faith and hope are in God."*
> 1 Peter 1:18-20

This passage from Peter links with the passage of Paul in Ephesians 1 where he describes the eternal plan of the Father in choosing us in Jesus,

> *"For he chose us in him before the creation of the world to be holy and blameless in his sight. In love he predestined us to be established as his sons through Jesus Christ, in accordance with his pleasure and will, to the praise of his glorious grace, which he has freely given us in the One he loves. In him we have redemption through his blood, the forgiveness of sins, in*

accordance with the riches of God's grace that he lavished on us with all wisdom and understanding." Ephesians 1:4-8

John the Baptist's recognition and designation of Jesus as the Lamb of God is a key part of the revelation in the heart of the Father in bringing about our redemption and placing us in the glorious position of his beloved sons.

THE FATHER RECOGNISES AND AFFIRMS HIS SON

It is between the two statements by John describing Jesus as the Lamb of God, first generally and second specifically to his two disciples, that Jesus is baptised. At the moment when Jesus stands in the waters of the River Jordan having been baptised by John a most amazing sound is heard. The voice of the Lord God Almighty breaks the silence of centuries and he speaks.

"This is my Son, whom I love; with him I am well pleased."

John says that the Father himself who had sent him to baptise had told him in advance, "The man on whom you see the Spirit come down and remain is the one who will baptise with the Holy Spirit." I have seen and I testify that this is God's Chosen One." John had seen the Holy Spirit descend on Jesus in the form of a dove and then he heard the Father speak. This confirmed to him that not only would he baptise with the Holy Spirit but that he was the Lamb of God.

All four gospel writers unanimously record the events of Jesus' baptism, the most explicit being the three synoptic gospels, Matthew, Mark and

Luke. Each of these record the words that the Father spoke over his Son. Luke's version has a more intimate feel than the others.

> *"And as he was praying, heaven was opened and the Holy Spirit descended on him in bodily form like a dove. A voice came from heaven, "You are my Son, whom I love; with you I am well pleased."* Luke 3:21-22

In this version the Father addresses Jesus personally rather than speaking generally about him. These words would have been a great personal encouragement to Jesus. The Father first confirms him as his very own Son. This is his true identity. Then the Father affirms and states his love for him. This is an unconditional statement of fatherly affection and love which many have never heard from their natural fathers. Finally he asserts his pleasure in him. This is not based on any activity or ministry or accomplishment it is based on who he is in himself.

It is notable that before and after his baptism and the voice of the Father speaking that John describes Jesus as the Lamb of God. These affirmations come after thirty years in waiting. Jesus has been known as the carpenter's son in Nazareth. In his own heart he knew he was God's own Son and that God was his true Father. He stated as much as a young boy in the temple eighteen years before. Now on the very brink of his public ministry and as the opening act of the drama of the next three years that is about to unfold, the Father himself is announcing who Jesus is, who he has eternally been and will be. The delight and pleasure that is in the heart of the Father as Jesus begins his great ministry of revealing the Father and bringing redemption to mankind is evident in the Father's words.

"You are my Son, whom I love; with you I am well pleased."

THE THIRD STORY TELLER

JAMES
THE BROTHER OF JESUS

"In many ways I think perhaps I knew him better than anyone. I grew up with him. He was my older brother of course. I looked up to him. He was the best brother anyone could have. After my father died Jesus very much took over the family business. My father Joseph had been a carpenter in the village where we lived, Nazareth in Galilee. All our family lived up there in Galilee except some relatives down in Judea. We didn't see much of them except John. His parents, Zachariah and Elizabeth had died when he was quite young.

As a young man Jesus was different from any of the boys I knew in the village. I felt in many ways he was like a father to me after my Dad died. I felt it deep within me. I remember one day when Jesus was about thirty years old, he told my mother and the rest of us that he was leaving home. I was pretty shocked and annoyed. I wondered what would happen to the business as none of us his brothers, me, Simon, Joseph or Jude had his skill or were anything like as good as him at carpentry. He said he was going off to Judea to hear what our relative John was saying down there. News was spreading all over Galilee that this new prophet had appeared, they were calling him after Elijah. It was very exciting. Some were also wondering if he was the Messiah. This was dangerous as many were hoping that the Messiah would come and liberate us from the Romans. Then Jesus announced he was off down south to see John. I was annoyed because I wanted to go but someone had to stay at home and look after mother and the rest of the family.

He was gone for quite some time. We heard from some people that he had been baptised by John. That so surprised me. I had heard that John was baptising people as a sign of the forgiveness of their sins. I would never have put my brother Jesus in that category. In fact, I can't ever remember him doing anything that I would remotely call sin! We didn't hear anything from him for a while. It is as if he just disappeared for a month or two. Later he told me that he had gone off on his own into the hills of Judea. He said he was deeply challenged and felt that the devil was attacking him and tempting him at every level of his being. I wondered what he meant as I know God wasn't tempting him, because God doesn't tempt anyone. I didn't really understand this when he first told me.

He came back home some time later. He was changed somehow when he came back. I could not put my finger on it. There was a seriousness in him that I had not seen before. He seemed focused on a new direction. He was not going to come back home to take up being a carpenter again that was clear. It seemed as if he was waiting for something. Now I know he was waiting to do the things that God was telling him to do. He began to refer to God as being his father. He had a few new friends with him who he got to know while he was in Judea. I knew some of them, they came from Bethesda, a town down on the lake. There were five of them including our cousins James and John.

Not long after that we had all been invited to a wedding in a town nearby, Cana. It would be quite a big gathering and a wonderful opportunity to catch up on all the family news. The cousins from Bethesda would be there too. Mother particularly wanted us all to go to the wedding. This was three days after Jesus had returned to Galilee. So off we went, it is only about five miles from home so we enjoyed the walk. His new friends, who called themselves his disciples, came too. They seemed to have taken him over and we family didn't seem to count as far as they were concerned. As the wedding feast got going there was all the usual dancing and celebrating but the big drama was that the wine ran out. My mother told Jesus that they had no more wine. He turned to her and asked her why she wanted to involve him because his time had not yet come whatever that meant. Mother, being mother, told the servants to do whatever he told them to do. Nearby were six very large stone water jars, the kind used for ceremonial washing. They must have held twenty to thirty gallons. To my surprise Jesus told the servants to fill the jars with water. I thought he was joking. The servants looked very confused but there was something about the way he spoke that made them do it and they filled them to the brim. Then he told them to draw some out and take it to the master of the banquet. I wanted to stop him because it would be so embarrassing for them all to be served water. The servants did so, and the master of the banquet tasted the water. I held my breath watching, but he smacked his lips, then burped loudly. He had no idea where it had come from, but he called the bridegroom aside and made the comment that everyone brings out the choice wine first and then the cheaper wine after the guests have had too much to drink. He was amazed that the bridegroom had saved the best till then.

When I look back at it now I realise that what Jesus did there in Cana of Galilee was the first of the various signs through which he began to reveal himself. His disciples seemed to believe in him because of this, but I was not so sure. I was confused. He was my brother. I had known him all my life and this was all very unexpected. After this we all went down to Capernaum including our mother and the rest of us and his disciples. We stayed there for a few days. He started to speak publicly and teach and soon everyone was talking about him. He was speaking with great authority and power. It was as if the very Spirit of God himself was on him. News about him was spreading through the whole countryside. Initially he was teaching in the synagogues, and everyone was speaking well of him.

Then he came back home to Nazareth, and on the Sabbath day we went into the synagogue, as we did each week. We men where all there together. Mother and the girls were there too but behind the screen that kept the women separate from the men. I was standing right there next to him when the rabbi invited him to read the scroll. Jesus stood up to read, and the scroll of the prophet Isaiah was handed to him. Unrolling it, he found the place where it is written:

"The Spirit of the Lord is on me, because he has anointed me to proclaim good news to the poor. He has sent me to proclaim freedom for the prisoners and recovery of sight for the blind, to set the oppressed free, to proclaim the year of the Lord's favour."

He read it out aloud to everyone then he rolled up the scroll, gave it back to the attendant and sat down. Everyone in the synagogue were staring at him. Then he said this to us all, "Today this scripture is fulfilled in your hearing."

Initially, I don't think we really heard what he said or rather the weight of the words and the very authority with which he spoke. There was a general murmur of approval of him and particularly the way his words were so....so....how shall I say it....gracious. I heard people saying, "Isn't this Joseph's son?"

Then Jesus said to everyone, "Surely you will quote this proverb to me:' Physician, heal yourself! ' And you will tell me, 'Do here in your hometown what we have heard that you did in Capernaum. Well I tell you, no prophet is accepted in his hometown. I assure you that there were many widows in Israel in Elijah's time, when the sky was shut for three and a half years and there was a severe famine throughout the land. Yet Elijah was not sent to any of them, but to a widow in Zarephath, in the region of Sidon. There were many in Israel with leprosy in the time of Elisha the prophet, yet not one of them was cleansed, only Naaman the Syrian."

Suddenly the whole mood changed, all the people in the synagogue were furious when they heard this. They started to angrily ask each other where Jesus got this wisdom and these so called miraculous powers. They knew our father was the carpenter and that Mary was our mother, and they were looking at me and our younger brothers, Joseph, Simon and Judas. They started pointing at our sisters too. It got very ugly. I wished the ground would open up beneath me. Then they got up, threw him out of the synagogue and the town, and took him to the brow of the hill on which the town is built, in order to throw him off the cliff. These were our friends and neighbours! We had no idea what had come over them. We tried to get to him to help him but they jostled us and pushed us. They were accusing him of blasphemy. I was convinced he would be killed, but he walked right through the crowd and went on his way out of town.

He did not come home hardly ever again after that. We heard all sorts of rumours about him and what he was saying. We heard about healings and things like that. At that time, I'm ashamed to say, I didn't believe the stories. One time we went down to Capernaum to find him and try to bring him home. We were worried about him. Mother insisted she come with us because she did believe the stories. She believed in him! She said he was unique and that she had known that from before he was born. She would get very mysterious when she talked like that. It was as if she knew something that no one else knew.

When we found where he was we could not reach him because of the crowd. We sent a message in to the house where he was. Someone told him that we were outside wanting to see him. The message that came back from him was that his mother and brothers were those who hear the word of God and do it! I was angry and offended. We only wanted to see him and talk to him about maybe coming home and stopping all this public stuff. Mother calmed us down and urged us to go home. I was so offended I refused to listen to any more of the stories. I just wanted to get on with my life. I did not want to be the younger brother of anyone famous or notorious.

After this, Jesus went around mostly in Galilee. He did not want to go about in Judea because the Jewish leaders there were looking for a way to kill him. I was not happy with all this talk and publicity he was receiving. However, when the Festival of Tabernacles was near, we brothers decided to go to Jerusalem and said to him very sarcastically to be honest, "Why don't you leave Galilee and go to Judea with us, so that your disciples there may see the works you do. After all, no one who wants to become a public figure acts in secret! Since you are doing these things here in Galilee, why not show yourself to the rest of the world." Sadly even we his own brothers did not believe in him at that point. It was a low point in our relationship. I think I may have been jealous. I don't know.

Well anyway, Jesus just looked at us and said that his time was not yet here; but we could go if we wanted to! He then went on about the world not hating us, but they hated him because he testify that its works were evil. He told us go to the festival and that he was not going because his time had not yet fully come. After this, he stayed in Galilee. However, after we had left for the festival, I found out he went also, not publicly, but in secret. I was quite annoyed with him for doing that. Now at the festival the Jewish leaders were watching for Jesus and asking where he was. Among the crowds there was widespread whispering about him. Some were saying he was a good man others that he was deceiving the people. No one would say anything publicly about him for fear of the leaders.

Well, you know all the terrible things that happened a couple of years later in Jerusalem. I was not there. Mother went up to the city, along with many others. I didn't, I stayed in Nazareth. By then I had met many who claimed to have been healed by him in Galilee. The evidence was overwhelming. I realised I had been so wrong about him. I wanted to see him and talk to him and ask him to forgive me for being so full of anger and jealousy. For not believing him. I planned to go to the city as soon as the Passover was over to talk to him.

Then the news came to us up in Nazareth. He had been arrested, tried and sentenced. He was crucified, not stoned, as I thought might happen if he was not careful. No! He was crucified on a Roman cross! Mother was there but I wasn't. I had not been there for him or for my mother. I left everything as quickly as I could and went to Jerusalem to find her. When I got to the city I found his disciples and my mother all gathered together in a friend's house. I expected to walk into grief and tears and pain. Instead I walked into a room full of joy, laughter and excited chatter. It seemed the world had gone crazy. Then they told me he had risen from the dead! I was speechless! They said he really had died and had been in a tomb for virtually three days. Then apparently he had appeared alive again and had walked in this very room we were in just a few days earlier. I did not know what to think. I had to get out of the room. The swirl of emotions I was experiencing were extreme. I fled the house. I went to the garden where he had been buried a week before. The tomb was there. It was empty. I walked back to the city past the place of execution. The cross he had been on was still there. It was blood stained. It was his blood that stained it. One of the other crosses had fallen over and the other still had a bloated body hanging on it. The stench of death was everywhere. Tears were streaming down my face. I fell on the ground and wept.

As I lay there with my face buried in my soaked arms, I felt a hand on my shoulder. I turned and the dazzle of the sun in my face hid the person from my eyes. Then he said my name. "James." It was him he was risen indeed!"

JAMES IN THE NEW TESTAMENT

James the brother of Jesus was one of a number of individuals with this name mentioned in the New Testament. He is specifically described as the brother of Jesus in Galatians 1:19 by the Apostle Paul who meets him on his first visit to Jerusalem after becoming a Christian. Paul distinguishes him from other individuals called James such as the Apostle, the son of Zebedee. The Hebrew version of his name would have been Yakov or the anglicised, Jacob. The Greek is Jacobus and the Latin version that is most widely used is James.

Hegesippus in the second Century refers to him as 'James the Just', others 'James the Righteous', 'James of Jerusalem', and 'James Adelphotheos', this latter meaning James the brother of God. In a letter addressed to James from Clement of Rome, James was described as the "bishop of bishops, who rules Jerusalem, the Holy Assembly of Hebrews, and all assemblies everywhere." Like the rest of the of the early church leaders information about his life is scarce and ambiguous.

There are a handful of references to him in the Gospels. He is presumably included a number of times generally and occasionally mentioned by name with the family of Jesus and as the brothers of Jesus.

> *"Now Jesus' mother and brothers came to see him, but they were not able to get near him because of the crowd. Someone told him, "Your mother and brothers are standing outside, wanting to see you." He replied, "My mother and brothers are those who hear God's word and put it into practice."*
> Luke 8:19-21, See also Matthew 12:46-50, Mark 3:31-35

When people are discussing Jesus' identity and describing him as the carpenter's son, James is included in the list of his siblings. This may be Matthew's version of the events described in much greater detail in Luke's account of a visit to Jesus' home town of Nazareth in Luke 4.

> *"Coming to his hometown, he began teaching the people in their synagogue, and they were amazed. "Where did this man get this wisdom and these miraculous powers?" they asked. "Isn't this the carpenter's son? Isn't his mother's name Mary, and aren't his brothers James, Joseph, Simon and Judas? Aren't all his sisters with us? Where then did this man get all these things?" And they took offence at him."*
> Matthew 13:54-57

In John's Gospel, John refers to the brothers of Jesus in a general way and makes the point that Jesus' siblings were almost cynical about his fame and Jesus' desire to keep his identity as the Messiah a secret. John's assessment of them was that they struggled to believe in him as the Messiah.

> *"Jesus' brothers said to him, "Leave Galilee and go to Judea, so that your disciples there may see the works you do. No one who wants to become a public figure acts in secret. Since you are doing these things, show yourself to the world." For even his own brothers did not believe in him."* John 7:3-5

There is no mention of the immediate family of Jesus being in Jerusalem for the last week of Jesus' ministry. Apart from Mary and her sister Salome, the family were notably absent from the cross or the resurrection lists.

A person called 'James' is mentioned in Paul's first letter to the Corinthians as one to whom Jesus appeared after his resurrection. It is generally accepted that this is James the brother of Jesus. This list of Paul's is the earliest mention of people who saw the risen Jesus, as Paul's letter was written before any of the other Gospels. It is interesting that Paul names only Peter and James among the disciples and others who saw Jesus.

> *"For what I received I passed on to you as of first importance, that Christ died for our sins according to the Scriptures, that he was buried, that he was raised on the third day according to the Scriptures, and that he appeared to Cephas, and then to the Twelve. After that, he appeared to more than five hundred of the brothers and sisters at the same time, most of whom are still living, though some have fallen asleep. Then he appeared to James, then to all the apostles, and last of all he appeared to me also, as to one abnormally born."*
> 1 Corinthians 15:3-8

Most commentators identify this James with the James who emerges as the leader of the church in Jerusalem who Paul identifies as the brother of Jesus. This would make this resurrection appearance to James as Jesus' brother a significant appearance. It would most certainly have been very important to James given his apparent indifference to Jesus before the resurrection.

The main sources for James' life after the resurrection are in Acts and Paul's letters. The Letter of James is traditionally attributed to him, and he is a principal author of the letter sent out after the Council of Jerusalem in Acts 15.

Hegesippus in his fifth book of his Commentaries, writing of James, says, *"After the apostles, James the brother of the Lord surnamed the Just was made head of the Church at Jerusalem."*

The emergence of the doctrine of the perpetual virginity of Mary which does not allow that she had children after Jesus, caused problems for Jerome, in the fourth century, when translating the New Testament into Latin. He considered that the term 'brother' of the Lord should be read 'cousin', and translated it accordingly.

We do not know at which point James became recognised as the leader of the church in Jerusalem. In the non canonical writings of the second century such as the Gospel of Thomas, Jesus names James his successor: *'The disciples said to Jesus, 'We know that you will depart from us. Who will be our leader?' Jesus said to them, 'Where you are, you are to go to James the Just, for whose sake heaven and earth came into existence.'* Like much, in these non canonical gospels, these references cannot be received with much certainty but reflect a widespread view held at the time.

In Galatians Paul recounts his first visit to Jerusalem where he meets James for the first time. By this time he was already recognised with some seniority and having some sort of leadership.

> *"Then after three years, I went up to Jerusalem to get acquainted with Cephas and stayed with him fifteen days. I saw none of the other apostles, only James, the Lord's brother."* Galatians 1:18-19

In Acts 15 is the account of the first attempt to resolve the growing issue of the integration of Gentile converts into the newly emerging Christian communities. Many from the Jewish background were insisting that all new converts needed to adopt Jewish customs and practices including circumcision. This was causing considerable confusion not only in Jerusalem but the confusion had spread to Antioch and also to the new churches in Galatia. In response to this Paul and Barnabas visited Jerusalem to present the case from the Gentile perspective. It is here that Paul met James again. There was considerable discussion among the leaders about how to respond to the challenges of the new non Jewish converts, if Paul's account in Galatians reflects an accurate assessment of the events. Paul says,

> *"...they recognised that I had been entrusted with the task of preaching the gospel to the uncircumcised, just as Peter had been to the circumcised. For God, who was at work in Peter as an apostle to the circumcised, was also at work in me as an apostle to the Gentiles. James, Cephas and John, those esteemed as pillars, gave me and Barnabas the right hand of fellowship when they recognised the grace given to me. They agreed that we should go to the Gentiles, and they to the circumcised."* Galatians 2:7-9

Luke's account of the events in Acts 15 gives James the brother of Jesus a prominent role and makes him the mouth piece of gathered assembly.

> *"The whole assembly became silent as they listened to Barnabas and Paul telling about the signs and wonders God had done among the Gentiles through them. When they finished, James spoke up. "Brothers," he said, "listen to me. Simon has described to us how God first intervened to choose a people for his name from the Gentiles"."* Acts 15:12-14

> *"It is my judgment, therefore, that we should not make it difficult for the Gentiles who are turning to God. Instead we should write to them, telling them to abstain from food polluted by idols, from sexual immorality, from the meat of strangled animals and from blood."* Acts 15:19-20

It is a strong statement that Luke records. James takes a very prominent role in the proceedings and it is his words that are described as being the judgment of the assembly.

In the light of the subsequent challenge presented by the 'judaisers' that Paul so vehemently opposes in his letter to the Galatians the letter sent by the leaders in Jerusalem seems very weak.

Sometime after Paul had returned to Antioch it was obvious that the issue was still not fully resolved. Peter had come to Antioch and was mixing with the gentile believers until some people supposedly sent by James arrived.

> *"..before certain men came from James, he (Peter) used to eat with the Gentiles. But when they arrived, he began to*

> *draw back and separate himself from the Gentiles because he was afraid of those who belonged to the circumcision group. The other Jews joined him in his hypocrisy, so that by their hypocrisy even Barnabas was led astray. When I saw that they were not acting in line with the truth of the gospel, I said to Cephas in front of them all, "You are a Jew, yet you live like a Gentile and not like a Jew. How is it, then, that you force Gentiles to follow Jewish customs."* Galatians 2:12-14

How much this behaviour was encouraged by James is difficult to say, but Paul took a very strong stand against it nonetheless. It was a major crisis for the early church and Paul's letter to the Galatians, which is most likely the first piece of Christian literature ever written, has this as its principle focus. The theme of his letter describes very fully the reality that being 'In Christ' and being redeemed by him, results in us being placed in the position of sons and daughters to God the Father. Paul declares that it is for freedom that Christ has set us free. It is debatable whether James the brother of Jesus fully saw this. The letter named after him in New Testament has always been viewed with some concern since the earliest days of the church. Many of the early church Fathers, whilst knowing the work, did not consider it to be "inspired" in the same way as the rest of the New Testament. Martin Luther, in the sixteenth century described it as an "epistle of straw." In reading through the epistle, its writer has a strong emphasis on obedience and good behaviour which are not in anyway wrong in themselves, but does not reflect the life and freedom that Paul is so eager to promote in Galatians and his other writings.

In contrast, in the New Testament is a letter by James' other brother, Jude who writes,

"Jude, a servant of Jesus Christ and a brother of James, To those who have been called, who are loved in God the Father and kept for Jesus Christ: Mercy, peace and love be yours in abundance." Jude 1:1

THE DEATH OF JAMES

We do not read of the death of James in the New Testament. Yet outside of the Bible Josephus records his death, which indicates the importance and knowledge there was of James as a leader in the Jerusalem church.

"Festus was now dead, and Albinus was but upon the road; so he assembled the Sanhedrin of judges, and brought before them the brother of Jesus, who was called Christ, whose name was James, and some others, [or some of his companions]; and when he had formed an accusation against them as breakers of the law, he delivered them to be stoned." Josephus Antiquities 20.9.1

JESUS KNOWS THE WORK THE FATHER HAS FOR HIM

Whether James the brother of Jesus had a personal revelation of God the Father or not he certainly believed that he was the Messiah and followed him and ultimately gave his life as a martyr for the faith. In his life he was present at some significant moments and heard Jesus say things that few others heard.

Jesus had returned full of the Holy Spirit from Judea having been baptised by John. The Spirit had come upon him and he had then gone out into the wilderness for some time and we are told he was tempted by the devil.

The nature of those temptations were significant in that each of the three attacks were aimed at undermining the identity that had just been confirmed to him by the Father. At the Jordan river, in his encounters with John and in his baptism, Jesus stepped out from waiting in obscurity in Nazareth to beginning his public ministry. He had heard the Father affirm him as his beloved son. He began from that day onwards to publicly live and walk in that identity. Immediately the devil began to lie to him and try to divert Jesus from living in that place as the Son. Each temptation began with a questioning doubt. "If you are God's son."

Each temptation was designed to make him follow another path rather than the one chosen by the Father for him. The first was supernaturally feeding the masses as a short cut to kingship. The Romans kept their hold over the people by providing bread and circuses. This was Satan's stratagem with Jesus. Feed the masses and then rule them. The second was a fantastic personal and public miracle that would have drawn people to him as a wonder worker and brought great personal fame and notoriety. The miracles that Jesus did perform were all in response to the expressed instructions given to him by the Father and were signs that people might believe in the one who sent him, that is the Father. They were not even his own works, they were the works the Father was doing through him.

> *"I tell you, the Son can do nothing by himself; he can do only what he sees his Father doing, because whatever the Father does the Son also does. For the Father loves the Son and shows him all he does. Yes, and he will show him even greater works than these, so that you will be amazed."* John 5:19-20

The third temptation was an offer of sovereignty over the whole world. Satan was offering his kingdom of the earth to Jesus in exchange for worship of him by Jesus. It was the same basic desire by Satan for worship that had led to his expulsion from heaven in the very beginning and ultimately led to the fall of all mankind. Satan was demanding for himself worship from God the Son.

Each temptation was rebuffed and resisted by Jesus. Finally this round of temptation ended.

> *"When the devil had finished all this tempting, he left him until an opportune time."* Luke 4:13

The first Adam in the garden of Eden was tempted and fell. All of his descendants have lived with the consequences of that temptation ever since. Adam's words to God in the garden were that he was hiding from him, that he was afraid of God because he knew he was naked. Genesis 3:10. The result was that all of humanity became afraid of God, hiding from him in our nakedness and shame. As a human being born of a woman Jesus too had to face that challenge every day. The writer to the Hebrews says he was tempted in every way as we are but did not sin. Hebrews 4:15. Every day Jesus was tempted to fear God and hide from him but every day he chose to resist and recognise that God was his real Father, who loved him, was pleased with him and he did not need to hide from him. Jesus broke the cycle of fear and hiding that all humanity has been living with ever since. These temptations by Satan of the Son of God, who Paul describes as the last Adam, in 1 Corinthians 15:45, failed because Jesus knew his true identity and was listening to his Father's voice.

Sometime after this season of temptation Jesus returned to Galilee and visited his home town of Nazareth and he went to the synagogue on the Sabbath day as would have been the custom for all male Jews at that time. The event in Nazareth happened very early in Jesus public ministry.

It is very possible that James, Jesus' brother was the source of the story that records Jesus speaking in the synagogue on that occasion. In many ways it marks the beginning of his public ministry. James is implied as being there in Matthew's gospel and as a Jew and a resident of Nazareth it is highly likely that he would have accompanied his brother there on that occasion. If not James, it was most likely another member of Jesus' immediate family. What is clear is that someone intimately connected to Jesus was there who saw and heard what happened. Luke's story has the ring of an eyewitness account to it.

Luke tells us that Jesus had been teaching in various synagogues in Galilee, and everyone was speaking positively about him. News of this would have reached Nazareth.

We are told it was this custom and on the Sabbath day he went into the synagogue. On this occasion he stood up to read, and the scroll of the prophet Isaiah was handed to him. Unrolling it, he found the place where it is written:

> *"The Spirit of the Lord is on me, because he has anointed me to proclaim good news to the poor. He has sent me to proclaim freedom for the prisoners and recovery of sight for the blind, to set the oppressed free, to proclaim the year of the Lord's favour."* Luke 4:18-19

Luke says he then rolled up the scroll, gave it back to the attendant and sat down. The eyes of everyone in the synagogue were fastened on him. In itself this was not remarkable in that he read an appropriate passage from the scroll. The fact that he then sat down in front of everyone indicated that he was going to teach on what had been read. He adopted the stance of a Rabbi. Then he spoke the astounding words,

"Today this scripture is fulfilled in your hearing." Luke 4:21

I wonder if they fully understood the implications of those words? Initially, they expressed amazed politeness, pointing out that this was Joseph, the carpenter's boy. Then Jesus went on to throw down the gauntlet to challenge them. He is not subtle. He makes it very clear the message he was bringing would not be welcomed in his hometown. He reminds them how the people of Israel rejected Elijah in his day and how their rejection led to the prophet going to pagans. This was not lost on the people in the synagogue in Nazareth. Their polite approval quickly turned to violent opposition and aggression.

In his reading of Isaiah 61 and then his announcement that this scripture was fulfilled in their hearing, Jesus is deliberately and pointedly identifying himself with the prophetic revelation that Isaiah spoke of centuries before. Isaiah was looking to a time when the sovereign Lord would reveal himself afresh to his people. It was to be a time of the restoration of Israel's fortunes. In Isaiah 59:20, there was the promise of the Redeemer coming to Zion and to those in Jacob who would repent of their sins. It was a promise of the Spirit of the Lord speaking through the mouth of his servant. It was a day of the glory of the Lord resting upon them. All of this would have been in the minds of the people who knew these scriptures. It was summed up in the longing for Messiah to come and restore Israel. The people would have not missed the implications of these words.

Jesus is clearing identifying himself with all this. The Spirit was upon him. He had experienced that filling in his baptism. He had been led by the Spirit into the wilderness where Satan had intensified his attack on him. Jesus had now returned to Galilee full of the Holy Spirit. Jesus knew that the anointing of the Father's Holy Spirit was fully on him and that anointing was in order for him to proclaim the good news to the poor. Each of the categories in this passage, the poor, the prisoners, the blind and the oppressed, represented the false identities that mankind had been living with and hiding in since the Fall. We are poor spiritually and physically on account of our fear of God and are hiding from him. We are prisoners in a world where we have projected onto the face of God our broken vision of him. He becomes the God we hide from and of whom we are afraid. We are in a prison of our own making. We are the blind who cannot see for the looking at the one who has come among us. As C.S.Lewis puts it so graphically, in The Last Battle, the dwarfs in the stable, which in reality was the entry into the new Narnia and Aslan's presence, refused to open their eyes. Lewis says they were so afraid of being taken in that they could not be taken out. This typifies those who are spiritually blind to the truth. Adam and his wife wanted to have their eyes opened by Satan instead they were tricked into spiritual blindness. They had become oppressed in the darkness of their disobedience and unbelief. Paul said it this way,

> *"As for you, you were dead in your transgressions and sins, in which you used to live when you followed the ways of this world and of the ruler of the kingdom of the air, the spirit who is now at work in those who are disobedient. All of us also lived among them at one time, gratifying the cravings of our flesh and following its desires and thoughts. Like the rest, we were by nature deserving of wrath."* Ephesians 2:1-3

In reading the passage from Isaiah 61 in the synagogue in Nazareth that day, Jesus was declaring the work that the Father had given him to do. It was to proclaim this good news, the gospel of freedom from oppression and captivity and the opening of spiritual eyes. It was the year of the Lord's favour. By saying this was fulfilled in their hearing, he was leaving no doubt to anyone that he saw himself as the bringer of the good news, the liberator of the prisoners and the oppressed and the healer of the blind. He was actively living in the favour and blessing of his Father.

Whether James or any of Jesus family fully understood this at the time the words were said, is not known. However, the Holy Spirit, who was on Jesus as he said these words, was poured out on the church on the Day of Pentecost. Jesus had told his disciples that one of the works of the Holy Spirit would be to remind them of what he had said.

> *"The Holy Spirit, whom the Father will send in my name, will teach you all things and will remind you of everything I have said to you."* John 14:25

In the writing of the gospels and the memories of the eyewitnesses the Holy Spirit has been carefully reminding and orchestrating the truth that reveals the heart of the Father to us through the words and actions and life of his Son, Jesus.

THE FOURTH STORY TELLER

ANDREW
THE FIRST DISCIPLE

"I had grown up in Bethsaida on the shore of the lake of Galilee. My family had been there for years throughout all the troubles. There were many troubles too. One army after another passed through Galilee, burning and destroying as they went. My grandfather told me once, how virtually the whole town was burnt to the ground including all the fishing huts along the lake shore. He was out on the lake when it happened and he thinks that is what saved our two boats. He sailed along the shore and hid them in the reeds so at least we kept our boats.

That was long ago but our fishing business prospered over the years. By the time my father died we were doing reasonably well. My older brother Simon, was married and his mother in law lived in Capernaum a town a little further down the lake also. When my father died, the business naturally became Simon's to manage and I was the junior partner. That is the way with Simon. He was the loud one who was always speaking his mind often without thinking, which regularly got him into trouble. He had an opinion about everything and everyone. Simon made the decisions and not always the right ones. One of his decisions nearly lost us the business too and we only managed to save it by going into partnership with Zebedee and Sons who were already one of the more successful fishing businesses on the lake. They even employed people. They were based down in Capernaum and Simon relocated the business there and moved in with his wife's family. If I am honest my heart was not really in it after we moved.

I have a good friend who I had known for years. His name is Philip. We both grew up in Bethsaida. We did lots of things together over the years, we were like brothers. Philip told me one day that he had heard that a new prophet had started teaching down in Judea and we started hearing interesting stories about what he was saying. We both decided we wanted to hear what this new prophet had to say for ourselves so planned to go to find him. I told Simon. He was none too happy with me. That was not new. He accused me of abandoning him and leaving him in the lurch. I was always offending him it seemed. He would just have to get over it and forgive me.

So Philip and I set off for Judea working our way down the Jordan valley where the river flows out of the Lake. We soon started meeting others heading south. It seems that many were going to hear this man whose name was John son of Zechariah. They were calling him the baptiser. He was preaching a baptism of repentance for the forgiveness of sins. The words of Isaiah the prophet were being quoted by people in describing what he was saying. They said he was like a voice of one calling in the wilderness to prepare the way for the Lord.

Philip and I were amazed at what he was saying and after a few days we approached him and asked if we could become his disciples. He looked at us oddly and said we could.

John was an amazing and outstanding direct preacher. I imagine it was because he was a true prophet. One time he called the crowds coming out to be baptised by him a brood of vipers! He wanted to know who warned them to flee from the coming wrath? He challenged them to produce fruit in keeping with repentance. He warned them not to begin to say to themselves, 'We have Abraham as our father. ' He said that out of the stones God could raise up children for Abraham. The ax was already at the root of the trees, and every tree that did not produce good fruit would be cut down and thrown into the fire. That was really hot stuff and got everyones's attention.

People started calling out and asking him what they should do and he replied that anyone who had two shirts should share with the one who had none, and anyone who had food should do the same. That was not what they expected!

Even tax collectors came to be baptised. They asked him also what to do and he went straight to the point by telling them not to collect any more than they are required to. Philip and I think we recognised one of them. We were sure it was one of the local tax collectors from Capernaum. We were surprised to see him there. I think it was Matthew son of Alphaeus, but I can't be sure.

Then some soldiers asked John the same question. He told them not to extort money and not to accuse people falsely, but to be content with their pay. I've never come across a soldier who wasn't on the make somehow so I think they were very challenged by these statements.

The people were waiting expectantly and were all wondering in their hearts if John might possibly be the Messiah. Everyone was talking about it. John answered them all that he baptised with water, but one who was more powerful than he would come, the straps of whose sandals he was not worthy to untie. This one would baptise with the Holy Spirit and fire. His winnowing fork would be in his hand to clear his threshing floor and to gather the wheat into his barn, but he would burn up the chaff with unquenchable fire.

The next day Philip and I were with him again. Suddenly he saw a man coming towards us. This was Jesus from Nazareth. He been around for a few days and had even been baptised by John. I had missed that but someone told me afterwards they had seen him in the water and a pigeon or dove or something landed on him in the water, then they said there was a rumble of thunder even though there were no storm clouds. There was a lot of discussion among the people because some people said it sounded like someone speaking from heaven. We asked John about it and he smiled one of his enigmatic smiles and said it was God speaking to Jesus. He told us that his ministry and preaching were preparing the way for the coming of this man. He said the voice of God declared that this was his own beloved son and that the Father was very proud of him.

As we were listening to this, John saw Jesus passing by close to us. John said, "Look, the Lamb of God!" When we heard him say this, we looked at John and he seemed to know what we wanted to do, he smiled at us and just said, "Go on boys!"

So we followed along after Jesus. Turning around, Jesus saw us following and asked us what we wanted. I looked at Philip and said to Jesus, "Rabbi where are you staying?"

He just told us to come and see. So we went and saw where he was staying. It was about four in the afternoon and we spent the rest of the day with him. That was the first day of the rest of my life! I have never been the same since.

A few days later I went back to Galilee. Philip stayed on for a few more days. Sometime later Jesus also went off somewhere. We didn't hear or see him for about a couple of months. When I returned from my visit I went straight to find my brother Simon in Capernaum who was staying at his mother in law's house. I told him that Philip and I had found the Messiah. He didn't comment at the time, I think he thought I was a bit crazy.

I eventually heard that Jesus was back in Nazareth and had been at a wedding in Cana where it was rumoured he had done something extraordinary and had saved the day when the wine ran out. I heard this from our business partners the Bar Zebedee brothers, James and John. They turned out to be Jesus' first cousins. John told me that Jesus had turned several jars of water into the most wonderful wine. He was very impressed. I told him about meeting him down in Judea and that I thought he might be the Messiah we had all been waiting for.

Well, when I heard that Jesus was back in the area and what had happened at Cana I told Simon. Then to my great surprise I bumped into Jesus that day in town. He was very pleased to see me and I asked him if he would come and meet my brother. I went off and found Simon and told him again I had found the Messiah. This time I asked him to come and meet him. Surprisingly, Simon agreed to, so I brought him to Jesus.

Jesus looked at him and said, "You are Simon son of John. You will be called Peter!" For once Simon did not know what to say. He just looked at Jesus who was holding his gaze. I saw Simon's eyes all well up with tears. Then Simon turned away. Simon was very odd with me for the next couple of days. He didn't really want to talk much which was completely out of character.

Then a few days later, as Jesus was walking beside the Sea of Galilee, he saw me and my brother. We were casting a net into the lake, doing some fishing. He stood there on the shore and said to us, "Come, follow me, and I will send you out to fish for people."

We both looked at each other. I knew what I wanted to do. I looked at Simon and there was no question about it, he wanted it too. Almost without a second thought we left our nets and followed Jesus. After a while there was a small group of us that went around with Jesus. There was Simon and me, also the Bar Zebedee boys, also my friend Philip. He brought along another friend of his called Nathaniel. There were a few others and eventually there were twelve of us. People started calling us 'The Twelve'. We felt very important!

Not long after this we got news that John the baptiser, Jesus' relative, who had been arrested and imprisoned by King Herod Antipas had been executed. Jesus was very saddened and distressed by this news. So he decided to cross to the far shore of the Sea of Galilee because he wanted to be alone with us. A great crowd of people followed him because they saw the miracles he had been performing by healing the sick. They walked around the lake following where our boat had gone. We landed on the other side and then Jesus went up on a hillside and sat down with us, his disciples. I think this was not long before the Passover Festival that year. We were listening to him and talking and were quite engrossed. When Jesus looked up he saw a great crowd coming toward him. Then he asked Philip where we could buy bread for these people to eat. Poor Philip looked at me then said to Jesus, "It would take more than half a year's wages to buy enough bread for each one to have a just one mouthful!"

By now there was a huge crowd around us and I could see a young boy with his lunch so I went over to the boy to see if others had any food. I decided to take him to Jesus to see what he would do. I told Jesus I had found a boy with five small barley loaves and two small fish but that wouldn't go very far among so many.

Jesus told us to organise the people and get them to sit down. There was plenty of grass in that place, and so we started to but it wasn't very easy as there must have been many more than five thousand of them. Jesus then took the loaves that the boy had given him, and started to give thanks to God. Then he told us to distributed the food to those who were seated, and to give them as much as they wanted. He did the same with the fish. I was amazed at what happened. My heart was racing as I realised that the bread and fish was multiplying as we passed it around. All the people seemed to get some and they were all eating! I had some too, we all did. I was stuffed!

When everyone had enough to eat, Jesus told us to gather the pieces that were left over. So we gathered them and we each filled a whole basketful. There were twelve baskets of leftovers after everyone had eaten. This was astonishing! I had no idea where all the food had come from as there had only been a tiny amount to start with. Jesus had done something extraordinary and the small loaves and the fish had fed them all. After the people saw this miracle Jesus performed, they began saying that he was the Prophet who was to come into the world.

There was huge excitement and people were talking about making him a king, especially a king that would fill their empty bellies. Jesus, knowing that they were thinking about making him king by force, said he wanted to withdraw again to a mountain by himself. Jesus told us to get into the boat and go on ahead of him to Bethsaida, while he dismissed the crowd. After leaving them, he went up on a mountainside on his own to pray.

It was very late when we set out and there was a strong westerly wind blowing. Later that night, the boat was in the middle of the lake, and he was still alone on land. He must have seen we were straining at the oars, because the wind was against us. Shortly before dawn he came out to us, walking on the lake! He was about to pass by us. Some of us thought he was a ghost after all no one had ever walked on water! We began to shout and cry out, because we all saw him and were terrified. There was pandemonium in the boat.

Immediately he spoke to us and told us to take courage and not be afraid because it was really him. Then he climbed into the boat with us, and the wind died down. We were completely amazed. We had not understood about the loaves, now this. It was as if our hearts were hardened and we could not take in these miraculous events. As for our heads, we had never seen anything like this before.

When we had crossed over, we landed at Gennesaret and anchored there. As soon as we got out of the boat, people recognised Jesus. They ran throughout that whole region and carried the sick on mats to wherever they heard he was. Wherever he went, into villages, towns or countryside, they placed the sick in the marketplaces. They begged him to let them touch even the edge of his cloak, and all who touched it were healed. These were astonishing and remarkable days for all of us.

I had watched Jesus praying many times. He seemed to so enjoy praying to God. On one occasion Jesus was praying in a certain place on his own. We used to watch him from a distance. When he finished I asked him to teach us to pray, just as John had taught us when we had been his disciples. It was just for us. He didn't give it to just anyone. I was hoping that Jesus would give us one too. Jesus then said that when we prayed this is what we should say.

"Father, holy is your name, may your kingdom come. Give us each day our daily bread. Forgive us our sins, for we also forgive everyone who is indebted to us. Also keep us safe when we are tempted." We all use this prayer now and teach it to all the new followers of the Way. We have added a bit more to it but essentially it is exactly as he taught it to us.

One time we were down in Jerusalem for one of the festivals. There were some Greeks among those who went up to worship at the festival. They were Hellenistic Jews more like but they spoke Greek. They came to Philip, who was from Bethsaida in Galilee where quite a few people spoke Greek. They had a request which was to meet Jesus. Philip came to tell me. We talked about it together and decided we would tell Jesus. So we went to Jesus with their request.

Sometimes Jesus would say things that seemed totally unconnected to what was happening. This was one of those occasions. Jesus just said to us that the hour had come for the Son of Man to be glorified. He continued that unless a kernel of wheat falls to the ground and dies, it remains only a single seed. But if it dies, it produces many seeds. Then he said that anyone who loved their life will lose it, while anyone who hates their life in this world would keep it for eternal life. Then looking straight at us he said that whoever served him must follow him; and where he was, his servants would also be. His Father will honour the ones who served him.

Jesus seemed very serious and was deeply troubled. He looked up and prayed, 'Father, save me from this hour'? He paused and then seemed to relax and change his mind. Then he said, "No, it was for this very reason I came to this hour. Father, glorify your name!"

Suddenly we heard a voice that seemed to come from heaven itself. It said, "I have glorified it, and will glorify it again." There was a great consternation in the crowd. The Greeks particularly looked very shocked. Some in the crowd said it had thundered; others said an angel had spoken to him. Jesus turned to Philip and me and said to us that this voice was for our benefit, not his. He said that now was the time for judgment to come on this world and from now the prince of this world would be driven out. He then said that when he is lifted up from the earth, he will draw all people to him. Later, we realised that he had said this to show the kind of death he was going to die.

Someone in the crowd spoke up and asked him that they had heard from the Law that the Messiah will remain forever, so what did he mean by 'The Son of Man must be lifted up'? They wanted to know who this 'Son of Man' was. Then Jesus told us that we were going to have the light just a little while longer, therefore we needed to walk while we had the light, before darkness overtook us. He said whoever walks in the dark does not know where they are going so we needed to believe in the light while we had the light, so that we may become children of light. When he had finished speaking, Jesus left and hid himself from them. That was the last time he spoke to the crowds. After this he only spoke with us his disciples. A few days later we were all together to celebrate the Passover. He opened up to us things that we had not properly understood.

There were many other things that I saw and heard Jesus say. Others can add their version of those events. As for me, well, I ran away like the rest from the garden that night. I did not see him die but I know he died and I know he knew exactly how he would die. He was indeed lifted up from the earth on that cross. I was there too in the upper room when he came back on the first day of the week. I saw him on a number of occasions. It certainly was him, he was no ghost as some have suggested. He ate with us. I was there too when he went 'up'. It was difficult to describe it. He just sort of ascended through the air up into the clouds. He said he was going back to his Father.

I was there too when the Holy Spirit fell on us when we were back altogether in Jerusalem. After that well, that's another story."

ANDREW IN THE GOSPELS AND BEYOND

Apart from the few references to Andrew in the Gospels we do not know much of Andrew's life. The Gospels recount that Andrew was the brother of Simon Peter, by which it is inferred that he was also a son of John, or Jonah. He was born in the village of Bethsaida on the northern shore of the Sea of Galilee. Both he and his brother Simon Peter were fishermen by trade and according to Luke 5 were partners with James and John in their fishing business.

John, in his Gospel, states that Andrew was a disciple of John the Baptist whose testimony first led him, and another unnamed disciple of John the Baptist to follow Jesus. Andrew recognised Jesus as the Messiah and went to introduce him to his brother. Sometime later the two brothers were called to a closer relationship, and then they left their fishing business to follow Jesus.

In the Gospels, Andrew is referred to as being present on some important occasions as one of the disciples more closely attached to Jesus. Andrew told Jesus about the boy with the loaves and fishes (John 6:8), along with Philip he told Jesus about the Greeks seeking him, and was present at the last supper together with all the others. He is not listed personally but was present as one of the remaining eleven disciples of Jesus who meet him after the resurrection. He is included in the list of the disciples in Acts that were present when the Holy Spirit was poured out at Pentecost.

The fourth century Church Father, Eusebius, in his church history quotes Origen writing in the early third century, as saying Andrew preached in Scythia, Asia Minor and along the Black Sea as far as the Volga River in modern day Russia. Scythia is difficult to locate but may be in the area of modern day Ukraine. The Chronicle of Nestor, a tenth century manuscript that records the origins and conversion of the east Slavic peoples, adds that he preached along the Black Sea and the Dnieper River as far as Kiev in the Ukraine and from there he traveled to Novgorod. Hence he became a patron saint of Ukraine, Romania and Russia. According to other traditions, he founded the church of Byzantium (Constantinople) in AD 38, installing Stachys as leader or bishop. Stachys was Bishop of Byzantium from AD 38 to AD 54. He seemed to be closely connected to Andrew and Paul. This church would later develop into the Patriarchal See of Constantinople having Apostle Andrew as its Patron Saint. It was not clear if Stachys was the same person as the one Paul calls "dear" in his letter to the Romans. (Rom. 16:9).

According to Hippolytus of Rome (235AD) Andrew preached in Thrace, and his presence in Byzantium is also mentioned in the apocryphal Acts of Andrew written in the second century. Basil of Seleucia (d.458AD) also knew of Apostle Andrew's mission in Thrace, as well as Scythia and Achaea.

Andrew is said to have been martyred by crucifixion at the city of Patras in western Greece. Early texts, such as the Acts of Andrew known to Gregory of Tours (594AD) who described Andrew as bound, not nailed, to a Latin cross of the kind on which Jesus is said to have been crucified. A tradition developed that Andrew had been crucified on a cross called 'Crux Decussata', an X-shaped cross, or "saltire", now commonly known as a 'Saint Andrew's Cross'. This was supposedly at his own request, as he deemed himself unworthy to be crucified on the same type of cross as Jesus had been.

The church tradition of Georgia regards Andrew as the first preacher of Christianity in the territory of Georgia and as the founder of the Georgian church. This was adopted by the 10th-century Georgian ecclesiastics and, refurbished with more details, a version was inserted into the Georgian Chronicles. The story of Andrew's mission in the Georgian lands endowed the Georgian church with apostolic origin.

Cypriot tradition holds that a ship which was transporting Andrew went off course and ran aground on the island. Upon coming ashore, Andrew supposedly struck the rocks with his staff at which point a spring of healing waters gushed forth. Upon drinking, the sight of the ship's captain, who had been blind in one eye, was restored. Thereafter, the site became a place of pilgrimage and a fortified monastery stood there in the 12th century.

The official stance of the Romanian Orthodox Church is that Andrew preached the Gospel in the province of Dobruja that is Scythia Minor to the Daco-Romans, whom he is said to have converted to Christianity. There have been some ancient Christian symbols found carved in a cave in that area. According to George Alexandrou's research, Andrew spent twenty years in the Dacian territories preaching and teaching. Alexandrou also supposed that Andrews felt very close to the Dacians because they were monotheists. During that period Andrew traveled around the Danube territories and along the coast of the Black Sea, but mostly he stayed in and around his cave in Dobruja. St. Andrew's cave is still kept as a holy place.

All of this tradition is quite detailed and across a wide spectrum of places and ages. They all seem to indicate a strong association with the Black Sea coast of Romania and the Ukraine so there may be some foundation in facts for these traditions as the area of operation for the post Acts adventures of Andrew the fisherman.

THE FATHER EXPRESSES HIS PLEASURE AT THE FAITHFULNESS OF HIS BELOVED SON

Very early on Andrew began to see that Jesus was the promised Messiah. Whether he saw this in political terms rather than that of Jesus being the anointed one - the Christ - is difficult to say. He certainly recognised, as did the other early disciples, that Jesus was different from anyone else he had ever met. Andrew seemed to be a man who shared what he believed with others and was eager for them to meet Jesus. He introduced his brother Simon to Jesus. It was Andrew who as an act of faith brought the boy with his lunch bag to Jesus. It was also Andrew who brought a group of Greeks to meet Jesus.

In this incident recorded in John 12:23f, when Andrew brings Greeks to meet him, Jesus replies in an unusual way. It is in the last days of the week leading up to his arrest and crucifixion. His heart is heavy and he is preoccupied with his coming passion and sacrifice yet within this he reveals something else about the Father. Andrew is there and is a witness to this revelation. Jesus says,

> *"The hour has come for the Son of Man to be glorified. Very truly I tell you, unless a kernel of wheat falls to the ground and dies, it remains only a single seed. But if it dies, it produces many seeds. Anyone who loves their life will lose it, while anyone who hates their life in this world will keep it for eternal life. Whoever serves me must follow me; and where I am, my servant also will be. My Father will honour the one who serves me."* John 12:23-26

In this passage, Jesus is thinking of his own coming death and sacrifice. He describes this as his hour when he will be glorified. His own life would be given and fall like a seed into the ground that then is resurrected in order to bring forth many more seeds. Jesus is talking about not holding on to the love of this life, instead looking forward to the life to come where true glory resides. He is going to be glorified because the Father's beloved son has followed each step of the plan that will lead to the freeing of God's children from the clutches of Satan and the kingdom of darkness. To the Greeks hearing Jesus talk they may not have grasped the implications of these statements. Jesus is giving them a very clear path for them to follow if they are to know him and the one whom he is revealing. It is a statement about discipleship that is recorded in the synoptic gospels. To follow him is to come and die with him in order to receive the greater reward of enjoying the Father's glory.

Paul describes this transaction by which we are glorified and redeemed in Colossians,

> *"giving joyful thanks to the Father, who has qualified you to share in the inheritance of his holy people in the kingdom of light. For he has rescued us from the dominion of darkness and brought us into the kingdom of the Son he loves, in whom we have redemption, the forgiveness of sins."* Colossians 1:12-14

After this, Jesus addresses those around him and those closest to him, with these stark words.

> *"Now my soul is troubled, and what shall I say? 'Father, save me from this hour'? No, it was for this very reason I came to this hour. Father, glorify your name!"* John 12:27

In the agony of heart that was building up inside of him as he approached the climax of the week, his ministry and his life on earth, Jesus expresses to his Father the natural pain and dread that he was experiencing in his humanity. Humanly speaking, it was a cry similar to that expressed in the garden of Gethsemane. It was not that he was unwilling to go through the process rather it was the understandable dread of the process itself. Instead of avoiding the hours ahead he declares this is the very reason why he came and in this he wants to bring glory and honour to his Father. For Jesus, his every thought and action is to glorify the Father and reveal his heart and nature.

As he utters the words of submission and sonship a voice is heard coming from heaven. The crowd that heard it said it had thundered;

others said an angel had spoken to him. It was the voice of his Father speaking audibly for the third time directly to his Son. The first time in his baptism in the Jordan at the commencement of his public ministry the Father speaks assuring his Son of his love and recognition of him. The second time was at the mount of transfiguration when he speaks again, affirming his love and calling his disciples to listen to him. Now on this last occasion the Father speaks to his son before the hours of his greatest trial and agony. The Father says to Jesus,

"I have glorified it, and will glorify it again." John 12:28

The Father is saying to Jesus that all that he has done so far in his ministry had brought glory to the Father. The life of the son and the Father are so intertwined, so one, that together glory and honour have been accruing to them. It is as if the Father is saying that in his work and life, as the Father's beloved Son, his name has already been glorified in him, and now in his approaching sacrificial agony in which he will complete his work as priest and King, and the author of eternal salvation, "I will glorify it again."

Jesus' whole life was committed not to draw attention to himself but to reveal his Father and to glorify him. John 4:34 states that Jesus came to, *"do the will of him who sent me and to finish his work."* And again in John 5:1, *"I tell you the truth, the Son can do nothing by himself, he can do only what he sees his Father doing."*

Through his life, Jesus glorified his Father by living obediently to the Father's will. In this passage, Jesus first explains that he must go to death to bear the fruit of his ministry. He does so because this is the request of his Father, and he will obey his Father.

After Jesus declares to the Father, 'glorify your name', the Father responded that he has glorified his name, meaning the name of the Father has been glorified in the obedient life of Jesus, and the Father says he will glorify it again in the death of Jesus. In fact, the ultimate evidence of obedience in Jesus' life was his obedience to go to his death willingly, even to the point of death on a cross as Paul says in Philippians 2:8-10.

So Jesus glorified the Father's name in his obedient life, and he was about to glorify God's name again in his obedient death.

John Piper said this of this passage,

> *"And what makes this such good news especially in the Gospel of John is that the glory of God is full of grace and truth. "And the Word became flesh and dwelt among us, and we have seen his glory, glory as of the only Son from the Father, full of grace and truth" John 1:14. The most glorious thing about God is that he is so completely, fully self-sufficient that the glory of the fullness of his being overflows in truth and grace for his creatures. He doesn't need us. And therefore in his fullness he overflows for us." Desiring God: Meditations of a Christian Hedonist,* Multnomah, 1996; 3rd edition, 2003

THE FIFTH STORY TELLER

THE WOMAN
JESUS MET AT THE WELL

"I can't honestly say I like the Jews. They always looked down on us Samaritans because we weren't pure bloods as they are. We worship the same Lord God as them but we are despised by them nonetheless. They are a funny lot those Jews. Anyway, that's not the point. On that particular day I was heading off to the well to fetch water for the day. I usually avoided going earlier in the day because that is when most of the women from Sychar, that's the name of our village, go to draw water. I knew them all of course, well most of them and they are a nasty bunch. At least they are with me. It's because I knew their husbands better! Yes that is what I said, that's how it was in those days for me. It was just easier and less hassle going to the well when the women from the village had all finished and gone home. That way at least I didn't have to put up with their cheap comments. The disadvantage was that it was mid day, boiling hot and there wasn't much shade but there weren't many people around. Just occasionally it was handy for making appointments for the evening if a man came by. You know what I mean.

I can't honestly say I like men either. I've known a few in my time.

The Fifth Story Teller

Technically I've been married to five over the years. Each time it all ended badly. I got put away, divorced by them. I, of course being a mere woman cannot divorce them. Some of them only married me for sex. With one or two it was different but their families got involved and I was viewed as damaged goods by them. Sometimes it is the women that are the nastiest. Imagine having five mothers-in-law! If you think having had five husbands is hard, you should think about going to the well in the morning and meeting five ex mothers-in-law and the occasional new wife of an ex husband. I used to say to myself that I was hard as nails. I wasn't really. Sometimes I longed to get away.

On that particular day I was heading off to the well as usual about noon. It's a very old well. They say it was dug by our ancestor Jacob, hundreds and hundreds of years ago. As I got nearer to the well I passed a whole group of Jewish men on the road into town. This often happened as sometimes Jewish travellers stopped in at Sychar on their way going to and from Galilee to Jerusalem. It is not usually the very religious ones, they tend to avoid passing through Samaria in case they became ritually unclean by being contaminated by us. Well, this group, there must have been about a dozen of them, they were mostly young and some of them were very good looking too. I wondered if this might mean extra business that evening. In those days I needed to make a living. That is of course before I had met him.

I kept looking over my shoulder, as you do, to see if any of them were interested in stopping for a chat. So I hadn't noticed that there was another one sitting down by the well. It was about noon. He made me jump as I hadn't expected to meet anyone there. He looked very tired. I guess he must have been about thirty. My first thought was this could mean work for me later so I put the water jar down and tidied up my hair.

Then to my surprise he asked me for a drink. My first thought was that this would definitely be a possibility of work. I thought I'd play and tease a bit to see what he wanted, so I said to him, "You are a Jew and I am a Samaritan woman. How can you ask me for a drink? He answered me, "If you knew the gift of God and who it is that asks you for a drink, you would have asked him and he would have given you living water." Now that was not what I was expecting. There was nothing slimy or salacious in the way he spoke to me. It really surprised me and took me off guard.

I thought for a minute and wondered if he knew somewhere I could get water that meant I wouldn't have to keep coming to this well. Then I noticed he didn't have anything to draw water with so I thought this must be a new chat up line. I decided to play along for a bit. "Sir," I said, "you have nothing to draw with and the well is deep. Where can you get this living water? Are you greater than our father Jacob, who gave us the well and drank from it himself, as did also his sons and his livestock?"

He answered me in a way that I did not expect at all. He said that everyone who drinks this water would be thirsty again, but whoever drinks the water which he will give them will never be thirsty. He insisted that the water he gives will become in them a spring of water welling up to eternal life. I was very confused by these things and I felt very flustered. I just blurted out and said to him, "Sir, give me this water so that I won't get thirsty and have to keep coming here to draw water." I know it sounds silly but I really thought that he had some magical water or something that meant I would not have to keep coming to the well.

Then he said this to me, "Go, call your husband and come back." Suddenly I felt very odd and I know I blushed deeply. I don't usually do that, well not back then. There was very little that made me blush.

He was looking straight at me. I am used to being looked at by men but nobody had ever looked at me like this before. There was a purity in his eyes that I had never seen in a man. I paused and looked down at the ground and told him I had no husband.

This man, who of course was Jesus of Nazareth, said to me, "You are right when you say you have no husband. The fact is, you have had five husbands, and the man you now have is not your husband. What you have just said is quite true."

I just didn't know what to say. I looked back at him and he was still holding me with his eyes. He was smiling and there was no judgment in them. I felt something, I thought it might have been pity, but it wasn't, it was love. Not the usual love I knew about or rather what passed off as love in my world. No, this man really loved me. I was confused and a little frightened at the same time. I also felt very embarrassed that he had seen through me and was so accurate with it. How did he know I had been "married" five times? Not that they were anything like real marriages. I thought perhaps he was a seer or something like that and I wanted to change the subject as it was getting far too personal. I paused, and wondered how can I get him to stop talking about my life? As he was a Jew I thought I would get him on his favourite topic, religion! So told him I thought he was a prophet and said that our ancestors worshiped on Mount Gerizim, but that the Jews claim that the place to worship is in Jerusalem.

He looked at me and said, "Believe me woman, a time is coming when you will worship the Father neither on this mountain nor in Jerusalem. You Samaritans worship what you do not know. We worship what we do know, for salvation is from the Jews. Yet a time is coming and has now come when the true worshipers will worship the Father in the Spirit and in truth, for they are the kind of worshipers the Father seeks. God is spirit, and his worshipers must worship in the Spirit and in truth." I had never heard anyone called God Father before. I wondered how he knew these things. Then a thought struck me. I said to him, "I know that Messiah is coming. When he comes, he will explain everything to us."

Jesus looked straight at me and said, "I, the one speaking to you, that's who I am!"

Just then his friends returned and were surprised to find him talking with me, a woman. Their faces were a picture! None of them asked me what I wanted nor did they ask him why he was talking to me.

I could not believe what he had just said to me. He had just said he was the Messiah! He had seen into my heart, he knew all about me and my life. My heart was racing within me. This day changed my life forever. I had to go back to the village. I had to tell them who was here in our village! So I just went. I forgot all about my water jar and went back to the town. I didn't know what to say but when I got into the centre of the village I said to the people, "Come, see a man who told me everything I ever did. Could this be the Messiah?" Some of them probably thought I had been drinking cheap wine but most of them saw my face and they knew I was absolutely serious. A number of them came out of the town and made their way toward the well were Jesus was. When I got back to the well I heard his disciples urging him to eat something.

He told them he had food to eat that they knew nothing about. They looked at each other and asked if someone had brought him food They looked at me thinking I had given him food. He then said to them that his food was to do the will of the one who sent him and to finish his work. He reminded them of the saying that it is still four months until harvest. Then he said, "Open your eyes and look at the fields! They are ripe for harvest. Even now the one who reaps draws a wage and harvests a crop for eternal life, so that the sower and the reaper may be glad together. Thus the saying 'One sows and another reaps' is true. I sent you to reap what you have not worked for. Others have done the hard work, and you have reaped the benefits of their labour."

There was quite a crowd of us at the well by that point. People were hanging on every word he said. You could say we were a harvest just waiting for this man. From that day many of us Samaritans from the town believed in him because of my testimony. We urged him to stay with us, and he stayed two days and because of his words many more became believers. They said to me, "We no longer believe just because of what you said. No! Now we have heard for ourselves, and we know that this man really is the Saviour of the world." They couldn't resist having a poke at me even in that!

My name? Oh you don't need to know my name, I was the woman at the well!"

PHOTINA, A TRUE LIGHT

Lots of people have wondered what her name was. Needless to say there are traditions. According to Greek tradition, her name was Photina which means Little Light. She was reputed to have been deeply moved by the experience and she began to preach the Gospel. As a result she was imprisoned, and was finally martyred at Carthage, which is a very long way from Samaria. Another tradition states that Photina was put to death in Rome after bringing the daughter of the Emperor Nero to faith along with one hundred of her servants. In this story she supposedly was martyred in Rome with her sons Joseph and Victor, along with several other Christians during the persecution of Christians initiated by Nero after the burning of Rome. She was included in the Roman list of martyrs owing to the widely held view that the head of Photina was preserved in the church of St. Paul's Outside the Walls, in Rome.

Whatever the truth, one thing is for sure, she told someone, most probably the writer of the fourth Gospel, the content of her conversation at the well with Jesus.

If someone wanted to travel from Jerusalem in the south to Galilee in the north, by the quickest route, the road taken would go through the area known as Samaria. This was the route taken by Jesus and his disciples on one occasion. They would have stopped, tired and thirsty by Jacob's Well, about a half mile away from the village of Sychar. Jesus' disciples went to the village to buy food while he sat down by the well. It was about noon, the hottest part of the day, and a Samaritan woman came to the well at this inconvenient time, to draw water.

Samaria was a non Jewish region surrounded by Jewish settlements and lands. The land had been settled after the fall of the Northern Kingdom of Israel when the Assyrians conquered the land. They replaced the dispersed Israelites with non Jews from other lands. 2 Kings 17:23f. These heathen intermarried with the remaining Israelites resulting in a nation of half-breeds, a most distasteful and evil thing for a devout Jew. Worse yet, the true religion of Israel became intermingled with heathen idolatry.

After the fall of the Southern Kingdom of Judah to the Babylonians, the Samaritans remained in the area. When the returning Jewish exiles set out to rebuild the temple and Jerusalem, the Samaritans offered to help them and were summarily refused. In about 400 BC, the Samaritans constructed their own rival temple on Mount Gerizim. At the end of the second century BC this temple was destroyed by John Hyrcanus, the Hasmonean ruler of Judea. This greatly increased hostilities between the Jews and the Samaritans.

The Samaritans professed to believe in the God of Israel and awaited the coming of Messiah. They accepted the first five books of the Law, but rejected the rest of the Old Testament Scriptures. Wherever they found it necessary to justify their religion and their place of worship, they modified the Law. The relationship between the Jews and the Samaritans was definitely strained.

In his encounter with the woman at the well, Jesus broke three Jewish customs. First, he spoke to a woman. Then second, she was a Samaritan woman, a group the Jews traditionally despised and third, he asked her to get him a drink of water, which would have made him ceremonially unclean from using her cup or jar. Not surprisingly, this shocked the woman at the well.

In the course of the conversation Jesus enigmatically told the woman he could give her living water so that she would never thirst again. Jesus meant eternal life by this, the gift that would satisfy her soul's desire was only available through him. At first, the Samaritan woman did not understand Jesus' meaning at all.

Although they had never met before, Jesus asked her to call her husband but he knew she had had five husbands and was now living with a man who was not her husband. Jesus now had her attention! To change the subject the woman tries to divert Jesus by discussing worship. As they talked about their two views on worship, the woman voiced her belief that Messiah was coming. Jesus answered by saying that was who he was.

As the woman began to grasp the reality of her encounter with Jesus, the disciples returned. They were equally shocked to find him speaking to a woman. Leaving behind her water jar, the woman returned to town, inviting the people to *"Come, see a man who told me all that I ever did."*

Meanwhile, Jesus told his disciples the harvest of souls was ready, sown by the prophets, writers of the Old Testament, and John the Baptist. Excited by what the woman had told them, the Samaritans came from the village and implored Jesus to stay with them.

So Jesus stayed two days, teaching the Samaritan people about the realm of the Father's love, the Kingdom of God. Whatever the opinion the locals had of this woman, she had been on the receiving end of some bad attitudes and behaviour by men. In the culture of the first century, husbands divorced their wives, but wives did not divorce their husbands. If this woman was married and divorced five times, it was because five men had divorced her. I have wondered how she thought about herself. And the man she was now living with was not her husband. She wasn't even married when she met Jesus, but just living with a man, perhaps another woman's husband. This woman has certainly been passed around by some of the male population of Sychar. Perhaps she was a prostitute, or perhaps she had just been used and abused. Jesus' words not only call the woman's attention to her sins but they call our attention to the sins of the men of that city.

John does not tell us the disciples are shocked to find Jesus talking to this Samaritan woman because she is a Samaritan, or because she is sinful, they actually don't know this. They are surprised to see him talking with her because she is a woman! There may be a race issue here, but there is certainly a gender issue. The Jews were inclined to hold a very demeaning view of women and the disciples seem to share this view.

THE FATHER IS SEEKING WORSHIPERS IN THE SPIRIT

The conversation between Jesus and the woman has many facets and one that is easily over- looked is that during their discussion of worship. Jesus says,

> *"Woman, believe me, a time is coming when you will worship the Father neither on this mountain nor in Jerusalem. You Samaritans worship what you do not know; we worship what we do know, for salvation is from the Jews. Yet a time is coming and has now come when the true worshipers will worship the Father in the Spirit and in truth, for they are the kind of worshipers the Father seeks. God is spirit, and his worshipers must worship in the Spirit and in truth."*
> John 4:21-24

Three times in this passage Jesus explicitly links the Father to worship. He foresees a time when worship of the Father will not be focused in a geographical locality either on Mt Gerizim or in Jerusalem. Jesus is saying this some forty years before the fall of Jerusalem in 70 AD and the burning of the Temple by Titus' troops. More to the point, he was disconnecting the worship of God the Father from one specific cultural or religious context. The worship of the Father would not be the special preserve of the Jews but for all those who would meet him in the Spirit and in truth. He is referring to the new community of those who would be filled with the Spirit of the Father. He goes one step further and says that the Father is seeking that sort of worshiper and that quality of true worship.

For many today, worship is a major part of Christian life and devotion. In many places this has been interpreted to be a passive activity, where "worshipers" watch and observe a group of professional, musically gifted people, who are leading worship from the front of a church or on a stage. Audience or congregational participation has been reduced to little more than the occasional sing-a-long to some catchy tunes, arm waving or clapping in time with the rhythm of the tune, or the adoption of a somewhat mystical, far away look, that seems to locate God somewhere up in the rafters. Invitations are issued to come and worship Jesus, who, in many places is the focus and object of the worship. This style of worship is widespread across the charismatic world. In some places there is enthusiastic congregational participation. I have witnessed an African expression of this where worshipers are called to a frenzied, almost hysterical fever pitch. There was a high emphasis on participants entering a trance like state. This was engendered by the rhythm, volume and screamed demands of participation by the worship leader. Many worship songs being sung today have an absence of biblical content and seem to be very self centred rather than God centred. The lyrics often consist of a pleading, like desperate orphans for God to come and do something. There is often a cry coming from our brokenness and need to be helped rather than from a heart that worships the Father, or from a place of being in the Spirit.

I once picked up a leaflet produced by a church styling itself "The Worship Centre". In the leaflet we were invited to come and, "Worship the Lord in spirit and truth." It misquoted John 4:23. The invitation was to worship the Lord not the Father and the worship was to be offered in spirit rather than 'The Spirit'. This is not just splitting hairs. Obviously the Lord refers to God but this seemed to not only typify the somewhat careless disregard for accuracy as far as the scriptures are concerned but also to be missing a fairly major point about the place of the Spirit.

So much of worship today is, at best, Jesus only focused and at worst, man centred and all about our feelings, our needs and includes a lot of unbelief and poor theology. Jesus, in these words to the woman at the well, was specifically saying that the focus of worship is to be the Father, his Father and that it would be in the power of his Spirit. This seems to be a more full and rounded expression of Trinitarian worship than what many are experiencing today. In these words the Son is calling for worship of the Father in the Spirit. This, Jesus says, is true worship.

We have a long way to go to get this revelation back into our hearts.

THE SIXTH STORY TELLER

SIMON
THE TERRORIST

"I hated the Romans. We all did. There were a few of us who said they had to be stopped after what they had done to our people. I remember when I was just a young boy maybe I was only about ten when it happened. What you may ask! I'll tell you about it. I didn't know what was going on the country in those days. We were only children. There was some sort of power struggle going on between Herod the King of Judea and the Romans. King Aretas of Arabia who has his capital in Petra across the Jordan was also involved. He was always looking for an opportunity to get favour with the Romans and hated the Jews. It made for dangerous times.

I was born in Galilee and lived in Cana. I had relatives in Sepphoris and some of the other towns. As tension mounted in the land we knew that we would be drawn into the conflict. When it began we had no idea how terrible it would be. There were Roman legions based up north in Syria and also in Judea. We Galileans were caught between them. Eventually troubles began and before we knew it there was fighting all over Galilee. Sepphoris became a centre of resistance but it was pointless as we were no match for the Romans or their allies, Aretas' troops from Arabia. I remember my parents waking us all up in the night and we went into the caves in the hills to hide. From the cave mouth we could see a glow in the sky in the direction of Sepphoris. We knew it was burning. My parents worried all night and my mother cried, she had many relatives in Sepphoris.

As soon as it was light my father decided to go with some others of the men to see if they could help anyone. I was not allowed to go and was told to look after my mother and sisters. However, I followed from a distance. I so wanted to be with my father. I kept well back away from him and the other men. I climbed to a small hill where I could get a view of what was happening. What I saw shocked me. The whole city was smouldering in ruins. A large contingent of Romans and Arabians were in the vicinity and to my horror I saw that they had captured my father and the other men who had come to see what had happened.

I saw groups of women and children bound and chained together. They were clearly going to be sold as slaves. Many of the soldiers were doing terrible things to the younger women. Things I did not understand as a child. I know now of course, it is what soldiers always do to women when they get a chance. As I watched something too terrible to describe happened. I saw them take my father and many of the other men and they forced them to make crosses and as I watched one by one they nailed them to the crosses. I was paralysed by the horror and the shock of it. I felt powerless and hid in the rocks in the hills. I did nothing. I just shook and cried. As night fell again I heard the agonising cries of the men who had been crucified. I heard women's screams and cries. I still hid and did nothing. I was so terrified and traumatised. As light came again I decided to go back home. It was very hard because the Romans and their allies were on the roads. Crowds of bound people were being marched away down the valley to the coast. Sepphoris was no more. The crosses were everywhere.

It was a scene I have never been able to forget. I hated the Romans and everything they stood for. As a young boy I made a vow that I would do everything I could to get the Romans out of Galilee. I decided I would kill any Roman that I could as soon as I got the chance.

Mercifully my home was not attacked and I could never tell my mother what I had seen. She knew that my father was dead. She eventually went with some other women and found his body. They were forbidden to take the bodies down but she stayed there, waiting. Waiting until the Romans left. Then eventually she took his remains and we buried him. I renewed my vow that I would one day get my revenge on those Romans.

When I grew older I found a number of friends who shared my hatred of the occupiers. One day we had contact with some older young men who started to talk to us. They quickly realised how much I hated the Romans and one of them took me aside and told me there was a way to get back at them. That was the beginning of it. I became a Zealot. Not that we called ourselves this in those days. We were just a group of young men who wanted our revenge. We knew that there were no good Romans and the only good Roman was a dead Roman. We started to practice using a knife. When I was asked by my mother to slaughter a kid or lamb for a meal I willingly agreed. I relished the chance of slitting the animal's throat. It was good practice.

Eventually, we boys joined up with a number of others who hated the Romans. Finally the day came when we had an opportunity to put our desires into practice. A small unit of Romans passed through the area and made camp one night along the main road. We were instructed to slip into the camp at night and to use the knife on the first Roman we found. This was to prove that we meant what we said. I was terrified and exhilarated at the same time. I agreed to go with two other boys. We slipped into the camp. I crawled along the ground to where the handful of Romans were sleeping. Their sentries were dozing as we managed to get into the camp. I found myself within a few paces of a sleeping soldier. The knife in my hand was slick with my sweat. My heart was pounding inside my chest. Suddenly one of the guards spotted us. All three of us made a run for it. I was the fastest and got away into the night but one of my friends stumbled and got caught. When we stopped at the top of the hill we could hear him screaming. Long high pitched screams that pierced the night. I renewed my vow. One day I would get one.

The problem with killing Romans was that for every one we killed they would kill five Jews. Soon even our own people hated us and did not want us to kill Romans. Instead we turned our attention to those who worked for the Romans. Jews who had sold themselves for money to work for the Romans. There were plenty of them too. Every tax collector in Galilee collected for the Romans, taking their cut of our money for themselves. I hated them too. We caught one once down a dark alley in the back streets of Tiberius down on the Lake. He didn't scream - we wouldn't let him. It felt good, but the pain never went away inside me. It just festered like a putrid wound in my heart.

When I became a grown man I was less active in the cause. In fact all over Galilee things had quietened down and there was a grudging co-existence between the Romans and their cronies and the people in general. I ended up just being a Zealot in my heart. I still hated Rome and everything it stood for. As I got older the pain did not get less, it never went away, ever.

One day I met Jesus of Nazareth. I had heard of him of course. Everyone had. They even said there was something peculiar about him. He was known as Joseph the carpenter's son, or that was the official line anyway. Some people whispered and said his mother had been raped as a girl by a Roman soldier and this Jesus was the result. Well, that story went around for years. Long after we knew better, the Jews used to say that about him to discredit him.

I don't really remember how I joined up with him. I think I just met him one day and he said I should follow him. So I did. Just like that. I don't know why. There was something so wonderful about being with him that I couldn't describe back then. I know now of course but I was so wounded and broken then. He was like a father to me even though we were about the same age. I felt when I was with him that that I was safe and he somehow understood the pain in my heart. Not that it was always easy.

I remember Jesus teaching one day when looking right at me he said, "You have heard that it was said, 'An eye for an eye and a tooth for a tooth.' But I say to you, Do not resist the one who is evil. Rather if anyone slaps you on the right cheek, turn to him the other also. Also if anyone would sue you and take your tunic, let him have your cloak as well. And if anyone forces you to go one mile, go with him two miles." That really got to me because we all knew that a Roman soldier could force you to carry his bags and you just had to do it. Here was Jesus telling us to carry those bastards bags twice as far. Inside I was screaming. I would rather kill him than do that.

Jesus knew it too.

One day the unbelievable happened, Jesus saw a man named Matthew sitting at the tax collector's booth. Jesus went up to him and asked him to follow him. Matthew got up and followed him. I couldn't believe Jesus would do that. Then to crown it all, this Matthew invited Jesus and us all to go to his house for dinner. I was all for sticking a knife in his back, not in his food. I refused to go in. I wouldn't do it, I couldn't. The house was full of Matthew's fat cat friends and neighbours including many tax collectors and sinners. Then to make matters worse a group of those smarmy religious Pharisees turned up and saw this. They asked me, because I was one of his disciples and happened to be outside sulking, why Jesus was eating with tax collectors and sinners?

Jesus came out just at that moment and overheard this and said to them that it was not the healthy who needed a doctor, but the sick. He then told them to go and learn what it means to desire mercy, not sacrifice. He said he had not come to call the righteous, but sinners. He said this to the Pharisees but as he turned back he looked right at me and smiled. He knew exactly what was going on.

Sometime later I remember walking along the road and I felt Jesus draw alongside me. He put his arm around my shoulder and I felt his comforting support. I was thinking about my father and the Romans. He didn't condemn me or judge me. He talked about forgiving people from the heart. It had come up earlier in the day. There had been some sort of altercation going on between Andrew and Simon Peter. These two brothers were arguing and Simon was holding forth about something that Andrew was supposed to have done and how he had magnanimously forgiven him. Then Peter turned to Jesus and asked him how many times he should forgive his brother or sister. As many as seven times? Jesus looked straight at Simon and said to him not seven times, but seventy-seven times! That rather took the wind out of Peter's sail! Then Jesus started to tell us one of his stories.

This one was all about a king who wanted to settle accounts with his servants. As he began the settlement, a man who owed him ten thousand bags of gold was brought to him. Since he was not able to pay, the master ordered that he and his wife and his children and all that he had be sold to repay the debt. At this the servant fell on his knees before him and begged him to be patient with him and he would pay back everything. The servant's master took pity on him, canceled the debt and let him go.

Jesus went on to say that then the servant went out and found one of his fellow servants who owed him a hundred silver coins. He grabbed him by the throat and began to choke him demanding that he pay back what he owed him. His fellow servant fell to his knees and begged him to be patient with him and he would pay it back. He refused and instead went off and had the man thrown into prison until he could pay the debt. When the other servants saw what had happened, they were outraged and went and told their master everything that had happened.

Jesus went on to describe the reaction of the master when he called the servant in. He was furious and called him a wicked servant. The King said that he had canceled all that debt because he begged him to. He told the servant that he should have had mercy on his fellow servant just as the king had on him. In anger the king handed him over to the jailers to be tortured, until he should pay back all he owed. That was quite some story.

We were all very quiet by now. Inside, my heart was pounding. Then Jesus got very serious with us all and told us that this is how his heavenly Father will treat each of us unless we forgave our brother from our heart.

I thought about the Romans. They were not my brother so this did not mean me. Jesus looked at me in his usual way as if he knew exactly what I was thinking. I knew that I needed to let go of those Romans who had killed my father. I had them by the throat. I so wanted to squeeze the life out of them. Yet the one who was suffering the most was me. I was in a prison of my own making. I was torturing myself.

That day something changed inside of me. Did I forgive the Romans? Indeed I did with his help."

SIMON THE ZEALOT AFTER THE GOSPELS

Much of what I have written about Simon the Zealot has been assumptions and musings. I have imagined what his background would have been. The only references to him are the mention of his name in the various lists of the disciples. What has always interested me has been his description as a Zealot. I have made more assumptions in his story than any of the others in this book and they are based on speculation and imagination. Within that I am conscious that the Spirit takes our thoughts and uses them to teach also.

I have started from the basis that he was a Zealot which means he was a member of the group of people who emerged in the first century Israel to resist the Romans. Not all have done that. For example the Eastern Orthodox Church tradition holds that it was Simon's wedding that Christ and his disciples attended in Cana of Galilee in which Christ turned water in six stone jars to wine. He is called zealot because in seeing this miracle, Simon left his home, his parents and his bride and followed Christ. In later tradition, Simon is often associated with Jude the younger brother of Jesus as an evangelising team. In Western Christianity, they share their feast day on 28 October. The most widespread tradition is that after evangelising in Egypt, Simon joined Jude in Persia and Armenia or Lebanon where both were martyred in 65 AD. Christian Ethiopian tradition claims that he was crucified in Samaria. Another tradition says he visited Britain. Another, doubtless inspired by his title "the Zealot" states that he was involved in the Jewish revolt against the Romans which was brutally suppressed and ended up with the sack of Jerusalem and the destruction of the temple.

Simon, like the other Apostles, is regarded as a saint by the Roman Catholic and Eastern Orthodox Churches, and the Anglican and Lutheran Churches.

The Zealots were a sect of Jews which originated with Judas the Gaulonite. They refused to pay tribute to the Romans, on the grounds that this was a violation of the principle that God was the only king of Israel. They rebelled against the Romans, but were soon scattered, and became a lawless band of mere brigands. One particularly extreme group of Zealots was also known in Latin as Sicarii meaning "violent men" or "dagger men" because of their policy of killing Jews opposed to their call for war against Rome. Probably many Zealots were also Sicarii.

According to historian H.H. Ben-Sasson, the Sicarii, originally based in Galilee were fighting for a social revolution, while the Jerusalem Zealots placed less stress on the social aspect.

In my imaginings about Simon the Zealot I have wondered what had led him to become a Zealot. In modern cultures young men who have grown up in occupied countries often become freedom fighters because of some traumatic event they have experienced. They are freedom fighters to their own people but terrorists to the oppressors.

Josephus recounts an event that happened to the city of Sepphoris in Galilee which was about ten miles north of Nazareth. This would have occurred during the infancy or childhood of Jesus and his disciples.

> *"As soon as Varus (the Roman General) was informed of the state of Judea by Sabinus's writing to him, he was afraid for the legions he had left there;... sent them upon an expedition into Galilee, made an attack upon the enemy, and put them to flight, and took Sepphoris, and made its inhabitants slaves and burnt the city. Upon this, Varus sent a part of his army into the country, to seek out those that had been the authors of the revolt; and when they were discovered, he punished some of them that were most guilty, and some he dismissed:*

now the number of those that were crucified on this account were two thousand." Antiquities. 17.10.9

I have drawn on all this background to reconstruct the life and times of Simon the Zealot. The Roman occupiers were brutal in all their occupied lands. Israel and the Jews suffered no worse than any other.

In the light of all this, Jesus teaching on forgiveness would have been extremely pertinent to all the disciples but particularly to a Zealot who most likely had issues with the Romans!

JESUS TEACHES THAT THE FATHER'S LOVE ENABLES US TO FORGIVE FROM THE HEART

Jesus taught and modelled forgiveness to his disciples. Even hanging on the cross he was forgiving those who had perpetrated his suffering. In this parable of Jesus, that is recounted in Matthew 18:21-35, he explores the issue of real forgiveness that comes from the heart not just as an act of the will.

Many have been taught that forgiveness is a choice, an act of the will, even a gift that we give to others that they do not deserve. Yet in his teaching in the parable, Jesus teaches about forgiveness as an attitude of the heart, not of the will, indeed a gift of grace that cannot be earned.

Jesus told this parable in response to Peter's question about how many times he should forgive his brother. He tells it to the disciples which would have included Simon the Zealot. Simon of all people may well have had reason to not forgive. If the life that he lived was remotely impacted by the events that took place in Sepphoris that I have described, he most certainly would have struggled with the issue of forgiving the Romans. If he had been a Zealot, a freedom fighter, he more than likely would have had issues in his heart about forgiving the Romans for some of the atrocities they had committed. Atrocities that some would consider unforgivable.

The parable is divided into two parts. The first half describes the true nature of forgiveness. The king in the story is not God, but us. We have been sinned against and need to forgive. This is seen by the somewhat arbitrary and high handed way the king behaves. This is not Jesus describing his Father as some have thought, rather it is the person who needs to forgive who is represented by the king.

In this case the king decides to take an account of who owes him money. One servant is found who owes a ludicrously large amount of money. The king demands payment and of course the poor servant can't pay. Instead he is threatened with being sold, along with his family as a slave, in a feeble attempt to recompense the king. This is clearly not the way God deals with us. Jesus' Father graciously forgives and makes this forgiveness and grace freely available to all who believe and respond to his son.

In the story the king is demanding full payment. The point that Jesus is making is that we need to make an account of what we are owed in order to even begin the process of forgiveness. This does not trivialise the thing that has happened or what is owed. It spells it out. It makes it very clear. It says it was serious and it does matter. For Simon the Zealot and those who have been grievously sinned against, what has happened to them does matter and cannot be simply ignored. Some would say that the Christian response is to just let it go and choose to forgive. We must not be angry or hold a grudge so the tendency is to bury the pain and say it doesn't matter. That is not quite how Jesus sees it here. He is saying we need to look at it fully for what it was and recognise what we are owed, what we have had happen to us. Like the king we are to take an account. If we do not do this we have not taken account of what we are owed and what we need to forgive.

For some this is the key issue as to why forgiveness is so hard. It is as if the pain of looking at what has been taken or stolen or has happened to us, is not embraced. This makes real heart forgiveness so hard. For some, when memories or feelings are suppressed they cannot begin to let go of the issues or the person who has sinned against them or the perpetrators of the offence.

This is not keeping a record of other wrongs as that is the antithesis of love as Paul says in 1 Corinthians 13. Instead, as a step in bringing real heart forgiveness it is essential. This is not to hold on to it but in order to let it go. The King makes his accounts up and finds just how much the servant owes him. It is a huge amount.

The servant cannot pay him back, it is just too much. The full scale of the man's debt is recognised first and foremost by the king. The servant pleads for mercy and promises to pay it all back. This is ridiculous but it is what happens. We tend to think we can fix it. He has a plan to work off his debts but it is just too much. He cannot pay the king back. It is at this point that the king realises the true nature of the situation. The man cannot ever pay him back and then the king decides to forgive him the whole amount. It is an astonishing act by the king. Jesus is showing the nature of the way we have been forgiven by God but in particular how we are to forgive those who have sinned against us. That was the fundamental point of the story.

For Simon the Zealot, or any one of us who have been sinned against, it begins with taking an account. For some this can take the form of writing it down. This can be very painful. It is not saying that what has happened does not matter, instead it says this does matter. Then it is followed by the realisation that we can never be paid back for what has happened to us. We cannot change the past. It is then after our hearts have fully embraced the situation that mercy can begin to triumph over the judgment that is often in our hearts.

To forgive in the way the king does in the story is to cancel the debt. This is only possible when our hearts are free and we know exactly what we are owed. This is much more than just choosing to forgive, it is embracing the whole issue and cancelling the debt. It is saying to the person, "You owe me nothing because I have set you free."

This is the stunning revelation in this story that Jesus brings. His Father has counted the cost of what he is owed and has set all mankind free from the debt we owe him. He brings freedom and life to us and in return he expects us to forgive others in exactly the same way as we have been forgiven.

In the second part of the story Jesus explains what happens to us if we do not forgive from the heart. The forgiven servant goes straight out from the presence of the king and finds someone who owes him a trivial amount by comparison. Instead of forgiving in the way he was forgiven, he refuses to forgive and grabs the man by the throat and wants to have him thrown into prison.

The result is that the king, on finding out what has happened, has the unforgiving servant thrown into prison and handed over to the torturers. Then Jesus says this is how his Father would treat those who refuse to forgive from the heart! What does he mean by this? Is he saying that God will torture us if we are unforgiving of others? If that were the case, the whole of the gospel would depend on us and our ability to forgive rather than the grace of God. So what is he saying? What happens to our hearts if we do not forgive those who have sinned against us?

Going back to the story we see the answer. The point of the story is how many times must we forgive those who have sinned against us? It is not keeping a tally of the times we have forgiven but letting our hearts be free from the accumulation of unforgiveness. Having described true heart forgiveness in the first part of the story Jesus moves on to show what happens to our hearts when we do not forgive from the heart.

The servant demonstrates his unforgiveness by trying to choke the man, by taking him by the throat. It is a powerful image because it pictures what we often do to people that we do not forgive. It is as if we want to squeeze the life out of them in order for them to know just what they have done to us. It is as if we won't let them go and we hope that they in some way will feel the pain that we have felt. This often happens when we try to forgive because we are told that we should or ought to forgive, through gritted teeth and not from the heart. Ultimately, what happens is that the person we are demanding recompense from and want to see punished, is sometimes oblivious to this. Instead of them realising their guilt, we become consumed with bitterness and judgment because we will not forgive, or as we more often put it, can't forgive.

The torture is what happens in our hearts. We are stuck in the torture chamber of our own unforgiveness. Jesus says that is what happens to us when we refuse to forgive from our hearts. The Father cannot take us out of that place of pain and self torture as long as we are refusing to forgive from our hearts. We are locked into our own prison cells. Jesus is not saying that the Father tortures us. A loving Father would not and could not do that, but he has given us free will and will not force us to change. He waits even if we are locked into our own pain. He does all he can in wooing us with his love and speaking truth to us but he will not violate our free will. He does not force us to forgive, to love or respond to him.

For Simon the Zealot and those like him, indeed for all of us, the issue of heart forgiveness is crucial. Our sins are forgiven through Jesus' death on the cross. We are then called to forgive others in the same way that we have been forgiven, from our hearts. It is one of the major reasons why we struggle in our Christian lives and are not able to relate to God as a Father when we have not forgiven those who have sinned against us.

The question raised earlier was, did Simon the Zealot forgive the Romans from his heart, if he had things that he needed to forgive them for? The answer is unquestionably, he did. He is among those named as being in the Upper Room in Jerusalem when the Holy Spirit was poured out on the day of Pentecost. With the other disciples he took the gospel to the Roman world and beyond. If tradition is to be believed he evangelised, along with Jude, around the eastern end of the Mediterranean right in the heart of the Roman Empire. I would not be surprised to find that there were a number of Romans who became Christians because of the zeal of Simon the Apostle.

THE SEVENTH STORY TELLER

SIMON
THE PHARISEE

"I was rather proud of being a Pharisee. I know that may sound odd but most of us were really proud of our achievements or rather what we considered our achievements. Our main objective was to keep the Torah as best we could. We did not interpret it literally as the Sadducees did rather we interpreted it in such a way as to make it liveable. It was something we lived by every day. This meant there was a rule for everything. Every eventuality was covered. Nothing was left to personal interpretation. It was this that really brought us into conflict with Jesus. He seemed to interpret everything by a new law of love. It was so irritating and he had a way of seeing through our inconsistencies so quickly. Maybe it was this that drew me to him.

I remember one day Jesus was teaching, and some of us Pharisees and teachers of the law were sitting there listening. We had come from every village of Galilee and from Judea and Jerusalem. There were all these rumours circulating about healings but I had not witnessed any myself. As he spoke there was a commotion outside caused by some men who came carrying a paralysed man on a mat. They were trying to take him into the house to lay him before Jesus. When they could not find a way to do this because of the crowd, they went up on the roof and lowered him on his mat through the tiles into the middle of the crowd, right in front of Jesus. I can't imagine what the householder would have thought about the damage to his roof.

When Jesus saw this, he said to the man that his sins were forgiven. I was stunned by this statement. It was blasphemous as only God can forgive sins. It was as if Jesus knew exactly what we were thinking. He looked straight at me and asked, "Why are you thinking these things in your hearts? Which is easier to say, Your sins are forgiven, or to say, Get up and walk? Yet, I want you to know that the Son of Man has authority on earth to forgive sins." Then he told the paralysed man, to get up, take his mat and go home. Immediately he stood up in front of us! He took up the mat that he had been lying on and went out the door praising God. We were completely amazed and some even gave praise to God. We were filled with awe. I told a friend that we had seen remarkable things that day.

Sometime later on another Sabbath, Jesus went into a synagogue and was teaching, and a man was there whose right hand was shrivelled. I knew that many of the Pharisees were already looking for ways to confront Jesus, so they watched him closely to see if he would heal on the Sabbath. Again, Jesus seemed to know what we were thinking and told the man with the shrivelled hand, to get up and stand in front of everyone, which he did. Then Jesus said to us, "I ask you, which is lawful on the Sabbath, to do good or to do evil, to save life or to destroy it?" He looked around at us all, and then told the man to stretch out his hand. He did so, and his hand was completely restored.

Many of the Pharisees and the teachers of the law were furious and began to discuss what they might do to Jesus. I was not sure. I had seen two very clear miracles that no one could deny. I wanted to meet Jesus myself and talk to him personally. So I decided to invite Jesus to have dinner with me. Jesus came to my house and was reclining at the table with me and a small group of personally invited friends.

The meal went well to start with. We were chatting and eating, then a woman suddenly burst into the room. We all knew who she was. She lived a sinful life. You know what I mean. How she got in my house I just don't know. Well, maybe I do, but that is not the point. Somehow she had learned that Jesus was eating at my house, so she came there with an alabaster jar of perfume. We were all very surprised and I was embarrassed that this should happen at my table. I was about to call my steward to have her removed when she went and stood behind Jesus at his feet weeping. She began to wet his feet with her tears. Then she wiped them with her hair, kissed them and poured perfume on them.

When I saw this, I was thinking to myself that if this man were a prophet, he would know who was touching him and what kind of woman she was, that she was, well you know, a sinner. I felt so indignant that she had done this in my house and Jesus had not stopped her.

Jesus turned to me and said, "Simon, I have something to tell you." I asked him to tell me so at least we could now ignore this woman.

Jesus then started talking about two people who owed money to a moneylender. One owed him five hundred denarii, and the other fifty. Neither of them had the money to pay him back, so he forgave the debts of both. Then came the question, which of them would love him more?

I said I supposed the one who had the bigger debt forgiven. "You have judged correctly," Jesus said to me. Then he turned toward the woman and said to me, "Do you see this woman, Simon? I came into your house. You did not give me any water for my feet, but she wet my feet with her tears and wiped them with her hair. You did not give me a kiss, but this woman, from the time I entered, has not stopped kissing my feet. You did not put oil on my head, but she has poured perfume on my feet.

Therefore, I tell you, her many sins have been forgiven as her great love has shown. But whoever has been forgiven little loves little." Then Jesus said to her, "Your sins are forgiven".

My other guests began to ask each other, "Who is this who even forgives sins?" I had heard him say this the first time I saw him heal the man. Now here he was saying it again to this sinful woman, right there in my home. Then to my amazement Jesus said to the woman, "Your faith has saved you. Go in peace."

I was deeply troubled by this. Jesus was unlike any other Rabbi or teacher that I had heard. I could not get these thoughts out of my mind. I was drawn to him and wanted to hear more but so many of my friends in the Pharisee party were against him.

A friend of mine wanted to invite Jesus to dinner too. It was my idea really. I thought if they just sat at a table and talked with him they might begin to see what I was seeing. So my friend, also a Pharisee, invited Jesus to eat with him. We all went in and reclined at the table. I hoped to make it easier by being there. What a disaster it was. The others were just out to criticise and attack him verbally.

First of all, my friend was surprised when he noticed that Jesus did not first wash before the meal. Then the Lord said to him, did you notice that I called him Lord! Well I didn't in those days but I do now. This is what Jesus said to my friend, the host, "Now then, you Pharisees clean the outside of the cup and dish, but inside you are full of greed and wickedness. You foolish people! Did not the one who made the outside make the inside also? But now as for what is inside you, be generous to the poor, and everything will be clean for you. Woe to you Pharisees, because you give God a tenth of your mint, rue and all other kinds of garden herbs, but you neglect justice and the love of God. You should have practiced the latter without leaving the former undone. Woe to you Pharisees, because you love the most important seats in the synagogues and respectful greetings in the marketplaces. Woe to you, because you are like unmarked graves, which people walk over without knowing it." There was a great silence in the room and then finally one of the experts in the law said to him, "Teacher, when you say these things, you insult us also."

Jesus turned to him and said, "And as for you, you experts in the law, woe to you, because you load people down with burdens they can hardly carry, and you yourselves will not lift one finger to help them.

Woe to you, because you build tombs for the prophets, and it was your ancestors who killed them. So you testify that you approve of what your ancestors did; they killed the prophets, and you build their tombs. Because of this, God in his wisdom said, 'I will send them prophets and apostles, some of whom they will kill and others they will persecute.'

Therefore this generation will be held responsible for the blood of all the prophets that has been shed since the beginning of the world, from the blood of Abel to the blood of Zechariah, who was killed between the altar and the sanctuary. Yes, I tell you, this generation will be held responsible for it all. Woe to you experts in the law, because you have taken away the key to knowledge. You yourselves have not entered, and you have hindered those who were entering."

With that Jesus got up and left! As I said the dinner was a disaster. The problem was Jesus had said it exactly as it was. No one had dared speak like that. We all knew it was true.

When Jesus left, all the Pharisees and the teachers of the law who had been at the meal began to oppose him fiercely and began discussing ways to catch him in something he might say. I left once I saw that this was the way it was going. There were a few of us who were secretly becoming followers of Jesus. I did not say anything publicly but I was aware of all the talk and the plotting. I even heard that Herod was trying to kill Jesus. So a few of us went to Jesus and told him to leave this area and go somewhere else because Herod wanted to kill him.

He said to us, "Go tell that fox, I will keep on driving out demons and healing people today and tomorrow, and on the third day I will reach my goal. In any case, I must press on today and tomorrow and the next day, for surely no prophet can die outside Jerusalem!"

Jesus eyes filled with tears as he continued, "Jerusalem, Jerusalem, you who kill the prophets and stone those sent to you, how often I have longed to gather your children together, as a hen gathers her chicks under her wings, and you were not willing. Look, your house is left to you desolate. I tell you, you will not see me again until you say, Blessed is he who comes in the name of the Lord."

One Sabbath, Jesus went to eat in the house of one of the most prominent Pharisees in Galilee. They were carefully watching his every move. I was invited to be a guest also. One of the guests was not well, he was a man suffering from abnormal swelling of his body. Jesus asked the Pharisees and experts in the law, "Is it lawful to heal on the Sabbath or not?" We all remained silent. So taking hold of the man, he healed him and sent him home.

Then Jesus asked us if one of us had a child or an ox that falls into a well on the Sabbath day, would we not immediately pull it out. We had nothing to say. It was going to be another one of those difficult meals. I wonder sometimes why we Pharisees kept inviting him to dinner. Maybe we were a bit jealous of the fact that he would also eat with very undesirable types. My heart was in such turmoil in those days. I was hearing things that challenged me to the core of my being. Jesus spoke like no one else I had ever heard and with such authority.

When Jesus noticed how the guests picked the places of honour at the table, he told them one of his stories. "When someone invites you to a wedding feast, do not take the place of honour, for a person more distinguished than you may have been invited. If so, the host who invited both of you will come and say to you, 'Give this person your seat.' Then, humiliated, you will have to take the least important place. So when you are invited, take the lowest place, so that when your host comes, he will say to you, 'Friend, move up to a better place.' Then you will be honoured in the presence of all the other guests. For all those who exalt themselves will be humbled, and those who humble themselves will be exalted."

Then Jesus said to his host, "When you give a luncheon or dinner, do not invite your friends, your brothers or sisters, your relatives, or your rich neighbours; if you do, they may invite you back and so you will be repaid. Rather, when you give a banquet, invite the poor, the crippled, the lame, the blind, and you will be blessed. Although they cannot repay you, you will be repaid at the resurrection of the righteous."

When one of those at the table with him heard this, he said to Jesus, "Blessed is the one who will eat at the feast in the kingdom of God." He sounded so sanctimonious, it made me almost gag on my food.

Jesus replied with yet another story: "A certain man was preparing a great banquet and invited many guests. At the time of the banquet he sent his servant to tell those who had been invited, 'Come, for everything is now ready.' However, they all began to make excuses. The first said, 'I have just bought a field, and I must go and see it. Please excuse me.' Another said, 'I have just bought five yoke of oxen, and I'm on my way to try them out. Please excuse me.' Still another said, 'I just got married, so I can't come.' The servant came back and reported this to his master. Then the owner of the house became angry and ordered his servant, 'Go out quickly into the streets and alleys of the town and bring in the poor, the crippled, the blind and the lame.' 'Sir,' the servant said, 'what you ordered has been done, but there is still room.' Then the master told his servant, 'Go out to the roads and country lanes and compel them to come in, so that my house will be full. I tell you, not one of those who were invited will get a taste of my banquet."

That was a very memorable meal!

On one occasion all the tax collectors and sinners were all gathering around to hear Jesus. A group of the Pharisees and the teachers of the law stood on the edge of the crowd and were muttering together about the fact that he welcomed sinners and eats with them. I was there with them, but by now I am not sure whether they considered me one of the sinners because I had eaten a number of times with Jesus myself. Again it was as if he knew exactly what they were all thinking. In answer to this he told three stories. The first was about a lost sheep. The second was about a woman who had lost a precious and valuable coin. Then the third story he told us that day changed my life forever. It was about a man who had two sons.

I told Luke the story and he recorded it in his account of the life of Jesus along with much I have spoken of today. It is the best story I have ever heard. I would say from that day I was truly his follower. As Jesus spoke I felt at times that I was just like the younger son who was coming home to his father. In the second half of the story I felt just like the self righteous older brother. I knew as he spoke that he was describing the way God was like a father to us. It was so clear. When he finished telling the story in my heart I stopped being a Pharisee. I lost all interest in that dead religious legalism. I withdrew from many of my former friends.

Much later after Jesus was arrested and executed I started to hear rumours that he had come back to life. I made my way up to Jerusalem and made contact with his friends and family there. One day there was a huge crowd of us, there must have been at least five hundred people, and he came and spoke with us. He really was alive. Not long after that I was with them again in the city at the time of Pentecost. You know what happened that day. It blew the last shred of my pharisaical mind to bits! I became a follower of the Way."

THE PHARISEES IN LUKE'S GOSPEL

Luke tells us in Acts 15 that a number of believers in the early church belonged to the party of the Pharisees. Paul himself had been of that group and the Gospels record the names of some of them. Most famous of all was perhaps Nicodemus who is mentioned in John's Gospel. More of him later.

A closer examination of all four gospels reveals some interesting detail about this group. Most notably there seems to be two different sources of information about them. There are a number of stories that centre around Jesus' encounters with Pharisees in the Jerusalem and Judea areas. These stories are in John and the later part of the synoptic Gospels. They depict great antagonism and resistance towards Jesus by the Pharisees and the Sadducees, two distinctly different groups within Judaism. These stories do not contain much detail but are mainly descriptive of the growing conflict that was emerging in Jerusalem.

There are other stories however, that relate to Pharisees, which have a different tone. These stories are recorded in much greater detail in Luke's Gospel. Much of the detail is unique to Luke and records incidents that happened when Jesus was in Galilee rather that Judea. The context of these accounts often involves eating a meal with Pharisees in their houses and they appear to be from their perspective rather than from one of the disciples. Indeed these stories make hardly any mention of the disciples. The conclusion that I have come to is that Luke, in his attempts to carefully investigate all things, could very well have met and talked with a number of these individuals at some point. I have noted the specific mention of Simon the Pharisee in Luke 7:36 - 44 and have based my story around this character. As before, I have speculated, but believe if this was not the person, Luke must have met and talked with someone very similar to him or known to him who provided this unique information. The fact that Luke mentions his name would suggest that he was known to the early Church and that his identity would not be compromised by mentioning him in association with Jesus.

The unique Lucan material is set predominantly in Galilee. The Pharisees in the area are free in inviting Jesus into their homes to talk with him and eat with him. The Jerusalem based Pharisees, like Nicodemus, are more covert and less public in their interactions with Jesus. Nicodemus' famous meeting happens at night.

The stories recounted exclusively by Luke provide unusually detailed information. They have everything about them that speaks of personal recollection by an eye witness.

In his encounters with the Galilean Pharisees, Jesus reveals more of his character and particularly the nature and character of God the Father. He continually emphasises the nature of forgiveness of personal sin. Illness and disease were seen as the result of individual sin and in particular a failure to keep the decrees of the Torah, the Jewish Law. Many Pharisees interpreted the difficulties of life experienced by the common people as the consequences of sin. Jesus addresses this in his discussions with them and in his healings. He declared the bed ridden man forgiven, and the so-called sinful woman who anoints his feet at Simon's house is declared forgiven also. He in turn describes in graphic language the hypocrisy of the Pharisees in their covering up of their own sin behind the facade of religious respectability. The Pharisees had been notoriously public about their piety but had also lived hidden lives like whitewashed tombs. The way the sinful woman who was able to come right into the home of Simon the Pharisee and appear at the dinner table indicates a familiarity with the house and most probably the household servants by the woman. Perhaps Simon was himself a whitewashed sepulchre. The older brother, in the Luke 15 story who had not met his returned sibling, famously announces to the father in the story that the boy had spent all his money on prostitutes. It was not necessary to go to a far country to find prostitutes. They were in every town and village in Galilee. The twinning of stories and the discussion of the activities of the sinners was a regular theme for these meetings with the Pharisees.

The most intriguing part of the story is in the account in Luke 15 of the story of the lost sons which is known popularly as the Parable of the Prodigal Son. No other gospel writer records this most famous and detailed of parables except Luke. He places the setting as an audience of tax collectors and sinners and also a group of Pharisees and teachers of the law. It is conjecture who told this story to Luke. Whoever did tell Luke recorded one of the most clear statements that Jesus made about the nature and character of his Father.

When Luke put these stories together each one carries the theme of the joy that erupts in heaven over the return and homecoming of those who had lost their way and their connection with where they belonged. In the first parable the sheep that had been in the flock and strayed away is found and restored by the shepherd. The coin in the second story is found once the woman who owned the coin lit a lamp and with the help of the extra light is able to find the coin in the dark house.

In the last story, the main character is the father who goes out to both the sons in the story and invites them home.

The three finders are the shepherd, the lighted lamp and the father. Each represents one of the three persons of the Godhead. The shepherd represents Jesus, the good shepherd. The lamp in the hand of the housewife represents the light of the Holy Spirit that enlightens every man and finally the patriarchal Jewish man who represents the Father himself.

THE FATHER OF JESUS IS THE FATHER OF COMPASSION AND THE GOD OF ALL COMFORT

The father in this story is a description of the character of Jesus' own Father. Jesus frequently says,

> *"I do nothing on my own but speak just what the Father has taught me."* John 8:28

and,

> *"For I did not speak on my own, but the Father who sent me commanded me to say all that I have spoken. I know that his command leads to eternal life. So whatever I say is just what the Father has told me to say."* John 12:49-50

In this parable he is giving the fullest and richest description of the Father. The father in the story responds to both boys who in their own ways have no heart relationship with their father. The younger has demanded his inheritance and has gone off and squandered it all without thought of how the father would feel. This so typified the behaviour of the tax collectors and sinners to whom the story is addressed. The older son has stayed at home being 'the good boy.' He does all the right things but his heart is empty and when he speaks he virtually stabs his finger in his father's face as he spits out the famous words,

> *"Look! All these years I've been slaving for you and never disobeyed your orders. Yet you never gave me even a young goat so I could celebrate with my friends. But when this son of yours, who has squandered your property with prostitutes, comes home, you kill the fattened calf for him."*
> Luke 15:29-30

This typifies the heart attitude of the other group listening to the story, the Pharisees. They had served God as slaves, afraid of disobeying orders. There was no joy in their service or their hearts. It was cold, heartless, religious duty and nothing more. They despised others who were less righteous than they were. The older son even despised the father and his extravagant giving heart.

The father in the story had treated both boys the same. He divided his property between them. According to the Jewish custom the older son would have received two-thirds of the estate. Hence the father's words to him, *"everything I have is yours."* When the younger son returns, the father goes out to him. When the older son refuses to come in to the party the father goes out to him also. His heart for them both is one that reaches out to them.

The actions of the father when he sees the younger son coming home are a vivid depiction by Jesus of the heart of God the Father.

> *"So he (the younger son) got up and went to his father. But while he was still a long way off, his father saw him and was filled with compassion for him; he ran to his son, threw his arms around him and kissed him. The son said to him, "Father, I have sinned against heaven and against you. I am no longer worthy to be called your son." But the father said to his servants, "Quick! Bring the best robe and put it on him. Put a ring on his finger and sandals on his feet. Bring the fattened calf and kill it. Let's have a feast and celebrate. For this son of mine was dead and is alive again; he was lost and is found." So they began to celebrate."* Luke 15:20-24

The father is described as watching for the son. On many days, dots on the horizon would have become people who passed by the house. Yet on one particular day the father recognised the dot as his son. He was expecting him. There is in this something of the longing in the heart of God the Father for his children to come home to him. In the Old Testament something of that longing can be heard through the words of the prophet Jeremiah who says,

> *"I myself said, (the LORD), "How gladly would I treat you like my children and give you a pleasant land, the most beautiful inheritance of any nation." I thought you would call me Father' and not turn away from following me."* Jeremiah 3:19

Since the fall of man in the Garden of Eden the desire of God's heart was to make a way back home for his wayward children. As he cursed the serpent in Genesis 3 he says the seed of the woman would crush Satan's head. Jesus would come and undo the work of Satan. The way back was prophesied in the very beginning. Here in the parable Jesus describes the heart of the Father who welcomes home the returning wayward son who is representative of all humanity.

Jesus says the father's heart was filled with compassion for the returning boy. This describes the emotion that was in the father's heart at the sight of the son coming home. In Exodus, Moses has asked the Lord God to show him his glory. So God hid Moses in the cleft of the rock and covered him by his hand while his glory passes by. Then the Lord spoke.

> *"The Lord passed in front of Moses, proclaiming, "The Lord, the Lord, the compassionate and gracious God, slow to anger, abounding in love and faithfulness, maintaining love to thousands, and forgiving wickedness, rebellion and sin."* Exodus 34:6-7

The first word he uses to describe himself is "compassionate". The same word is used by Jesus in the parable in describing the emotion of the father at seeing his son. Paul uses the same word in 2 Corinthians in his introductory exclamation of praise.

> *"Praise be to the God and Father of our Lord Jesus Christ, the Father of compassion and the God of all comfort, who comforts us in all our troubles, so that we can comfort those in any trouble with the comfort we ourselves receive from God."* 2 Corinthians 1:3-4

It is the father who runs to his son with a heart full of compassion. Jesus deliberately chooses this word in describing his Father. He knew him to be a God of comfort and the Father of compassion. He is the source of compassion, the bringer of comfort. This is what the father in the story is about to do. He is going to comfort his son.

The father runs to his son. The father wants to get to the boy before anyone else does. It would have been a different story if the older brother had got to him first. Yet this is only a story so I don't want to read too much into it. The main point that Jesus is making is that the father is very proactive in running to the returning son. We can make much of the fact that the father does not know what the boy has done with the money or where he has been. That is all speculative, but the primary issue is that the father is running to the son. He is not waiting for the boy to come to the house.

I can remember a time when my son was due back home after some misdemeanour had occurred and I waited at the door to maximise the psychological effect of displaying my disapproval. The father in the story is not like that. This father represents God the Father who comes running to us to welcome us home. It is as if as soon as he sees a sign of return in our hearts he runs to us to comfort us with a heart full of compassion.

To the first hearers of this story, they would have been scandalised by the very thought of an elderly Jewish patriarch running in a very undignified manner to the boy. Jesus is not saying God is like an elderly Jewish patriarch. Instead he is describing a passionate Father who runs arms outstretched to welcome the son home.

Much has been made of this rich parable. One particularly good book is Henri Nouwen's book *'The Return of the Prodigal'* which is based on the picture painted by Rembrandt which hangs in The Hermitage Museum in St Petersburg, Russia. The front cover of the book displays the painting by Rembrandt. I enjoyed reading the book and highly recommend it. However the painting shows the father embracing the son surrounded by various other characters in the story. I am not convinced that this is what Jesus had in mind because the father running to the son means that he met the boy on his own, away from the house. The exchange that follows is just the two of them, alone in the field being reconciled and reunited. The boy would have been covered in shame and a sense of failure. He is very conscious of his sin and he has his speech prepared that emphasises his sense of unworthiness and guilt.

There is a strong sense in this parable of the forgiving and caring heart of the Father. The boy is repentant and will attempt to make his speech but before he is able to do so the father runs to the boy, throws his arms around his neck and kisses him. This is a passionate embrace by the father, it is not half hearted or weak. It is the father demonstrating a strong, welcoming and passionate reaction to the son. The highly significant part of the meeting and the embrace is the kiss given to the son by the father.

Pictures of fathers kissing their sons and the acceptance that the kiss means are rich in the Old Testament. Isaac kissed his son Jacob in Genesis 27:27. Laban welcomes Jacob into his home with a kiss and declared him his own flesh and blood. Genesis 29:13. When Esau meets his brother Jacob after years of separation they kissed.

> *"Esau ran to meet Jacob and embraced him; he threw his arms around his neck and kissed him. And they wept."*
> Genesis 33:4

Jesus' hearers would have known these stories and the reconciliation that occurred between them. All these images are in this parable. The kiss symbolised acceptance and reconciliation.

In many ways the kiss of the father on the cheek of the son is the most powerful gesture of acceptance in the story. God the Father is one who welcomes his children home with the kiss of love and acceptance. Our worship of God begins with his accepting kiss. The Greek word for worship is 'proskuneo' which means literally to "kiss toward". In our worship we return the Father's kisses with our kisses. As Jesus had said before, these are the worshipers the Father is seeking.

In the midst of the father's embrace the son begins to speak his preplanned speech. He recognises his sin and failure in its fullest sense. He has sinned against his father and that also means he has sinned against "heaven" and therefore God. Sin not only separates those affected by the sin, but also separates us from God in heaven. The boy then says something that is so typical of our broken and fallen view of ourselves and God. He says, *"Father, I have sinned against heaven and against you. I am no longer worthy to be called your son."* Luke 15: 21

These words put into his mouth by Jesus, the master story teller, describe what we all feel when confronted by our sin and failure. We feel unworthy and we believe the lie that we are disqualified by God because of our sin and brokenness. This attitude of heart goes right back to the Garden of Eden where Adam in his sin and failure can no longer see God as his Father but projects onto the Father's face his own broken image of God, the God that he is now afraid of and hides from. All of humanity has responded to God in this way ever since. The fact that Jesus puts these words into the son's mouth shows how seriously flawed our perception of God is.

Instead of letting him finish his speech with his concluding statement of a request for a job as a servant, the father interrupts his son. He calls for the servants, who have by now caught up with the father, he tells them to quickly bring the best robe to put on the son. The boy has just returned from the far country where he has lost everything. He has been working as a hired hand on a pig farm where he has been so hungry that he was tempted to eat the pig swill. He is tired, dirty, stinking of pigs, ashamed and expecting rejection and more humiliation. Yet the father wants to cover up all the signs of dirt and failure by covering him with his best robe. It would probably have been his own garment. The father does not want anyone to see the broken spectacle of his humiliated son so instead he covers him with the very best that he has. He covers not only his physical dirt and filth, the father covers the shame that he would have felt. It is as if he wants to lead him back into the house dressed in his best. It is such a powerful demonstration of his love.

God our Father treats us, his wayward and broken sons and daughters, in exactly the same way when we come home to him. Jesus carefully uses words in the story that describe his Father. He wants us to know the loving compassionate heart that the Father has for us. We have been blinded by our fear and terror of the god who we have perceived as fearful, constantly demanding and judgmental. Jesus presents a Father so different that it is utterly shocking.

The son's shame is covered by the father in the story.

Then the father calls for a ring to be placed on his finger. The son would have left wearing a ring that denotes his authority as a son and like everything else it was sold or lost in the riotous life he had led. He literally came home empty handed. Here is another powerful symbol that is being used by Jesus. Only sons and heirs wore a ring that proclaimed their status as a son. Here this act is a reinstating and repositioning of the boy back in his rightful place as a son within the family and the household. To have a ring placed on his finger by his father amounted to a public proclamation that this is his beloved son.

The Greek word in the New Testament which is often inaccurately translated adopted is 'uiothesia', which means literally 'to place a son.' This is what the father has done to the boy. This word appears in Galatians 4:5 and Romans 8:14 and three other places where it is often translated 'adopted'. Early bible translators struggled to find an English word for this legal term and came up with adoption as an equivalent. The context however, is the process of making us sons of God is redemption, and the end result is that we are placed in a new position as his sons. This is what the father in the story has done. He cannot adopt the boy as a son since he is already his son. Instead he has welcomed him home and placed him back in the family as a son wearing the ring of sonship on his finger. Paul's use of the term in Galatians and Romans is exactly the same. God the Father has rescued us from the kingdom of darkness by means of redemption and placed us back into our rightful position of sonship which had been lost in the fall.

> *"For he has rescued us from the dominion of darkness and brought us into the kingdom of the Son he loves, in whom we have redemption, the forgiveness of sins."* Colossians 1:13

Then Paul writes in Galatians about what has happened to us a result of being redeemed. We are placed back in our rightful positions as son.

> *"God sent his Son, born of a woman, born under the law, to redeem those under the law, that we might receive the full rights of sonship (uiothesia)"* Galatians 4:5

and,

> *"The Spirit you received does not make you slaves, so that you live in fear again; rather, the Spirit you received brought about your placement in sonship. (uiothesia)"* Romans 8:15

Like the son in the story we have always been God's offspring but when we come home to him as Father and are redeemed by the blood of Jesus we are repositioned in our rightful place of sonship.

After the ring comes a new pair of shoes. Again, sons wore shoes. Slaves and servants would have gone about bare footed. Now the father wants shoes for his son's feet. It is as if everything about him would have spoken publicly of the father's very clear intention of restoring the boy to his former status and place in the family. He is leaving no one in any doubt about the acceptance and belonging that were being given back to the boy.

To the listeners, such as the Pharisees, the point of the story would not have been lost on them. Simon the Pharisee had seen Jesus treat people like this all the time. When Simon saw Jesus heal the lame man, Jesus had declared his sins forgiven. In the minds of the Pharisees the man was lame because of his sins. God was punishing him. The woman who anointed Jesus has her sins forgiven also. The Father that Jesus is revealing is one who forgives, redeems and restores the lost and places them back where they belong as his beloved and precious sons and daughters.

THE FATHER IS HAPPY AND FULL OF JOY

One last point that cannot have been missed by the listeners when this story was first told was the extravagant and joyful nature of the father that Jesus describes. After bringing the restored son back into the household he throws a party. The sheer joy of the father explodes on the whole household. He orders a fattened calf to be barbecued. Not just a goat or a lamb but the very best that he has. The fattened calf was the animal that was slaughtered for only the most special of occasions. It is no wonder that the older son hears the music, sees the dancing and smells the food cooking as he approaches the house. Yet he doesn't get to go in and taste the food because he is wounded and broken just as much as his younger brother. He is acting just like the Pharisees.

The sheer joy in the heart of the father in this story is what Jesus knows and experiences himself. The father says,

> *"But we had to celebrate and be glad, because this brother of yours was dead and is alive again; he was lost and is found."* Luke 15:32

It is as if the father cannot help but celebrate and rejoice at the return of his lost son. It is such a different picture of the angry and fearsome God who was the object of Jewish worship. The God who they were afraid of, who they believed was out to trick them and would punish them for the slightest little misdemeanour. This was the God that Simon the Pharisee served and lived for. This is why Jesus was such a challenge to the Pharisees. He completely upset the traditional adamic view of God that they, and ultimately all of us, had before we came to know God as our real Father.

The God that Jesus came to show us is part of the joyful trinity, Father, Son and Holy Spirit who have existed together in joyful harmony bound together in love for all eternity. The Father that Jesus reveals in the Gospels is a happy Father, who delights in his son and in his children.

Luke seemed to have realised this and included some sayings of Jesus that demonstrate this truth. He speaks to the seventy-two on their joyful return from their first preaching mission. He rejoices with them in their joy.

"At that time Jesus, full of joy through the Holy Spirit, said, "I praise you, Father, Lord of heaven and earth, because you have hidden these things from the wise and learned, and revealed them to little children. Yes, Father, for this is what you were pleased to do." Luke 10:21.

Then later he gathers his disciples together and says to them,

"Do not be afraid, little flock, for your Father has been pleased to give you the kingdom." Luke 12:32

In Luke 15, the joy that Jesus describes in the three parables increases exponentially as first, one lost sheep of one hundred is found. Then the housewife throws a party to celebrate the finding of her lost coin, one of ten. Finally the father throws a party at the return of his son.

Jesus' revelation of his Father is that he is a Father full of joy and celebration.

THE EIGHTH STORYTELLER

NICODEMUS
THE COUNCIL MEMBER

"From my earliest days I have been a seeker after truth. I grew up in Jerusalem. I became a Pharisee because I wanted to know the truth about Adonai. I read and studied the Torah and wanted to live my life based on its instructions. We were passionate about Israel and longed to see our land free from Roman domination. Jerusalem was full of Pharisees and then there were also the Sadducees. They were different from us. They represented the ruling classes in Israel and many of them were in the priestly classes and were aristocratic. In our opinion they had sold themselves out to the Romans maintaining the status quo for their own ends.

So I was a Pharisee. I was elected to the ruling council in the city therefore I knew most of what was going on. Jerusalem was a political city as well as a religious centre and anyone who challenged the order of things came in for special scrutiny. When John the baptiser appeared down in the Jordan news reached Jerusalem very quickly. We sent people down to find out what he was saying. I went once. He said we were a brood of vipers! Of course the people loved that. Some of them clapped and applauded when he called us Pharisees this. When he turned his critical attention to Herod and his family his days were numbered.

I digress. Round about that time I heard about the latest messianic claimant up in Galilee and didn't pay much attention to it. There were always lunatics who called themselves the Messiah. Soon everyone was talking about this one though. He was from Nazareth. A friend of mine, Nathaniel, even became one of his followers. He surprised himself because he would often tell us what he has said when he first heard at the time, "Can any good thing come out of Nazareth!" However, this Jesus was different from the rest. There were stories of healings too and of course we sent some of our people to find out if there was any truth in these rumours and claims. The reports were mixed. Some started to say that he spoke with an authority the like of which they had never heard before. Others said he was the son of Beelzebub! No one was neutral about this Jesus of Nazareth.

At some point he appeared here in the city of Jerusalem itself. I heard him speak on one occasion and I was dumbfounded. Indeed, Jesus spoke in a way that I had never heard anyone speak before. When he spoke it was as if he was speaking just to me. Once he caught my eye, just for a moment. I felt he looked deep into my soul. My eyes just welled up with tears. In that moment I knew I needed to meet him to talk to him one to one. So I sent a message to him via my friend Nathaniel and arranged a meeting. I did not want a crowd so I asked if we could meet one evening after dark. Yes, I know, I didn't want anyone else to know I was meeting him.

So I went to meet Jesus one evening. I told him that we thought he was a Rabbi and a teacher who has come from God because no one could perform the signs he was doing if God were not with him. I wasn't trying to flatter him, I did mean that.

Jesus looked earnestly at me and said that he really meant it when he said that no one can see the kingdom of God unless they are born again. He went straight to the issue, no small talk. I asked him how could someone be born when they are old? I could not see that we can enter a second time into our mother's womb to be born!

Jesus' answer was enigmatic. He said, "I tell you the absolute truth, no one can enter the kingdom of God unless they are born of water and the Spirit. Flesh gives birth to flesh, but the Spirit gives birth to spirit. He said I should not be surprised by him saying that we needed to be born again. The wind blows wherever it pleases. We hear its sound, but we cannot tell where it comes from or where it is going. This was the same for those born of the Spirit."

I wondered how this could be so I asked him to explain it. Then he questioned me as one of Israel's teachers, why I didn't understand these things. "I tell you the truth" he said, "we speak of what we know, and we testify to what we have seen, but still you people do not accept our testimony. I have spoken to you of earthly things and you do not believe; how then will you believe if I speak of heavenly things? No one has ever gone into heaven except the one who came from heaven, the Son of Man. Just as Moses lifted up the snake in the wilderness, so the Son of Man must be lifted up, that everyone who believes may have eternal life in him."

He continued, "For God so loved the world that he gave his one and only Son, that whoever believes in him shall not perish but have eternal life." I was amazed by this statement. I had not considered that God loved the world in the way he suggested. It seemed to me he was saying that he was this son! I can see why some accused him of blasphemy. Then he continued, "For God did not send his Son into the world to condemn the world, but to save the world through him. Whoever believes in him is not condemned, but whoever does not believe stands condemned already because they have not believed in the name of God's one and only Son." He continued by saying that this was the verdict, light had come into the world, but people loved darkness instead of light because their deeds were evil. Everyone who did evil hated the light, and would not come into the light for fear that their deeds would be exposed. But whoever lived by the truth came into the light, so that it may be seen plainly that what they have done had been done in the sight of God." I had never been spoken to by anyone like this before. We chatted about many things that evening but this is the main thing that has stayed with me to this day.

After I left him that night and went home I felt that I would never be the same again. It took many days and long nights as I sifted these words in my heart. He came to Jerusalem a number of times over the coming months for about two years. I went to hear him whenever I could. I have told most of what happened over the next few months to John bar Zebedee. He put it into his book about the life of Jesus.

Towards the end it became very difficult. There were all sorts of plots and plans afoot to catch Jesus out and eventually there were plans made to arrest him and have him tried for blasphemy. The Council and the priests just didn't want to see what was really happening and who Jesus was. They denied the evidence when it was staring them in the face. There were some of us though who thought he was indeed the Messiah.

On one of Jesus' visits to Jerusalem for one of the festivals, the crowds were all talking about him everywhere he went. When the chief priests and the leading Pharisees heard the crowd whispering about him being the Messiah, they sent temple guards to arrest him. This happened on the last and greatest day of the festival. There was Jesus in the temple amid the people standing there, speaking in a really loud voice, so that everyone could hear him. He called out, "Let anyone who is thirsty come to me and drink. Whoever believes in me, as Scripture has said, rivers of living water will flow from within them." At the time we had no idea what he meant but now we know he meant the Spirit, whom those of us who believed in him were later to receive. Up to that time the Spirit had not been given, since Jesus had not yet died and been raised. Only much later on the Day of Pentecost would I begin to understand what the living water meant.

There was great discussion in the crowd on hearing his words. Some of the people said that he was the Prophet. Others said that he was the Messiah. Still others asked how could the Messiah come from Galilee? They thought that the Scripture said the Messiah will come from David's descendants and from Bethlehem, the town where David had lived. Thus the people were divided about Jesus. Some wanted to seize him, but no one laid a hand on him. Incidentally I thought this was a very important question about his birth. Coming from Nazareth, as my friend Nathaniel had said raised doubts. It was only later that I found out that he had really been born in Bethlehem!

Anyway, eventually the temple guards went back to the chief priests and the Pharisees without having arrested Jesus. The Council members were furious and demanded why they hadn't arrested him.

The guards answered very sheepishly that no one ever spoke the way this man did. Not surprisingly the Pharisees were not happy and one of the leading Pharisees shouted at them, "You mean he has deceived you also? Have any of the rulers or any of the Pharisees believed in him? No of course they haven't! Yet this mob that knows nothing of the law says these things. There is a curse on them!"

This was too much for me. Finally I stood and spoke up for Jesus and asked if our law condemned a man without first hearing him to find out what he has been doing? They turned on me, "Aren't you from Galilee, too? Look into it, and you will find that a prophet does not come out of Galilee."

It was the way he seemed to ignore parts of the Law that we hold to so tightly, such as not working on the Sabbath that caused such a lot of trouble. So, because of this, doing these things on the Sabbath day, that the leaders of the Council began to persecute him. In his defence Jesus said to them, "My Father is always at his work to this very day, and I too am working."

For this reason they tried all the more to kill him; not only was he breaking the Sabbath in their opinion, but he was even calling God his own Father, making himself equal with God and this they saw as blasphemy.

Jesus gave them this answer, "I tell you the truth, the Son can do nothing by himself. He can do only what he sees his Father doing, because whatever the Father does the Son also does. For the Father loves the Son and shows him all he does. Yes, and he will show him even greater works than these, so that you will be amazed. For just as the Father raises the dead and gives them life, even so the Son gives life to whom he is pleased to give it. Moreover, the Father judges no one, but has entrusted all judgment to the Son, that all may honour the Son just as they honour the Father. Whoever does not honour the Son does not honour the Father, who sent him." I have told most of this to John as I said earlier and he has recorded it faithfully word for word.

One morning at dawn Jesus appeared again in the temple courts, where all the people gathered around him, and he sat down to teach them. On that particular occasion, I'm ashamed to say some of them did something that I think was utterly disgusting. The teachers of the law and some of the Pharisees brought in a woman caught in adultery. It was dawn and they had dragged this poor woman from her lover's bed and they made her stand before the group. They said to Jesus, "Teacher, this woman was caught in the act of adultery. In the Law of Moses, we are commanded to stone such women. Now what do you say?"

They were using this question as a trap, in order to have a basis for accusing him. Jesus bent down and started to write on the ground with his finger. When they kept on questioning him, he straightened up and said to them, "Let any one of you who is without sin be the first to throw a stone at her." Again he stooped down and wrote on the ground. At this, those who heard began to go away one at a time, the older ones first, until only Jesus was left, with the woman still standing there. Jesus straightened up and asked the woman where her accusers were and if anyone was there to condemned her.

She looked at him and said there was no one. "Then neither do I condemn you. Go now and leave your life of sin."

That day in my heart I was no longer a Pharisee. It took me a long time to walk away but in my heart I knew I did not want any part of them anymore. I wanted to be one of his followers but I was so afraid.

Over the coming months, every time he spoke in Jerusalem it caused uproar. Sometimes they tried to stone him and every time he seemed to just melt away into the crowds. Eventually Jesus went back across the Jordan to the place where John had been baptising in the early days. There he stayed and many people went to him. They said that they thought that even though John never performed a miraculous sign, all that John said about this man was true. Many believed in Jesus at that time.

The last time he came to Jerusalem, Jesus stopped in Bethany and we heard that he had been at the home of Lazarus who had just died. The city was full of the news. Jesus had stopped there and raised Lazarus from the dead even though he had been in the tomb for four days! The Council called a special meeting to discuss it. I attended and discovered there was a very specific plan to silence him, permanently. One of Jesus' own inner circle had even come forward to offer to hand him over to them for a trial. While we were meeting, a messenger burst in to say that Jesus was coming into the city along with a huge crowd. The Sadducees were so afraid that the Romans would think it was a rebellion and would call out their troops and there would be great bloodshed. We dissolved the meeting and we went out to see what was happening. I was with a friend of mine, Joseph from Arimathea, who was also a secret disciple of Jesus. We went out to the city gate along with hundreds of others and saw him coming with a great group of his followers. It was not a riot but there was damage going on. The people were tearing down palm branches and were all shouting out the old Hebrew word, 'hosanna' which means "save us" Then I heard them saying, "Blessed is he who comes in the name of the Lord! Blessed is the king of Israel!"

I expected to see Jesus riding a horse surrounded by an armed gang of thugs. Instead, Jesus was sitting on a young donkey surrounded by happy singing crowds and children. To my horror, they were calling him the king of Israel. I knew that would be his undoing. The Sadducees and the Priests did not want a king. They were content to be ruled by Rome. They remembered the tyranny of Herod and did not want a king like him again. Now there was all this crowd because he had called Lazarus from the tomb and raised him from the dead. They were telling everyone. Many people, because they had heard that he had performed this sign, went out to meet him. The group of Pharisees I was with said to one another that this was getting them nowhere because the whole world had gone after him.

Well, you know what happened by the end of the week. It is so painful to talk about it. Others can give you the details. For me, I was so ashamed I did not speak up for him or try to dissuade the Council from arresting him and putting him on trial. I never thought they would go as far as they did. As soon as they sent him to Pilate with the charge of claiming to be a king his fate was sealed. He had no chance. I never imagined it would be crucifixion.

I made my way to the execution site just outside the city wall, ironically called the place of the Skull or Skull Hill. There were many people there, mostly the curious and those mentally defective people who have to be there to see the gore and gratuitously watch the suffering and eventual death of the victims. I was shocked to see a number of my colleagues from the Council gleefully chatting and laughing together. I kept away from them because I was angry and sickened by what they had done. They occasionally jeered at him and shouted insults at him as he hung there nailed to the cross. He said something and they jeered louder. I don't know what he said.

I also saw a few of those who had followed him from Galilee. There was young John bar Zebedee and his mother Salome, and to my amazement and great sorrow there was Jesus' mother too. She was holding on to her sister Salome. They were all in a huddle near the foot of the cross. There were a couple of other women too. One of them was Mary, the wife of my friend Cleopas, but there was no sign of any of the other so called disciples. I wondered what had happened to them. Perhaps they had been arrested also. I kept my distance from all of them. I remember sitting on a rock and burying my head in my hands. Those words he had spoken to me those two or so years ago have never left me. The Father sent his son into the world because he loved the world so much. How the Father must hate the world now after what the world had done to his son. I also recalled that he had said, "Light has come into the world, but people loved darkness instead of light because their deeds were evil." This was evil indeed. He had also said, "Just as Moses lifted up the snake in the wilderness, so the Son of Man must be lifted up, that everyone who believes may have eternal life in him." Suddenly, an incredible thought penetrated my heart. He was being lifted up at this very moment! All who looked at the bronze serpent that Moses had held were healed. I opened my eyes and looked up at Jesus hanging there on the cross. He was looking right at me. Those eyes that had looked into my heart long ago looked at me again. I believed in him, I knew in that moment he was really was the son of God. His eyes looked deep into me and it seemed, ...it seemed, that, ...that he was loving me. My eyes were raw with weeping but something in my heart was warmed by his gaze. He looked away and appeared to say something to John and his mother.

Then I noticed someone standing next to me. It was the Roman Centurion who was overseeing the crucifixion. I knew him. I had met him and a few of Pilate's officers at some civic event. He had been originally posted to a Roman fort in Galilee and there were rumours that one of his servants had become ill and Jesus had healed him. It was probably someone's sick idea to put him in charge of Jesus' execution. I looked at him and we exchanged glances. His face was contorted with a mixture of grief and shame, anger and sadness. I reached out my hand to him and I said to him, "He really was the son of God, you know." He looked at me and nodded. "I know" he said. "What have we done?"

Suddenly we were startled by a loud cry coming from the cross. Everyone turned and looked in his direction. Even the Council members and Priest stopped and stared. It was difficult to hear what he said but it sounded like, "It is finished!". Then as clearly as anything he said, "Father, into your hands I commit my spirit." With that, he bowed his head and gave up his spirit. At that moment there was a violent earth tremor and many people screamed and some even fell to the ground. Then the Centurion who had been next to me said loudly so that even some of the soldiers and others looked round at him, "Truly this man was the Son of God." One of the priests heard him and spat at the ground in front of him and said he was a blasphemous Roman pig, and ran off down the hill.

It was getting late and the Sabbath was approaching and I knew that unless we took him down and buried him he would be left there for another twenty-four hours. I went over to John and the women and told them that I would help and get permission to have him taken down and buried. I mustered up my courage. I went and found my friend Joseph and together we went to ask the Roman Governor, Pilate if we could take the body of Jesus and arrange for his burial. Joseph, like me, was a disciple of Jesus, but secretly because he feared the Jewish leaders just like I did. When we got to the Governor's palace I bumped into the Centurion who had been at Skull Hill coming out from the Governor's offices. He came and spoke to us to say that he had reported to the Governor that Jesus was already dead. He was now being sent back to instruct the soldiers to finish off the other two criminals who had been crucified, by breaking their legs.

When we went in to speak to Pilate he was talking with his wife who was extremely upset with him. It looked like they had been arguing. He demanded to know what we wanted. When we told him, Pilate seemed almost relieved and his wife spun round and came towards us. She told us to wait a moment and she ran out returning in a few moments with a large jar of myrrh and aloes in her hands. She gave it to me and said. "It is the least I can do." She then gave Pilate a look that almost destroyed him and she left the room.

So with Pilate's permission, we went and took the body away. I brought the mixture of myrrh and aloes, and added more so that it must have weighed about seventy-five pounds, with me for the burial, it took two of us to carry it all. With the help of two of the women, we took Jesus' body, wrapped it with the spices in strips of linen in accordance with our burial customs. Near to the place where Jesus was crucified there was a garden, and in the garden a new tomb, in which no one had ever been laid. As it was the day of Preparation and since the tomb was nearby, we laid Jesus there. The two women who had been with John and his mother and Jesus' mother who had helped us, had stayed waiting for us and they saw where we had placed his body. One was my friend Cleopas' wife, Mary, and the other one was a Galilean woman also called Mary of Magdala.

You know what happened after that, others will tell you. As for me, I was there with the others at the Feast of Pentecost. I was there when the Holy Spirit fell on us. I have been following the Way ever since."

NICODEMUS IN THE NEW TESTAMENT

Nothing is known outside of the Bible of this man. He is mentioned only three times in the Gospel of John. The Eastern Orthodox Church recognises a Saint Nicodemus but there are no traditions associated with him. In the fourth century a Gospel of Nicodemus appeared but it contains nothing that is considered significant or factual.

All we know about him is what the Gospel of John records. Like much of the latter half of John the action takes place in and around Jerusalem. Most of the people mentioned by name in the gospel either live in the city or nearby. This includes Lazarus and his two sisters in Bethany, Joseph of Arimathea, Nicodemus and various others. It is widely believed that John was drawing heavily on eye witness accounts from that area as he constructs the various visits made to the city by Jesus.

Unlike the Pharisees in the Galilee area that Luke seems to have knowledge of, the encounters and interactions with the Jerusalem based Pharisees are much more aggressive and hostile towards Jesus. The exception is of course Nicodemus. He is described as a member of the Jewish ruling Council in Jerusalem. It is extremely likely that it is Nicodemus that gives John so much inside information about the workings, thoughts and plotting of the Council to trap Jesus and their opinions of so much that he says and does. As with so much of the material in the gospels, we can hear the voices of eye witnesses speaking to us of what they heard and saw.

GOD THE FATHER LOVES THE WHOLE WORLD

We know nothing about Nicodemus other than what John records in his Gospel. It is inconceivable that he was not part of the early church. His personal and private late night conversation with Jesus has become one of the most quoted parts of the Bible. It is to Nicodemus that Jesus reveals the most astonishing truth of all. Only Nicodemus hears these words. Nicodemus the Pharisee, the man who perhaps was the least likely to have thought about this truth. The Jewish religious leader who had spent all his life trying to keep the demands of the Law. The man who was also intrigued by Jesus and who recognised in this apparently uneducated carpenter from Nazareth something that drew him and touched his heart.

Nicodemus does not try to flatter Jesus, instead he blurts out something that God had revealed to his heart, that this Jesus was a teacher, a rabbi who had come from God. He, nor any of the Pharisees, knew God as Father. He saw God as the fearsome, angry God, who demanded obedience and absolute adherence to a Law that was completely impossible to keep. For the Pharisees, they had constructed an approach to God that kept him at a distance. They tried to keep all the rules and had found ways around the rules that they could not keep that everyone recognised was unbelievably hypocritical. They longed to see the Kingdom of God in Israel but for them it was all about strict obedience to the Law. Like Adam they were afraid of God. They covered their nakedness with a religious set of fig leaves, the like of which the world had never seen before. They had become masters at hiding behind their religious masks, so afraid to look at the face of the Lord God.

Jesus speaks to Nicodemus and goes straight to the heart of Nicodemus' greatest longing. Jesus says to know the realm of the Father's love, the kingdom of God, he needs to be reborn, to be born again. Nicodemus' immediately responds from his head and not his heart. He responds as a Pharisee. He asks Jesus how is it possible to be reborn when he is already old. His head is trying to understand. He is not seeing with the eyes of his heart but with the eyes of his understanding based on his fallen adamic way of thinking. Jesus however, is wanting to open Nicodemus' spiritual eyes, the eyes of his heart, to see things differently, from heaven's perspective, rather than his fallen earth bound perspective. Jesus responds with the language of the Spirit. He is talking about a rebirth that is not physical but one that is of the Spirit. The challenge for Nicodemus is that he cannot see the truth when he is only looking through his pharisaical mind set. Jesus tells him that the Pharisees cannot see even earthly things and believe. So Nicodemus is going to struggle to believe when Jesus speaks of heavenly things.

Jesus continues to speak directly to Nicodemus' heart and draws him into the place of revelation. Amid the evening's conversation Jesus is about to reveal the most astonishing statement that has ever been made in the history of the world. We are so familiar with this statement, we have heard it so much. For many, hearing this statement was the doorway to our own personal encounter with God. For many it is the great moment of divine transaction when they personally experience spiritual regeneration, when they are born again by the Spirit of God. For the vast majority of us who know this verse, it is the last part of the verse that we have focused on and loved. This is of course John 3:16.

> *"For God so loved the world that he gave his one and only Son, that whoever believes in him shall not perish but have eternal life."*

We have focused on the last part of the verse that it is through believing in Jesus that we receive the gift of eternal life. This is seen as a summary of the whole Christian message, it is the very heart of the gospel. There is so much truth in this but this is the second part of the verse. What Jesus says in the second part is totally built on the first part of the verse. In the first half of the statement Jesus tells Nicodemus that God, his Father, really, really loves the world.

The whole reason for the coming of the Son to save us for eternal life is because the Father himself loves the whole world. It is the revelation that the Father has continually and consistently loved the world since before creation. It is not that he just loves those who are religious, or who seek him or who respond to him, but all men, all mankind, whether they believe in him or not.

Paul, when addressing a group of pagan Greek philosophers at the Areopagus in Athens, quotes from Greek philosophers and poets. He said,

> *"For in him we live and move and have our being. ' As some of your own poets have said, We are his offspring."*
> Acts 17:28-29

It is surprising that the lyrical thought of a pagan poet would become the word of God through the lips of Paul and into the New Testament. "We are his offspring" means that all of humanity are God's offspring, his created children. This is not through some universal insemination by a deity but the result of a loving creator God who is revealed as Father. The notion that God becomes our Father when we are saved or born again does not hold up in this passage from John. This is not adoption, it is premeditated planning by a loving father to bring all his wayward offspring home so that they might receive the full rights of sons. The Father loves us before we are capable of believing in him or loving him or knowing him or receiving the salvation that his Son brings. This loving fatherhood of all mankind by God precipitates the coming of Jesus the Son and is the reason why he comes. The Son comes to save and bring new birth because the Father loves the world in all its fallenness, brokenness and rebellion.

It is this description of his Father that makes this statement totally revelatory. He is a Father who loves so passionately that he is prepared to not just stand by and do nothing but send his unique Son into the world to die in order to bring us back into relationship with him. This is the first time that Jesus specifically says that God loves the world. As the story and revelation unfolds this will increasingly characterise God the Father's attitude and heart toward us. He is a Father who passionately loves his children, his offspring, who he planned before the creation of the world to be his sons and daughters. The eternal life that he gives is spoken of again by Jesus in his high priestly prayer in John 17. Jesus says to the Father,

> *"Now this is eternal life: that they know you, the only true God, and Jesus Christ, whom you have sent."* John 17:3

Eternal life is knowing the Father and the Son Jesus, whom he has sent into the world.

As Jesus spends time teaching and instruction his disciples he begins to show them more of the loving heart that God the Father has. Jesus himself loves them and he only does what he sees his Father doing. In the final evening in the upper room Jesus says to his disciples,

> *"As the Father has loved me, so have I loved you. Now remain in my love."* John 15:9

Jesus was fathering the disciples as he loved them in the same way as the Father loved him. They knew that love. Late in his life John, the one Jesus loved, summed up this understanding in a very simple but profound statement in his first letter. He declares simply that God is love. 1 John 4:16. He summarises this truth thus:

> *"Dear friends, let us love one another, for love comes from God. Everyone who loves has been born of God and knows God. Whoever does not love does not know God, because God is love. This is how God showed his love among us, he sent his one and only Son into the world that we might live through him. This is love, not that we loved God, but that he loved us and sent his Son as an atoning sacrifice for our sins. Dear friends, since God so loved us, we also ought to love one another. No one has ever seen God; but if we love one another, God lives in us and his love is made complete in us."* 1 John 4:7-12

THE NINTH STORYTELLER

THOMAS
THE TWIN

"When you are one of a set of twins you are always labelled as 'a twin' or worse, 'the twins'. It's as if you don't have a separate personality. My twin and I grew up together but we were so different from each other. I have my own mind and quite early on in my life I decided that I would not take anything at its face value. Just because my twin thought it, it did not mean I would think it too. So I grew up with a reputation for saying things that no one else was willing to say. It worked well for me but I have noticed I have a tendency to be cynical at times.

A friend of mine called Nathaniel was a bit like that too. He became one of Jesus' followers. When someone told him that Jesus from Nazareth was the Messiah he commented, "Can anything good come out of Nazareth?" It was a classic comment. It did make me laugh. It was so true. Nazareth is such a dump. Eventually, I met this so called Messiah from Nazareth myself. From the very first I knew my life would never be the same again. He really impressed me. Every time he spoke he cut through all the rubbish that most of the Rabbis spoke with all their fancy words.

At times he was more than cynical, he was direct, to the point of being rude! The things he said about the Pharisees were priceless. I loved it when he called them 'whitewashed tombs.' So did the crowd.

Eventually his continual criticism of the Pharisees and the religious elite in the nation brought him into open conflict with them. There were times when I was convinced that they were going to stone him. We got wind of plots and plans so much so that we managed to persuade him to withdraw from Jerusalem and Judea as it was just too dangerous. His usual attitude was one of, "My time has not yet come!"

One time we were up in Galilee and we received word that his friend Lazarus, who lived down south just outside the city of Jerusalem, was really sick. The message came from Lazarus' two sisters. They wanted him to go down and heal him. We kept telling him how dangerous it was and that he shouldn't go. He seemed to listen to us and we stayed up in Galilee for a couple of days then he suddenly announced he was going to Judea. We told him again they wanted to stone him down there. Then he just said that Lazarus was asleep and he would go and wake him. Well, I thought this was ridiculous. If he was asleep then let him sleep, it would do him much more good than all of us turning up at his house and eating them out of house and home.

So, when he told us that Lazarus was asleep, I thought that would settle the matter. Instead he said outright that Lazarus was dead and that he would go to them and we would believe as a result of this. Well, what was there to do but go with him? I said to the others, "Come on boys, we might as well go and die with him!" It was a classic cynical comment from me.

We had been to Lazarus' house before and it was very embarrassing as his sister, Martha got very upset with everyone, especially with her rather pretty young sister Mary. Martha was clattering around in the kitchen making an obvious point that she needed help. Mary was oblivious to all this and was sitting at Jesus' feet just drinking in every word he was saying. I made a point of sitting as close to Mary as I could. Suddenly, in barged Martha, up to her elbows in flour, bright red in the face. She looked around the room, glared at Mary, then she really had a go at Jesus. She wanted Jesus to tell Mary to come and help her with the food. She virtually accused him of deliberately ignoring her and all the work she was doing by letting Mary just sit there. Jesus was so kind to her. He didn't tell her off, he just encouraged her by saying one dish was enough and that Mary had chosen the better part.

You know what happened when we got there to Bethany that next time. On his arrival, Jesus found that Lazarus had already been in the tomb for four days. Now Bethany was less than two miles from Jerusalem, and many Jews had come to comfort Mary and Martha in the loss of their brother.

When Martha heard that Jesus was coming, she came out to meet him. We were all there and gathered around Martha. I wanted to see Mary as I thought she was such a lovely girl and would have been very upset by her brother dying, but Mary was back at their home. Martha told Jesus that if he had been there her brother would not have died. Yet she insisted she knew that even at that point God would give Jesus whatever he ask for. Jesus said to her, "Your brother will rise again." She said to him, "I know he will rise again in the resurrection at the last day." As I listened to this exchange I didn't for one minute think that Jesus was about to raise Lazarus from the dead. Then Jesus said this to Martha, "I am the resurrection and the life. The one who believes in me will live, even though they die; and whoever lives by believing in me will never die." He asked her if she believed this. I saw his eyes, I saw the way he looked at her and she said, "Yes Lord, I believe that you are the Messiah, the Son of God, who is to come into the world." It was very touching. But I was thinking what a shame we had not got there earlier. I wondered how Mary was and wanted to see her.

Now Jesus had not yet entered the village, but was still at the place where we had met Martha. Martha went back to tell Mary that Jesus was there. I went with her to support her and comfort her. The house was full of official mourners and friends. Mary got up quickly and I took her to where Jesus was waiting. When the Jews who had come to mourn with them and had been with Mary back at the house noticed how quickly she got up they all came out too. They followed her, supposing she was going to the tomb to mourn there. When they reached the place where Jesus was and saw him, they all started wailing and crying and I remember Mary fell at his feet and tearfully told him that if he had been there, her brother would not have died.

You should have heard the noise of all that wailing! Some of it was genuine, but a lot was the usual fake stuff. When Jesus saw how much Mary and the Jews who had come along with her were weeping, he was deeply moved. He asked where the tomb was. So they showed him the way to the tomb. We all followed.

Then Jesus wept. This was not fake emotion he was very deeply touched. Everyone was saying that Jesus had really loved Lazarus. I was weeping too and I put my arm around Mary as we all stood there.

They weren't all like that. I heard some of them saying, "Could not he who opened the eyes of the blind man have kept this man from dying?" That was not very comforting I must say! So we all went with Jesus to the tomb. Once more, deeply moved, Jesus wept as we arrived at the tomb. It was a cave with a stone rolled across the entrance in the usual fashion in Israel. Then he said something none of us expected. He said, "Take away the stone." I was shocked and Martha was too, she told him that by that time there would be a terrible smell for he had been there four days.

Then Jesus said, "Did I not tell you that if you believe, you will see the glory of God?"

So they took away the stone. Then Jesus looked up and said, "Father, I thank you that you have heard me. I know that you always hear me, but I said this for the benefit of the people standing here, that they may believe that you sent me." When he had said this, Jesus called in a loud voice, "Lazarus, come out!"

It went very quiet. No one moved or said a word. No one seemed to breathe. We watched the dark entrance then suddenly I thought I saw a movement in the shadows of the cave. Someone called out, "Something moved in there!" Everyone gasped, somebody screamed, I even saw a woman faint! Then it happened. Lazarus came out, his hands and feet were still wrapped with strips of linen, and a cloth around his face. The whole crowd drew back thinking it was a ghost or a demon, or one of those Egyptian mummies. Some even ran away in fear. We just all stood there with our mouths open. Then Jesus smiling, turned and said to us, "Don't just stand there. Take off the grave clothes and let him go!" What a day!

It was not about dying it was about the opposite, he raised the dead, in front of our very eyes. When Lazarus came out of that tomb, I could not find words to describe the effect that had on me. My cynicism evaporated. I knew he was the Son of God.

Then about six days before the Passover, we were invited to a special dinner in Jesus' honour at Mary's home in Bethany. Martha as usual was doing all the cooking and Lazarus was the host. Lazarus was not just alive, he was different, we were all a bit in awe of him. Lazarus was among those reclining at the table. I am not sure where Mary was. I had caught sight of her when we first arrived she came over and especially greeted me. That made my heart miss a beat but then she left saying she had things to do. I thought she must have gone off to help Martha with the food.

Soon after the start of the meal Mary came into the room. She had with her about a pint of pure nard, it was one of the most expensive perfumes. She came up to where Jesus was reclining at the table. Then she poured it on Jesus' feet and wiped his feet with her hair. It was so lovely. The whole house was filled with the fragrance of the perfume. I was reclining next to Judas Iscariot, who started objecting and said in a rather loud voice so that Jesus could hear, "Why wasn't this perfume sold and the money given to the poor? It was worth a year's wages."

That was typical of him. He did not say this because he cared about the poor, but as keeper of the money bag he was always grumbling on about money. We found out later that he used to help himself to what was put into it because he was a thief. They should have asked Matthew to look after the money, but he had insisted his days of counting cash were long over.

However Jesus said to us, "Leave her alone, it was intended that she should save this perfume for the day of my burial. You will always have the poor among you, but you will not always have me."

Within a few days we were all together sharing the Passover meal in Jerusalem. The whole week was full of drama. It began with Jesus entering the city at the head of a huge crowd of his followers. It was as if he was challenging not just the Council but the Romans too. Then he went straight into the temple and nearly caused a riot by throwing out the money changers. From that point on it went downhill fast. The tension mounted all week. By the night of the Passover I wondered how it would end. We gathered together, just the twelve of us and Jesus. At the beginning of the evening Jesus got undressed and washed our feet for us just like a humble servant. Then he told us that one of us would betray him. I was mortified! Did he mean me? Would I betray him? Could I, after all this time? Soon after that, old money bags Iscariot left for some reason which we found out later was to collect his blood money from the Priests. Then Jesus told Peter that he would also deny that he knew him not just once but three times. It was turning into a very depressing evening.

Then Jesus told us to cheer up! To believe in God and believe also in him. He told us that his Father's house has many rooms. He said if that were not the case, why would he have told us that he is going there to prepare a place for us? He then said that if he goes and prepares a place for us, he would come back and take us to be with him that we would all be where he is. This was new to us. Then he said, "You know the way to the place where I am going don't you?"

I looked around the room at all the others reclining there. Did any of them have a clue where he was going? I didn't. There were blank looks and confusion on most people's faces. So I didn't think they knew any more than I did. I said to him, "Lord we don't know where you are going so how can we know the way?" Someone had to say it. It was what I was thinking. There was no point him saying anything else if we didn't know where he was going. His reply was astonishing. He said, "I am the way and the truth and the life. No one comes to the Father except through me. If you really know me, you will know my Father as well. From now on, you do know him and have seen him."

It was a long night. We had much to learn. John has written it down so well in his account. Others have told much of their experiences over the next few days so I don't need to say too much more.

Late that night I fled from the garden too, just like the rest of them. I was very ashamed of myself for running away. I decided to go away into the country and just lay low for a few days on my own. I went to Bethany to Mary's house. When I came back into Jerusalem I heard first that Jesus had been killed and was already buried. That was a terrible shock in itself. Then I heard that he was now supposed to have come back from the dead. I wondered if he had really died and hadn't just become unconscious. I went and found some of the women who had been there at his crucifixion, who had seen him die. They told me he really was dead. They described seeing the nails being hammered into his hands and feet. They even said that at the end, to make sure he was really dead a soldier had thrust a spear into his side. They said the fluid that flowed from his side had already begun to separate. They said he was really, really dead. There was absolutely no doubt at all. He had died.

Then there were these apparent sightings and meetings with his ghost or something. I was not going to have any of this. These were just the babblings of a group of grief-crazed and hysterical women and guilt ridden cowardly men who had denied and deserted him, just like I had. I became very angry with them. I finally shouted at them that I would not believe Jesus was alive until I put my finger into the nail wounds in his hands and feet and thrust my hand in the spear wound in his side. I was nobody's fool. I was not going to be taken in by silly stories. Tears of anger and sadness were pouring down my face as I spoke. Someone came to put their arms around me but I pushed him away. I fled again. I went back to Bethany because I needed to see Mary again.

A week later Mary persuaded me to go back into the city as she said she believed the stories were true. So I went back and found them. I felt so wretched. The stories hadn't died down. In fact, the whole demeanour of everyone who was supposed to have seen Jesus alive had radically changed. We were all together that evening. I had thrown out my challenge a week before and I felt almost foolish about it. As we were talking suddenly the atmosphere changed.

Then it went very quiet in the room. Though the doors were locked, Jesus came and stood among us and said, "Peace be with you!" Then he turned to me and gave me one of those wonderful smiles of his. He said to me, "Put your finger here Thomas, see my hands. Reach out your hand and put it into my side. Stop doubting and believe." All I could say to him was, "My Lord and my God!" I just cried and cried. He very tenderly took me in his arms and held me. Then Jesus told me, "Now that you have seen me, you have believed. How happy are those who have not seen and yet have believed." That was it! No more doubts for me. I had seen him and I believed.

Jesus appeared to us over a period of about forty days and spoke about the kingdom of God. He was not a ghost, he was a real flesh and blood man who would often eat with us. I remember some of us were up in Galilee and we had gone fishing and were out nearly all night on the lake. I'll let Simon Peter tell you that story, it was very significant for him.

On another occasion, while he was eating with us, he gave us this command: "Do not leave Jerusalem, but wait for the gift my Father promised, which you have heard me speak about. For John baptised with water, but in a few days you will be baptised with the Holy Spirit." We were all gathered around him not wanting to miss a thing he said so we asked him if at this time he was going to restore the kingdom to Israel. He told us that it is not for us to know the times or dates the Father has set by his own authority. But we would receive power when the Holy Spirit comes on us; and we would be his witnesses in Jerusalem, and in all Judea and Samaria, and to the ends of the earth.

I realised then, that I would go anywhere he wanted me to go to tell people about him, to the ends of the earth wherever that was, or further, even India if necessary."

THOMAS THE TWIN IN THE GOSPELS AND BEYOND

Thomas is referred to as the twin by both Matthew and Mark in Matthew 10:3 and Mark 3:18, and his name is the Hebrew word for twin. He was also called Didymus by John on two occasions. John 11:16; 20:24, Didymus is the Greek equivalent of the Hebrew name. All we know regarding him is recorded in the fourth Gospel. In the lists of the apostles he is always mentioned along with Matthew, who was the son of Alphaeus, and that these two are always followed by James, who was also the son of Alphaeus, it has been supposed that these three, Matthew, Thomas, and James, were brothers but this is only a possibility. Who his twin was is not known.

He is included in the list in the upper room in Acts and was there for the outpouring of the Spirit on the day of Pentecost. Eusebius of Caesarea (320AD) quotes Origen as having stated that Thomas was the apostle to the Parthians but Thomas is better known as the missionary to India through the Acts of Thomas perhaps written as late as about 200 AD. Ephrem, a doctor of the Syriac church writes in the forty-second of his "Carmina Nisibina" that the Apostle was put to death in India, and that his remains were subsequently buried in Edessa, brought there by an unnamed merchant.

A Syrian ecclesiastical calendar of an early date confirms the above and gives the merchant a name. The entry reads: *"3 July, St. Thomas who was pierced with a lance in 'India'. His body is in Edessa having been brought there by the merchant Khabin. A great festival."*

The Thomas traditions became embodied in Syriac liturgy, thus they were universally credited by the Christian community there. There is a legend that Thomas had met the biblical Magi on his way to India.

Thomas is believed to have left northwest India when invasion threatened and travelled by vessel to the Malabar Coast, possibly visiting southeast Arabia and Socotra en route. He then landed at the former flourishing port of Muziris(c. 51–52 AD) in the company of a Jewish merchant. From there he is said to have preached the gospel throughout the Malabar Coast. The various churches he founded were located mainly on the Periyar River and its tributaries and along the coast where there were Jewish colonies. He reputedly preached to all classes of people and had about 17,000 converts, including members of the four principal castes. Later, stone crosses were erected at the places where churches were founded, and they became pilgrimage centres. In accordance with apostolic custom, Thomas ordained teachers and leaders or elders, who were reported to be the earliest ministers of the Malabar Church.

Remains of some buildings in the area where he is supposed to have been active, influenced by Greek architecture, are believed to indicate that he was a great builder. Although little is known of the immediate growth of the church, Bar-Daisan (154–223) reports that in his time there were Christian tribes in India which claimed to have been converted by Thomas and to have books and relics to prove it. But at least by the year of the establishment of the Second Persian Empire (226), there were bishops of the Church of the East in northwest India with laymen and clergy alike engaging in missionary activity.

The historian Vincent Smith says, "It must be admitted that a personal visit of the Apostle Thomas to South India was easily feasible in the traditional belief that he came by way of Socotra, where an ancient Christian settlement undoubtedly existed. I am now satisfied that the Christian church of South India is extremely ancient...". The Oxford History of India.

According to tradition, Thomas was killed in 72 AD. The accounts of Marco Polo from the 13th century state that the Apostle had an accidental death outside his hermitage in Chennai by the badly aimed arrow of a fowler who, not seeing the saint, shot at peacocks there! Later in the 16th century, the Portuguese in India created a myth that Thomas was killed in Chennai by stoning and lance thrust by local priests. Other early Christian literature states that Thomas died a martyr, in the east of Persia.

In his encounters with Jesus, Thomas heard and witnessed revelation about the Father.

JESUS INCLUDES US THROUGH HIS RESURRECTION LIFE WITH THE LIFE OF THE GODHEAD.

When Jesus went to Bethany in response to the request of Mary and Martha, he was going according to the Father's timetable. On hearing their request he told his disciples that this sickness would not end in death rather, it would be for God's glory so that God's Son would be glorified through it.

The delay confused the disciples especially as after two days Jesus announced he was going to Bethany because Lazarus was 'asleep'. Jesus explained that he meant Lazarus was dead. If Jesus had gone and found Lazarus sick then no doubt he may have healed him. But Jesus listened to his Father, and Father had said, "wait". Father had a bigger plan and a bigger miracle in mind. The previous resurrections from the dead performed by Jesus had taken place in Galilee far from the eyes of the Jerusalem elite. Now the Father was going to bring glory to his Son and to himself right under the noses of the religious establishment of Israel. Bethany was barely two miles from the city. Many people knew Lazarus. There would be no doubt that an extraordinary miracle had taken place right on their own doorstep.

John tells us that Jesus declared to Martha that he is the resurrection and the life. This is significantly more than Jesus raising Lazarus from the dead, however wonderful that is. He is making a declaration about himself. "In him was life and that life was the light of all mankind", John had written at the beginning of his Gospel in John 1:4. Fallen man had entered the kingdom of darkness by eating the fruit of the tree of the knowledge of good and evil in the garden of Eden. Death, sin, destruction and darkness had entered the human experience and all mankind was overwhelmed by this. Here was the beloved Son of the Father, who has entered our darkness, declaring life, resurrection life is in him. Not only was he bringing back Lazarus to life but in himself he was the resurrection life. Within a few days, he would burst out of the kingdom of darkness into the resurrection life that he brought. Mankind is brought back to the Tree of Life, to Jesus, the incarnate Son, where we can also enter into this new resurrection life.

Jesus is preparing the way for his own resurrection. By raising Lazarus from the dead he is putting resurrection right at the top of everyone's agenda. Jesus says that the one who believes in him will live, even though they die; and whoever lives by believing in him will never die.

Athanasius, the great Father of Church writing in the turn of the fourth century said,

> *"For the Word, perceiving that no otherwise could the corruption of men be undone save by death as a necessary condition, while it was impossible for the Word to suffer death, being immortal, and Son of the Father; to this end He takes to Himself a body capable of death, that it, by partaking of the Word Who is above all, might be worthy*

to die in the stead of all, and might, because of the Word which was come to dwell in it, remain incorruptible, and that thenceforth corruption might be stayed from all by the Grace of the Resurrection. Whence, by offering unto death the body He Himself had taken, as an offering and sacrifice free from any stain, straightway He put away death from all His peers by the offering of an equivalent. For being over all, the Word of God naturally by offering His own temple and corporeal instrument for the life of all satisfied the debt by His death. And thus He, the incorruptible Son of God, being conjoined with all by a like nature, naturally clothed all with incorruption, by the promise of the resurrection."
Athanasius On the Incarnation

The resurrection of Jesus was the proof positive for the early church that Jesus was the Son of God. After Pentecost the resurrection of Jesus was the starting point of their preaching and teaching. It could not be denied or refuted as the evidence was overwhelming. The lamest of explanations put forward by the Jewish leaders was that the disciples had stolen the body and hidden it. The vibrant life of the apostles and the early church was an amazing proof of the transformation that had taken place within them. We are living in the reality of Jesus' resurrection life. As we grow in this knowledge and resurrection life we began to see that this means that we are now included in Christ's life within the Godhead. His resurrection life means that we too are now sons and daughters through faith in Christ. Truly, his Father is our Father.

Jesus' prayer of thanksgiving to the Father at Lazarus' tomb has a scope far beyond the moment when Lazarus is raised.

"Father, I thank you that you have heard me. I knew that you always hear me, but I said this for the benefit of the people standing here, that they may believe that you sent me." John 11:41-42

JESUS IS THE WAY INTO RELATIONSHIP WITH THE FATHER

Thomas is perhaps best remembered in the upper room for his candid admission of ignorance. Jesus had just told his disciples that in his Father's house there were many rooms. He had told them that he was going there to prepare a place for them and he would come back and take them to be with him where he was, or rather, is.

The location he was speaking from was the upper room but where he was at the very moment was within the Trinity, in the Father's embrace. John at the beginning of his Gospel said that Jesus was at the Father's side or as some translations read, in the Father's bosom. He is saying that he is intimately and personally connected to the Father in loving relationship. That is where he is, as he speaks, and that he will take them to exactly the same place as him. His intention is to bring all mankind home to our true Father, to that place of intimacy and personal connection. His intention is inclusion in him with the glorious Father and the Holy Spirit.

Jesus perhaps saw their blank looks and incredulous faces, so he asked them if they knew the way to the place where he is going. It is Thomas who finally says what probably all the others wanted to say. Thomas said to him that they don't know where he was going, so how can they know the way in John 14:6.

Jesus' answer is probably one of the most quoted parts of the Bible. Also it is probably the most misquoted or at least half quoted. So many have memorised and spoken about the wonderful truth but stop short of its full glory. Jesus answered, "I am the way and the truth and the life." It is at this point that many stop. They have become 'stuck on the way' as Derek Prince once famously put it. The focus of this statement is not the way, the truth or the life in Jesus alone, rather the focus on the way to what or to whom, the truth about what or whom, and the life of what or whom. Jesus says specifically, intentionally and categorically, that no one comes to the Father except through him. It could be translated equally that no one turns towards the Father, comes face to face with the Father except through Jesus. The focus of it all is the Father. The place he is going to is the Father and Jesus is the way or the means to get there, to be able to be face to face with the Father. This is not a diminution or neglect of Jesus. It is an elevation of Jesus to his rightful place at the Father's side. It is a revelation of the Father by Jesus and a revelation of Jesus by the Father.

In coming into this place of intimacy that Jesus inhabits in the Father, we come to know the Father as intimately as Jesus does. Jesus says immediately after this,

> *"If you really know me, you will know my Father as well.*
> *From now on, you do know him and have seen him."*
> John 14:7

The verb here 'to know' is the verb that describes experiential knowledge through relationship. It carries the same meaning as the word used in Genesis where Adam 'knew' his wife. It speaks of encounter and heart connection, of deep intimate joining rather than cold facts. Yet there is also a Greek word for "to know' that is absolute factual knowledge. This is the second verb used here.

It is as if Jesus is saying, "If you have an intimate experiential heart relationship with me you will absolutely, without a doubt know my Father as well because that is how I am towards him. To know Jesus is to know the Father as they are inseparably of the same substance. They are truly one.

Later Jesus says we are where he is. *"In that day you will know that I am in my Father, and you in me, and I in you."* John 14:20

Jesus' disciples spent the best part of perhaps three years with him. Yet, the four gospels record maybe only fifty or so days. We do not know what happened on the many other days. John, at the conclusion of his gospel says that if everything Jesus said and did were written down the world could not contain all the books.

> *"But these are written that you may believe that Jesus is the Messiah, the Son of God, and that by believing you may have life in his name."* John 20:31

Luke tells us that Jesus appeared to them over a period of forty days and spoke about the kingdom of God in Acts 1:3. We don't know what he taught them over those forty days. One thing is clear, they were living in a new reality, they were experiencing resurrection life on a day to day basis. They had entered into the dynamic relationship of the Father Son and Holy Spirit. They were just beginning to live in that reality and to find words to express it. It would take many years for the full implications of the revelation that they had experienced to be articulated. It would take a person like Paul to express it most powerfully and clearly. When next the disciples speak after the filling of the Holy Spirit on the day of Pentecost, they have a deeper and fuller revelation of who Jesus is as the Son of God, who God is as their Father and they are beginning to live in the anointing and life of the Spirit. They embark on a mission that continues to this day listening to what the Father is saying and doing what the Father is doing.

THE TENTH STORY TELLER

SIMON
THE FISHERMAN

"The first time I really heard anything about Jesus was when my brother Andrew turned up back from one of his trips down to Judea with his friend Philip. Those two were always off somewhere or other, especially when there was work to be done. He had always been like that! I continually had to make excuses for him if he wasn't around. It drove my parents crazy. This time he heard some tale about someone preaching down the Jordan Valley. Next minute, off he goes and that was the last we saw of him for weeks. I was trying to run a business in those days. He was always asking me to forgive him and promising it wouldn't happen again. All that stuff. He was so unreliable! Well, that is what I used to think.

Anyway, this time, when Andrew decided to show up again, he had some story about meeting the Messiah! Now that was a new one. I thought it was just another one of his excuses. Yet this time he was much more serious and didn't make any promises. He just looked me straight in the eye and said this Messiah was a man from Nazareth called Jesus. I ask you! How ridiculous is that? I was about to yell at him to stop talking nonsense and to come and help me with the nets but he just grabbed my arm and looked at me again and said nothing. I had never seen him that serious.

For the next few weeks Andrew stayed at home and worked so hard I was amazed. It was as if the meeting with the man he called the Messiah had, in some way, deeply affected him. Then one day he came rushing to find me to say that this so called Messiah, Jesus, was in town and he asked me if I would like to meet him. The earnestness and seriousness in his voice and the excitement in his eyes were unlike anything I had seen before. So I agreed to go and he brought me to meet this Jesus.

I was expecting some raving lunatic with a death wish. There were Roman soldiers in town and they had a simple way of dealing with messiahs! When we found him, he was just an ordinary man, about thirty, nothing remotely messiah like about him. He was sitting with his feet up outside somebody's house near the lake, chatting with a few children. Not even a crazed look in his eyes. It was quite the opposite. Jesus looked at me and said, "So you are Simon son of John. From now on you will be called Cephas." Jesus didn't say anything else, he just kept looking at me which made me feel awkward. It was as if he was looking right into me. Cephas is the Aramaic version of my name, but of course mostly I get called Peter these days. It is easier for the Greek speakers!

One day, some time later, Jesus was back in town and was standing down by the Lake. The people were crowding around him and listening to him speak. He looked along the beach at our two boats that we had left while we were washing our nets. He waved and came strolling up to me and asked if he could use one of the boats, and then asked me to put out a little from shore so he could sit down and teach the people from my boat.

When Jesus had finished speaking, he said to me, "Put out into deep water, and let down the nets for a catch." I thought for a moment and wondered why this carpenter, who knows nothing about fishing, would have the gall to tell me how to do my job. I decided it was best to humour him for a while rather than embarrass him in front of all the people. So I said to him, "Master, we've worked hard all night and haven't caught anything. But because you say so, I will let down the nets." I tried to hide my sarcasm. It was going to be a huge waste of time, but if nothing else, it would be a little boat trip away from the crowds.

So we pushed off from the shore. Surprisingly, Andrew hopped in the boat with us and helped us row. We were not far off from the shore and we put our nets in the lake to show Jesus how we did it. When we had done so, within moments a large shoal of fish swam by and before we knew it we caught such a large number of fish that our nets began to break. Jesus looked at us with one of those looks that didn't say, "I told you so!", more a smile of…of… of joy. Yes, it was sheer joy and delight!

We had to signal our partners in the other boat to come and help us, and they came and we filled both boats so full that I thought we might sink. When we landed and got the catch ashore I was full of confusion. We had just landed the biggest catch of the season. It would keep us in bread for months. We were astonished at the catch of fish we had taken, all of us, including James and John, the sons of Zebedee, our partners. The crowds were already asking how much we were going to charge for the fish. We made a fortune that day.

When I realised this, I went and found Jesus. He was sitting with some children and playing skim stones with them in the lake. I fell at his knees. All I could think to say was, "Go away from me, Lord; I am a sinful man!" Then Jesus told me not to be afraid but from now on I would fish for people. He asked us to follow him. So we pulled our boats up on shore, left everything and followed him. Just like that! That was the beginning of it all for me.

The following weeks and months took us all over Galilee, and back and forth to Jerusalem for the festivals. Mostly it was a wonderful time. I say mostly because up in Galilee he was something of a local hero. Everyone wanted to meet him. We got invited to dinner at some really nice houses. People soon saw that I was his right hand man. Down in Judea it was another story. There were some nasty people down there. Wherever we went I saw things happen that I didn't think were possible. Healings and miraculous signs. My own mother in law was healed from a fever too. I even got some teasing about that from the rest of the disciples!

Then there were the things Jesus was saying and teaching. Sometimes it made such sense and other times he would tell one of his odd little stories. He loved telling those stories, it was almost as if he didn't expect people to get what he was saying and that didn't seem to worry him in the slightest. He kept saying he was only telling us what his Father wanted to tell us. After a short while it became clear to us that he meant his Father in heaven. He talked about his Father so naturally.

One time he compared himself to bread that was from heaven and this made people begin to mutter about him. He said this while teaching in the synagogue in Capernaum. They were saying things like, "Isn't this Jesus, the son of Joseph, whose father and mother we know? How can he now say, that he has come down from heaven?"

Jesus turned to them and told them to stop muttering among themselves. He went on to say, "No one can come to me unless the Father who sent me draws them, and I will raise them up at the last day. It is written in the Prophets: 'They will all be taught by God.' Everyone who has heard the Father and learned from him comes to me. No one has seen the Father except the one who is from God; only he has seen the Father. It's really true what I am telling you, the one who believes has eternal life. I am the bread of life. Your ancestors ate the manna in the wilderness, yet they died. But here is the bread that comes down from heaven, which anyone may eat and not die. I am the living bread that came down from heaven. Whoever eats this bread will live forever. This bread is my flesh, which I will give for the life of the world."

Well, that caused a real stir! The Jews began to argue sharply among themselves So Jesus said to them, "It's really true what I am telling you, unless you eat the flesh of the Son of Man and drink his blood, you have no life in you. Whoever eats my flesh and drinks my blood has eternal life, and I will raise them up at the last day. For my flesh is real food and my blood is real drink. Whoever eats my flesh and drinks my blood remains in me, and I in them. Just as the living Father sent me and I live because of the Father, so the one who feeds on me will live because of me. This is the bread that came down from heaven. Your ancestors ate manna and died, but whoever feeds on this bread will live forever." This was really hard to understand and some people said all sorts of nasty things about him as a result.

Many of these hangers on said that his was too hard a teaching. Aware that these so called disciples were muttering about this, Jesus said to them, "Does this offend you? Then what will you think when you see the Son of Man ascend to where he was before! The Spirit gives life; the flesh counts for nothing. The words I have spoken to you, they are full of the Spirit and life. Yet there are some of you who do not believe." For Jesus seemed to know from the beginning who did not believe and who would betray him. He went on to say, "This is why I told you that no one can come to me unless the Father has enabled them."

From this time many of those who had just come along for the excitement, turned back and no longer followed him. There had been quite a crowd of disciples around him in those days. They loved all the miracles and drama and the free bread! I watched many of them drift off. After a while there were just us twelve and a few women and Jesus spoke directly to us and said, "So what about you? You do not want to leave too?"

I immediately jumped in with my usual bravado, "Lord, to whom shall we go? You have the words of eternal life. We have come to believe and to know that you are the Holy One of God."

We had, you see. Well, I had. I had come to believe that he was the Holy One, the Messiah. It wasn't just because my brother Andrew said it. I saw it for myself.

One really busy day in Capernaum Jesus was asked to go to the home of Jairus, the most important man in the synagogue. His daughter was very ill and he had sent for Jesus. On the way to his house a woman got healed just by touching the edge of Jesus' robe. As usual Jesus stopped to speak with her. While Jesus was still speaking, some people came from the house of Jairus, the synagogue leader, who was anxiously hopping from foot to foot waiting for Jesus to come to his house, and told him that his daughter was dead and he shouldn't bother him any more.

Overhearing what they said, Jesus told him, "Don't be afraid Jairus; just believe." When we got to the house Jesus did not let anyone follow him except me, James and John. There was a great commotion, with people crying loudly and carrying on as they do when someone has died. He went into the house and said to them, "Why all this commotion and wailing? The child is not dead but asleep." They all laughed at him! They were all the professional wailers who always show up when someone dies. We threw them all out. I'm good at doing things like that. Nothing like a bit of a punch up! After we put them all out, Jesus took the child's father and mother and us three who were with him, and went in where the child was. There she was, a sweet beautiful young girl about twelve years old. Stone cold dead. Jesus took her by the hand and said to her, "Talitha koum!", which means "Little girl, I say to you, get up!". Immediately the girl got up and began to walk around. At this we were completely astonished. He gave strict orders not to let anyone know about this, and told her parents to give her something to eat. As

God is my witness, that is what happened. I saw it with my very own eyes. 'Talitha koum', I have remembered those words ever since.

A few days later Jesus and all of us, his closest disciples, went on to the villages around Caesarea Philippi up to the north of Galilee. On the way he asked us who people were saying he was. Someone said, "Some say John the Baptist; others say Elijah; and still others, one of the prophets."

"But what about you?" he asked us. "Who do you say I am?"

I didn't hesitate. I said it straight away before any of the others came up with some silly answer. I said, "You are the Messiah, the Son of the living God."

Jesus replied, "Blessed are you, Simon son of John, for this was not revealed to you by flesh and blood, but by my Father in heaven. I tell you that from now on you are Peter. On this rock I will build my assembly, and the gates of Hades will not overcome it. I will give you the keys of the kingdom of heaven; whatever you bind on earth will be bound in heaven, and whatever you loose on earth will be loosed in heaven."

I felt very pleased with the way that had gone. Not only had I said the right thing, but he obviously recognised that I had some sort of gift and I was one of the most important men in his group. I'm not sure what he meant by saying that his Father had revealed this to me. I was not quite sure if I knew who his father was or what he meant by his Father in heaven. Anyway, I was not just one of the crowd, but I was going to get the keys of the kingdom heaven, whatever that meant. It was bound to be good. If there was a fight coming, we were going to win by the sound of things. He called me Peter. Then he did one of those little play on words things he was so fond of. He said on this 'petra,' that's a little bit of gravel, he would build his assembly. I wondered if he meant me by that, he couldn't have meant me as I was more than a bit of gravel. I was Rock! He used a different word that sounds like rock. I thought about it a lot after that and I realised he meant the truth he had been talking about would be the foundation stone. The truth, that the Father was revealing, would be the very foundation of his church.

Then Jesus warned us not to tell anyone about him. To my shock and surprise, he then began to tell us that the Son of Man must suffer many things and be rejected by the elders, the chief priests and the teachers of the law, and that he must be killed and after three days rise again. He spoke very plainly about this.

So, in my new role, I took him aside and began to have a little word in his ear. I told him bluntly he shouldn't talk like that, it was bad for morale. Jesus turned and looked at us all, and in front of everyone he rebuked me! "Get behind me, Satan!" he said to me. "You do not have in mind the concerns of God, but merely human concerns." I was devastated. He had just said I was his rock who had heard from God now he was calling me Satan's mouth piece! I felt quite offended and upset by this. To make matters worse he called the crowd to him along with the rest of the disciples and told them that, whoever wanted to be his disciple must deny themselves and take up their cross and follow him. For whoever wanted to save their life would lose it, but whoever loses their life for him and for the gospel would save it. What good would it be for someone to gain the whole world, yet forfeit their soul? What can anyone give in exchange for their soul? If anyone is ashamed of him and his words in this adulterous and sinful generation, the Son of Man would be ashamed of them when he came in his Father's glory with the holy angels.

There were quite a few smirks from the other disciples aimed in my direction that afternoon. I felt like knocking their blocks off! Jesus smiled at me a lot over the next few days as if he knew what I was going through. He never said anything. He just smiled. I felt very churned up inside for days.

After six days Jesus took me, James and John with him and led us up a mountain, where we were all alone. Then something quite strange happened. His clothes became dazzling white, whiter than anyone in the world could bleach them. And Jesus' face shone like the sun. In some way he seemed to be completely changed, like he metamorphosed as those Greeks call it. Something very, very unusual and magnificent happened to him. Then, there appeared before us two people who were talking with Jesus. We asked who they were and we were told it was Moses and Elijah! These were perhaps the most famous names in our history and Jesus was talking to them. I felt I had arrived! I was seeing the ghosts of these two famous people. I remember thinking that I couldn't wait to tell the others about this. This would wipe the smirks off their faces. As usual I had to say something and I blurted out, "Rabbi, it is good for us to be here. Let us put up three shelters, one for you, one for Moses and one for Elijah." The other two, James and John just stood there looking terrified with their knees knocking. Then a cloud appeared and covered them, and a voice came from the cloud: "This is my Son, whom I love, with him I am well pleased!"

Suddenly, when we looked around, we no longer saw anyone with us except Jesus. I am not making up cleverly devised stories when I talk to you about Jesus. We were eyewitnesses of his majesty. As I have thought about this over the years I realised that up on that mountain, he received honour and glory from God the Father when the voice came to him from the Majestic Glory, that said, this was his Son, whom he loved; and that he was so pleased with him. We ourselves heard this voice that came from heaven when we were with him on the sacred mountain. There was no doubt about it, it was the voice of God himself. It was another amazing moment.

As we were coming down the mountain, Jesus gave us orders not to tell anyone what we had seen until the Son of Man had risen from the dead. So we kept the matter to ourselves, but we did discuss what "rising from the dead" meant.

In the last week before he was crucified he said so many things. John has written a lot of them in his account of Jesus' life. Some stick in my mind so powerfully. I remember the last evening meal we had together. It was just before the Passover Festival. Jesus seemed to know that the hour had come for him to leave this world and go to the Father. The evening meal was in progress. We found out later that the devil had already prompted Judas, the son of Simon Iscariot, to betray Jesus. Jesus had told us that the Father had put all things under his power, and that he had come from God and was returning to God. To our surprise, he got up from the meal, took off his outer clothing and wrapped a towel around his waist. After that, he poured water into a basin and began to wash our feet, drying them with the towel that was wrapped around him.

He came to me, it was my turn, so I told him that he was not going to wash my feet. Jesus responded by saying that I did not realise now what he was doing, but later I would understand.

I told him he shall never wash my feet. Jesus answered, "Unless I wash you, you have no part with me." Oh me and my mouth! I had almost blown it again. My eyes filled with tears and I said, "Then, Lord, not just my feet but my hands and my head as well!"

When he had finished washing our feet, he put on his clothes and returned to his place. "Do you understand what I have done for you?" he asked us. "You call me 'Teacher' and 'Lord,' and rightly so, for that is what I am. Now that I, your Lord and Teacher, have washed your feet, you also should wash one another's feet. I have set you an example that you should do as I have done for you. It's really true what I am telling you, no servant is greater than his master, nor is a messenger greater than the one who sent him. Now that you know these things, you will be blessed if you do them".

As we were eating together Jesus told us that one of us would betray him. We stared at one another, at a loss to know which of us he meant.

John bar Zebedee, who called himself 'the disciple whom Jesus loved,' was reclining next to him. That description really used to annoy me, but many things used to annoy me in those days. Anyway I got his attention and said, "Oi! Johnny. Ask him which one he means."

Leaning back against Jesus, John asked him, "Lord, who is it?"

Jesus whispered to John and I could just make out that he said something about the one to whom he will give a piece of bread to when he has dipped it in the dish. Then, dipping the piece of bread, he gave it to Judas, the son of Simon Iscariot. As soon as Judas took the bread he looked very odd and got up to leave. So Jesus told him that what he had to do, do quickly. None of us at the meal understood why Jesus said this to him. Since Judas had charge of the money, some thought Jesus was telling him to buy what was needed for the festival, or to give something to the poor. When Judas had taken the bread, he went out. It was night by then. After he had left Jesus said, "Now the Son of Man is glorified and God is glorified in him. If God is glorified in him, God will glorify the Son in himself, and will glorify him at once. My children, I will be with you only a little longer. You will look for me, and just as I told the Jews, so I tell you now: Where I am going, you cannot come." He said he was giving us a new command to love one another. We were to love one another in the same way that he loved us. By this everyone would know that we were his disciples.

I was mystified. I interrupted him and asked him, "Lord, where are you going?" Jesus replied, "Where I am going, you cannot follow now, but you will follow later." I asked, "Lord, why can't I follow you now? I will lay down my life for you." I added, "Even if all fall away, I will not!" Then Jesus turned and looked straight at me, "Will you really lay down your life for me? I tell you the truth, before the cock crows, you will disown me three times."

I thought there was no way that was going to happen! This was Peter the Rock who he was talking to. After all this time I thought he would have known me better. I insisted emphatically, "Even if I have to die with you, I will never disown you." And all the others said the same. We were his men after all. We even had swords!

It was a tense evening and we all felt very low and sad about all this. He carried on talking and some of the others asked questions about where he was going. I felt very upset too to think he thought I would deny him. It was absurd. I'd never do that, is what I was thinking.

He went on to say that he would not leave us as orphans, that he would come to us. It was a strange thing to say as most of us had parents who were still living. I wasn't an orphan.

Jesus came back to the subject of loving us. He continued, "In the same way the Father has loved me, so have I loved you. Now remain in my love. If you keep my commands, you will remain in my love, just as I have kept my Father's commands and remain in his love. I have told you this so that my joy may be in you and that your joy may be complete. My command is this: Love each other as I have loved you. Greater love has no one than this, than to lay down one's life for one's friends. You are my friends if you do what I command. I no longer call you servants, because a servant does not know his master's business. Instead, I have called you friends, for everything that I learned from my Father I have made known to you. You did not choose me, but I chose you and appointed you so that you might go and bear fruit, fruit that will last, and so that whatever you ask in my name the Father will give you. This is my command: Love each other."

When I was with him I always felt loved by him no matter what I had said or done. At the end of the evening he prayed to his Father and he prayed for us too, his disciples. He said something quite surprising to me that I have thought about ever since. He said, "I have revealed you to those whom you gave me out of the world. They were yours; you gave them to me and they have obeyed your word." He was talking about us his disciples but he says we belonged to his Father before we met Jesus and that the Father gave us to Jesus. It was as if he was saying we had always belonged to God even before we knew it. I had never seen it like that. Then he said something that really amazed me, "All I have is yours, and all you have is mine. And glory has come to me through them." He was saying we had brought glory to him! I could see that the miracles and the teaching had brought glory to him, but how could a bunch of losers like us have brought glory to him? This really surprised me.

Soon after this we left. I think John Mark told you what happened after that. We all went off with Jesus to the garden on the Mount of Olives. You know what happened there. I took a sword with me, just in case. I got it from Simon the Zealot. He always knew where to find knives and swords. When the arrest happened and that bunch of thugs from the temple arrived with that wretched turn coat Judas, I decided it was time to act. So I whipped out my sword and swiped at one of them. I took his ear clean off. Blood went everywhere! Then Jesus stopped me and picked up the bloody ear and healed the man! He put the ear back on this man's head! Then it was all over.

We all gave up at that point, well, I gave up. I didn't know what to do. There was shouting and such and well, I, I, well, I just ran, I am ashamed to say. I just ran away.

After I got clear of the guards and the garden I bumped into one of the other disciples and we realised that no one was following us. We decided we would follow from a distance and because this disciple was known to the high priest, he followed Jesus into the high priest's courtyard, but I had to wait outside at the door. The other disciple came back, spoke to the servant girl on duty there and brought me in. As I was going through the gate she asked me,

"So you are one of this man's disciples too, are you?"

I denied it before I had a chance to think. While I was below in the courtyard, another one of the servant girls of the high priest came by. When she saw me warming myself, she looked closely at me. "You also were with that Nazarene, Jesus," she said.

I told her I had no idea what she was talking about and went out into the entryway. After a little while, those standing near said to me, "Surely you are one of them, for you are a Galilean." I began to call down curses, and I swore at them, told them to ****** off. I shouted that I didn't know this man they were talking about.

Immediately I heard a cock crowing. Then I remembered the word Jesus had spoken to me, "Before the cock crows you will disown me three times." I broke down and wept. I disappeared off into the night.

I went away on my own. I don't know where I went now. I virtually lost the next two days in absolute despair and agony. I finally resurfaced early on the morning of the first day of the week. I met up with some of the others who told me what had happened. Of course I knew he was dead but I had no idea where they had buried him. Some of the women were going to finish off preparing his body for a proper burial because it had all been rushed at the end on account of the Sabbath.

These women, Mary Magdalene, another Mary and John's mother, Salome went off to the tomb and I stayed with John and some of the others. I felt so ashamed of myself. I didn't want to talk to any of them. I listened to John when he told us what had happened on the day they crucified Jesus. I was at least glad that his mother was being looked after and her sister Salome was helping her sort out the burial arrangements. John said Jesus had asked him to look after his mother Mary now, as if she were his own mother. That made sense, they were relatives after all. I was angry at everyone but mostly myself. We had a terrible argument about nothing at one point. I just exploded. It was just the grief and the shame of it all. I decided to go back to Galilee, to get out of the city and to go and try to salvage what was left of my fishing business. My good for nothing brother Andrew turned up and it was clear he wasn't too thrilled with the idea of going home to take up fishing again. To be honest at that point I just didn't care what he did.

As I was packing to leave, the women burst into the house with ridiculous stories about an empty tomb and angels and Jesus being alive again. I shouted at them that they were just being hysterical. Then Salome put her hand on my arm and looked me in the eye and said that the angel had specifically said they were to tell his disciples and me! She said the angel mentioned me by name and called me Peter, not Simon as if somehow that was significant. Again I burst into tears. I felt like a grain of sand rather than a rock.

Mary Magdalene was insistent that we go and look for ourselves. So John and I went to the tomb. She showed us where it was. Sure enough the tomb was empty and there were the grave clothes. I didn't know what to think. John and I came back and a little while later a very excited Mary returned saying she had met Jesus in the garden and he was very much alive. She said she had spoken with Jesus! She did not sound crazy but I didn't know what to think. All day there were rumours and comings and goings. Two people turned up who said they had met him on the road to Emmaus. Perhaps it was a ghost or someone who looked like him. They were absolutely convinced it was him.

On the evening of that first day of the week, a number of us former disciples were together, with the doors locked for fear of the Jewish leaders. We were all talking and wondering what to make of these things. Mary was adamant that she had spoken with Jesus and that she was to give us the message that he was risen and he was going to ascended to his Father. She added that Jesus had called us his brothers. I didn't feel much like a brother. I felt a coward and would not be surprised if I never saw Jesus again. We also heard that Judas had hung himself. That shut everyone up for a while. Then someone said. "Good riddance too." Several of them agreed. Then they started making furtive looks in my direction. I just started crying again. In a few moments the room went very quiet, there were a few audible gasps. I blew my nose on my sleeve and dried my eyes. To my amazement he was there in the room with us. Jesus was standing among us! I burst into tears again and buried my face in my hands. I heard him say, "Peace be with you!"

After he said this, he showed us his hands and side. After we got over the initial shock we were overjoyed when we saw the Lord and it wasn't a ghost. Again Jesus said, "Peace be with you! As the Father has sent me, I am sending you." He looked right at me when he said this. My eyes filled up. I wanted to say something. I wanted to tell him that I was so sorry. Then with that he breathed on us and said, "Receive the Holy Spirit. If you forgive anyone's sins, their sins are forgiven; if you do not forgive them, they are not forgiven." An amazing sense of peace filled the room. More to the point it filled my heart. I think he was saying that he had forgiven me and that I needed to forgive the rest of them, even my poor little brother Andrew. At that point I put my arm around Andrew's shoulders and hugged him to me. When we looked around Jesus was no longer there. I hadn't heard him leave.

A week later he came back again, this time we were all there, even Thomas who had been in a tremendously bad mood all week. He hadn't been there that first night and was really upset. He didn't believe any of us. On this occasion Thomas was with us and Jesus came and the two talked. It was a very touching moment in every sense of the word! I felt a little envious of Thomas. Inside I still felt I had failed him so badly.

Sometime later we left Jerusalem and went back to Galilee. There were seven of us, the Zebedee boys, Thomas, Nathanael from Cana in Galilee, two other disciples and me. I had told them that I was going out to fish and they came with me. So we went out and got into the boat, but that night we caught nothing.

Early in the morning, we saw someone on the shore who had a fire burning. It was Jesus but we did not realise that at first. A voice we recognised called out to us, "Hey boys, haven't you got any fish?"

"No," we answered. How did he know that? He said, "Throw your net on the right side of the boat and you will find some." When we did, we were unable to haul the net in because of the large number of fish.

Suddenly this felt familiar, I remembered another big catch like this a few years ago! Then John said to me, "It is the Lord, Simon!" As soon as I heard him say, "It is the Lord," I tied my clothes around my waist because I was naked and jumped into the water and waded to the shore. The others followed in the boat, towing the net full of fish, for they were not far from shore, about a hundred yards. When I got on the beach I saw a fire of burning coals there with fish on it, and some bread. I stood there dripping, looking at the fish and the fire and Jesus.

Jesus said to us, "Bring some of the fish you have just caught." So I climbed back into the boat and dragged the net ashore. It was full of large fish, but even with so many fish the net was not torn. Jesus said to us, "Come and have breakfast." None us dared ask him, "Who are you?" We knew it was him.

Jesus came, took the bread and gave it to us, and did the same with the fish. When we had finished eating, Jesus turned to me and looked straight into my eyes and asked me if I loved him more than the others. I instantly remembered my proud boast that even if this lot abandoned him I would not. I felt uncomfortable but I answered, "Yes, Lord, you know that I am a loving friend to you." Somehow the word just wouldn't come out of my mouth. I had not loved him. I had denied him! I couldn't say I loved him, at best I was his friend.

Jesus said, "Look after my lambs." There was a long silence as we gazed into the burning embers of the fire. Again, Jesus asked me if I loved him. He didn't call me Peter, just Simon. This time he was not asking me to compare myself to the others. It was a straight question from him to me. Inside I was in agony. My shame and my guilt at my denial were flooding my heart.

I answered him again, "Yes, Lord, you know that I have the love of a friend for you." I felt so churned up. I remembered looking into the embers of a fire on that fateful night when I denied that I knew him. I was struggling to hold back my tears again. Jesus said, "Be a shepherd to my sheep." There was another long silence.

Then the third time Jesus said to me, "Simon son of John, are you my loving friend?"

I was heartbroken because Jesus asked me the third time. I said, "Lord, you know all things; you know that I love you like this." By now the tears were pouring down my face. After quite some time, I felt him reach out and put a hand on my shoulder. "Feed my sheep." He said. Then he went on to say that it was really true that when I was a young man I dressed myself and went where I wanted to go but when I am old I would stretch out my hands, and someone else would dress me and lead me where I did not want to go. I wondered what he meant by that.

Then he said to me, "Follow me!" It was just like that day I had first really met him on the beach there in Galilee. I had seen a huge catch of fish that day too and I felt a sinful man then, but he asked me to follow him. Now again on the beach, a great catch of fish. He asked me if I was his friend three times. Three times I had denied him. Three times he asked me if I loved him. Each time I felt he gave something back to me. Before, he said we would become fishers of men, now, he was telling me there was a change of job coming. I was going to be a shepherd. This time he asked me to follow him again. So I did. No more denials, just me being me with him. I think you know how the rest of the story unfolds."

PETER IN THE GOSPELS

Simon Peter ran a fishing business in Bethsaida in Galilee. He was named Simon, son of Jonah or John until renamed Peter by Jesus. Matthew, Mark and Luke all recount how Peter's mother-in-law was healed by Jesus at their home in Capernaum, which, coupled with Paul referring to his wife in I Corinthians clearly depict Peter as a married man. His wife is known in the Orthodox Church as Febronia and her feast is celebrated on June 28. In the Synoptics, Peter (then Simon) was a fisherman along with his brother Andrew and the sons of Zebedee, James and John.

In Luke, Simon Peter owns the boat that Jesus uses to preach to the multitudes who were pressing on him at the shore of Lake Gennesaret. Jesus then amazes Simon and his companions, James and John, by telling them to lower their nets, whereupon they catch a huge number of fish. Immediately after this, they follow him. The Gospel of John gives a comparable account in which we are told that it was Andrew and an unnamed disciple who heard John the Baptist announce Jesus as the "lamb of God" and then followed Jesus. Andrew then went and fetched his brother Simon, saying, "We have found the 'Messiah'. He then brought Simon to Jesus.

The three Synoptic Gospels all mention that, when Jesus was arrested, one of his companions cut off the ear of a servant of the High Priest. The Gospel of John also includes this event and names Peter as the swordsman and Malchus as the victim. Luke adds that Jesus touched the ear and miraculously healed it. This healing of the servant's ear is the last of the thirty-seven miracles performed by Jesus in the Bible.

Later that evening Peter denied that he was a follower of Jesus and as had been predicted by Jesus, the cock crowed. Peter flees from the scene distraught and does not appear again until the morning of the resurrection.

In John's gospel, Peter is the first person to enter the empty tomb, although the women and the beloved disciple see it before him. In Luke's account, the women's report of the empty tomb is dismissed by the apostles, and Peter is the only one who goes to check for himself. In fact, he runs to the tomb. After seeing the grave clothes he goes home, apparently without informing the other disciples.

Paul's first letter to the Corinthians contains a list of resurrection appearances by Jesus, the first of which is to Peter. Historically, this is the first written mention of a list of resurrection appearances as the gospels had not been written when Paul wrote First Corinthians around 55AD. It includes some appearances not mentioned in the Gospels such as the group of five hundred and the sole appearance to James the brother of Jesus. Here, Paul apparently follows an early tradition that Peter was the first to see the risen Christ, which however, did not seem to have been included when the Gospels were written.

In the final chapter of John, Peter, in one of the resurrection appearances of Jesus, three times affirmed his love for Jesus balancing his threefold denial, and Jesus reconfirmed Peter's position.

PETER IN THE ACTS OF THE APOSTLES AND BEYOND

Peter is listed first among the twelve disciples in the Gospels and in the Book of Acts. He is also frequently mentioned in the Gospels as being a part of a special group within the Twelve, along with James and John, who were present at incidents at which the others were not present. He often confesses his faith in Jesus as the Messiah.

Peter is often depicted in the Gospels as spokesman of all the disciples. Luke, the author of Acts, portrays Peter as an extremely important figure within the early Christian community, with Peter delivering a significant sermon on the day of Pentecost. According to Acts, Peter took the lead in selecting a replacement for Judas. He was twice arraigned, with John, before the Sanhedrin and directly defied them. He undertook a missionary journey to Lydda, Joppa and Caesarea, becoming instrumental in the decision to evangelise the Gentiles having preached to and baptised the Roman Cornelius and his household.

About halfway through, the Acts of the Apostles turns its attention away from Peter and to the activities of Paul, and the Bible is mostly silent on what occurred to Peter thereafter.

Acts 12 tells how Peter was put into prison by King Herod but was then released by an angel. At the Council of Jerusalem in about 50AD, Paul and the leaders of the Jerusalem church met and decided to embrace Gentile converts. Acts portrays Peter as successfully opposing the Christian Pharisees who insisted on circumcision of the gentile Christians.

Peter, referred to as Cephas, is mentioned briefly in Paul's Letter to the Galatians which describes a trip by Paul to Jerusalem where he meets Peter, and a trip by Peter to Antioch where Paul rebuked him for treating Gentile converts as inferior to Jewish Christians. These are the earliest references to Peter since Galatians is the first piece of Christian literature written.

Church tradition ascribes the letters First and Second Peter to the Apostle Peter, as does the text of Second Peter itself.

Papias (130AD) reported that the Gospel of Mark was based on Peter's memoirs, a tradition accepted by most scholars today. *"Mark,"* says Papias (according to the testimony of Eusebius, [Ecclesiastical History, 3. 39]), *"becoming the interpreter of Peter, wrote accurately, though not in order, whatever he remembered of what was either said or done by Christ; for he was neither a hearer of the Lord nor a follower of Him, but afterwards, as I said, [he was a follower] of Peter, who arranged the discourses for use, but not according to the order in which they were uttered by the Lord."*

To the same effect Irenaeus [Against Heresies, 3,1]:*"Matthew published a Gospel while Peter and Paul were preaching and founding the Church at Rome; and after their departure (or decease), Mark, the disciple and interpreter of Peter, he also gave forth to us in writing the things which were preached by Peter."* And Clement of Alexandria is still more specific, in a passage preserved to us by Eusebius [Ecclesiastical History, 6. 14]:*"Peter having publicly preached the word at Rome, and spoken forth the Gospel by the Spirit, many of those present exhorted Mark, as having long been a follower of his, and remembering what he had said, to write what had been spoken; and that having prepared the Gospel, he delivered it to those who had asked him for it; which, when Peter came to the knowledge of, he neither decidedly forbade nor encouraged him."*

Eusebius continues, *"The apostle, when he knew by the revelation of the Spirit what had been done, was delighted with the zeal of those men, and sanctioned the reading of the writing (that is, of this Gospel of Mark) in the churches "*[Ecclesiastical History, 2. 15]. And giving a similar statement in another of his works , he says, *"Peter, from excess of humility, did not think himself qualified to write the Gospel; but Mark, his acquaintance and pupil, is said to have recorded his relations of the actings of Jesus. And Peter testifies these things of himself; for all things that are recorded by Mark are said to be memoirs of Peter's discourses."*

In a strong tradition of the Early Church, Peter is said to have founded the church in Rome with Paul, and served as its bishop. He wrote two epistles, and then met martyrdom in Rome along with Paul. Peter might have visited Corinth as a party of "Cephas" existed there.

In the epilogue of the Gospel of John, Jesus hints at the death by which Peter would glorify God,…"*when you are old you will stretch out your hands, and another will dress you and take you where you do not want to go."* This is interpreted by some as a reference to Peter's crucifixion. The death of Peter is attested to by Tertullian at the end of the second century, and by Origen in *Eusebius*, Church History III.1. Origen wrote: *"Peter was crucified at Rome with his head downwards, as he himself had desired to suffer."*

Early church tradition also says Peter probably died by crucifixion with arms outstretched at the time of the Great Fire of Rome in the year 64AD. According to the apocryphal Acts of Peter he was crucified head down. Tradition also locates his burial place where the Basilica of St Peter was later built, in the Vatican, directly beneath the Basilica's high altar.

Clement of Rome in his *Letter to the Corinthians* (Chapter 5), written between 80–98AD, speaks of Peter's martyrdom in the following terms, *"Let us take the noble examples of our own generation. Through jealousy and envy the greatest and most just pillars of the Church were persecuted, and came even unto death… Peter, through unjust envy, endured not one or two but many labours, and at last, having delivered his testimony, departed unto the place of glory due to him."*

THE KINGDOM OF GOD IS THE FATHER'S REALM OF LOVE

Peter is one of the most complex characters in the New Testament. We read and know much about him. From the earliest days of the church, Mark's gospel has been linked to Peter as mentioned above. Mark's gospel does not sanitise or hide Peter's failings and stumbling. This makes him a vulnerable and accessible eyewitness.

A great emphasis in Peter's early teaching in Acts is the resurrection of Jesus as a powerful sign of the presence and power of the Kingdom of God breaking into the world. In the Gospel of Mark the initial thrust of Jesus' ministry is about the kingdom. In looking at the other gospels there is a clear connection with the Father to the kingdom. In the prayer of Jesus that he teaches his disciples, he addresses the prayer to his Father. Surprisingly, Mark does not record this prayer which from very early on became widely used by the church. This prayer inclusively draws the disciples into addressing God as Father which we have seen was his usual practice. In the prayer Jesus calls for the coming of the Father's kingdom in terms of the will of God being done on earth as it is in heaven. Jesus' teaching on the kingdom is an expression of the realm or sphere of the Father's love in action in the world and the lives of all men.

The first specific mention of the Father in Mark's gospel is in 8: 38 where Jesus speaks about his return when he comes in his Father's glory with the holy angels. This is after Peter's confession that Jesus is the Anointed One, The Messiah, The Christ. We are left wondering if this was the beginning of a new revelation for Peter in which he begins to see more clearly the relationship of Jesus with the Father.

JESUS, THE FATHER'S SON, IS THE FOUNDATION ON WHICH THE CHURCH IS BUILT.

Very shortly before this we read how Jesus questioned the disciples about who people were saying he was. Mark records Peter's response, that Jesus is the Messiah. However, in Matthew's version of the same account that additional detail is added.

> *Simon Peter answered, "You are the Messiah, the Son of the living God." Jesus replied, Blessed are you, Simon son of Jonah, for this was not revealed to you by flesh and blood, but by my Father in heaven. And I tell you that you are Peter, and on this rock I will build my church, and the gates of Hades will not overcome it. I will give you the keys of the kingdom of heaven; whatever you bind on earth will be bound in heaven, and whatever you loose on earth will be loosed in heaven."* Matthew 16:17-19

Matthew's Gospel was written with the intention of giving teaching to the early church based on the life and ministry of Jesus, therefore this may reflect issues being raised within the early church. Perhaps there was a degree of modesty in Peter that the revelation he received which Jesus says came from his Father, so is not fully included in Mark's gospel. Perhaps that realisation occurred to him later as the truth took deeper hold of his heart and mind.

The play on words used by Jesus when he called Simon Petros, and the word petra, which he uses to describe the foundation of the church, is significant. Roman Catholic tradition has long held this means it is the Apostle Peter as a person, on which the Church is built. Protestant tradition on the other hand has been reluctant to give credence to the resulting Catholic claims for the priority of the church of Rome over all other churches. They have seen this 'petra' to mean that it is the declaration of Peter, that is the rocklike foundation of the church. The declaration is that Jesus is the anointed one, the Messiah and indeed the Son of the living God. Therefore the rock is the revelation that God who is Father, has declared that his one and only beloved Son Jesus, is both Lord and Christ. On the day of Pentecost as Peter concluded his first sermon he declared this truth unequivocally,

> *"God has raised this Jesus to life, and we are all witnesses of it. Exalted to the right hand of God, he has received from the Father the promised Holy Spirit and has poured out what you now see and hear"......"Therefore let all Israel be assured of this: God has made this Jesus, whom you crucified, both Lord and Messiah."* Acts 2:32-33; 36

THE GLORY OF THE FATHER IS HIS LOVE

When Jesus went up with Peter, James and John to the mountain an event occurred which deeply impacted Peter. It is recorded by Mark and Peter writes about this himself in his second letter.

In his personal memory in the second letter, Peter begins by saying he wants to remind his readers of the truth and that his intention is to do that as long as he is alive. 2 Peter 2:12 - 14. Peter then says, *"I will make every effort to see that after my departure you will always be able to remember these things.*" It has been suggested that this a reference to "my son Mark," referred to in 1 Peter 5:13 who, as we have seen, is believed to have based his gospel on the memories and teaching of Peter.

He continues in his second letter,

> *"For we did not follow cleverly devised stories when we told you about the coming of our Lord Jesus Christ in power, but we were eyewitnesses of his majesty. He received honour and glory from God the Father when the voice came to him from the Majestic Glory, saying, "This is my Son, whom I love; with him I am well pleased." We ourselves heard this voice that came from heaven when we were with him on the sacred mountain."* 2 Peter 1:16-18

Peter is describing what he saw and heard personally on the mountain. After years of reflection he writes as an eyewitness of how the Father spoke and affirmed Jesus as his son whom he loves and is so proud of. This, says Peter, was Jesus receiving honour and glory from his Father. The glory he received was this loving affirmation of his Sonship and the pleasure and pride the Father felt in him.

The Apostle John, who was also there on the mountain at the beginning of his Gospel says, *"The Word became flesh and made his dwelling among us. We have seen his glory, the glory of the one and only Son, who came from the Father, full of grace and truth".* John 1:14.

John, like Peter, had seen the glory of God in and on Jesus. It was not so much the dazzling whiteness on the mountain but the declaration of the Father's love for Jesus. In his final prayer when Jesus has prayed for himself and then his disciples, he turns to pray for all of us.

> *"My prayer is not for them alone. I pray also for those who will believe in me through their message, that all of them may be one, Father, just as you are in me and I am in you. May they also be in us so that the world may believe that you have sent me. I have given them the glory that you gave me, that they may be one as we are one. I in them and you in me, so that they may be brought to complete unity."* John 17:20-23

The wonderful truth here is that Jesus has given us his glory. The same glory that the father had given him. This is being prayed by Jesus before he goes to the cross. It describes something that the disciples had already been experiencing. It is given to us in order to unite us together with Father, Son and Holy Spirit. It does not mean that we go around with halo-like gold discs on our heads. It does not mean we suddenly have mouths full of gold teeth, or are sprinkled with gold dust, however exciting a manifestation of his presence that may be. Instead we have received the weight of his glory. The very substance of his love poured into us. The disciples had been on the receiving end of that love as Jesus fathered them. Jesus says to them in John 15:9. *"As the Father has loved me, so have I loved you. Now remain in my love."* They knew what love looked like and felt like. They had received his love in the same way as the Father had declared his glory over his Son.

THE FATHER HAS NOT LEFT US AS ORPHANS

In the upper room on that last evening together, Jesus was challenging the disciples and comforting them in their distress. He promised them that he would not leave them comfortless but he would send another comforter, the Holy Spirit, who would remind them of all his words, comfort and come alongside them in their distress and be with them forever as his abiding presence within them. Paul confirms this in his writings as he describes the Holy Spirit pouring the love of the Father into our hearts by saying that God's love has been poured out into our hearts through the Holy Spirit, who has been given to us. Romans 5:5

Jesus said to them that he would give them another comforter. This implies that they had been comforted by someone already. Indeed, Jesus had been a comforter to them and had fathered them. He had walked with them and poured the love of the Father, which he had received, into them, day by day. They knew Jesus as a comforter and they would soon know the Holy Spirit as a comforter. Then Jesus said to his disciples that he will not leave them as orphans, he will come to them. These are words that Jesus was hearing his Father speak and he shared them with his friends. John 14:18. The Father would come to them as a comforter also. They would not be left as orphans without comfort. Some of the disciples may have been physical orphans whose parents had died, but not all. Certainly James and John were not orphans. So Jesus' intention must have been more than just a physical comforting but something deeper.

When Adam and his wife listened to Satan's lies in the Garden of Eden and started to distrust God, they took the fruit from the tree of the knowledge of good and evil and sin like a virus tore through their hearts and minds. They fell and they lost connection with God as their Father. It was as if from that day the whole human race had entered into an orphan-like condition in relation to God. They could no longer see him through the eyes of a son but as the broken and separated orphan-like offspring who no longer had any idea of what their father was like or indeed who he was.

Now in those last hours with his disciples, Jesus is telling them they are no longer going to be left with orphan-like hearts. They have a Father who is coming to them. The revelation that Jesus had spent three years explaining in and through his life was becoming deeper and richer.

Peter spent the rest of his life not as a broken orphan but as a son to God his Father, comforted and loved by him, living in union with Jesus, walking as Jesus walked, full of the Holy Spirit. The final words on this are from Peter himself.

> *"Praise be to the God and Father of our Lord Jesus Christ! In his great mercy he has given us new birth into a living hope through the resurrection of Jesus Christ from the dead, and into an inheritance that can never perish, spoil or fade. This inheritance is kept in heaven for you, who through faith are shielded by God's power until the coming of the salvation that is ready to be revealed in the last time."* 1 Peter 1:3-5

THE ELEVENTH STORY TELLER

JOHN MARK
THE GOSPEL WRITER

"I had been helping my mother all evening. We had a house in Jerusalem at that time. Our home had been used a lot in the first few years when the Followers of the Way were active in the city. My mother Mary was one of several women who were in the group. She was not the Mary who was his mother or Mary Magdalene, though we knew all those women. We had a large house with enough room for people to regularly gather when they wanted to talk and meet together.

On that particular evening, Jesus and a group of his disciples had asked to use our house to celebrate the Passover meal. We had a large upstairs room that we sometimes used for these sort of events. I had been walking home from the well with a large water jar when I was met by Simon Peter and John. They followed me home and asked if they could use the room. They did most of the preparations themselves but I helped take things up to the room and later helped serve the meal. As was the custom I took large jugs of water and bowls up to the room so that they could wash when they all arrived. I expected that I would need to wash their feet for them. When evening came, Jesus arrived with his twelve disciples. He told me that I did not need to do that. It was taken care of.

They were reclining at the table eating. I was placing more food on the table when I heard him say that one of them would betray him, one who was eating at the table with him. I could see that they looked very alarmed and saddened by this, and one by one they said to him, "Surely you don't mean me?" He then said that it was one of the Twelve. He leaned close to John and told him that the one who dipped bread into the bowl with him would be the one. I stood back in the shadows and listened carefully to every word. He said that the Son of Man would go just as it was written about him. But woe to that man who betrayed the Son of Man! It would be better for him if he had not been born. The atmosphere became very tense in the room after that. I brought more bread to the room for them. While they were eating, Jesus took some of the bread, and when he had given thanks, he broke it and gave it to his disciples, and said, "Take it; this is my body." Then he took a cup of wine, and when he had given thanks, he gave it to them, and they all drank from it. "This is my blood of the covenant, which is poured out for many". He went on to say, "I tell you, I will not drink again from the fruit of the vine until that day when I drink it new in the kingdom of God."

I heard all this from the shadows and after that I cleared away the cups and left them to it. The evening was a long one. Most of my family had gone to bed and I lay on a mattress waiting for them to finish so I could blow out the lamps when they left. I must have nodded off to sleep because I woke up to the sound of them singing a hymn. It was quite late into the night. The group left and went out into the darkness. I so much wanted to follow them so I grabbed a linen garment and slipped out after them into the night. They walked a short distance through the city and out of the gate and down into the Kidron Valley. They then followed the path that led them up into the olive groves and gardens along the far side of the valley. It looked like they were heading for the Mount of Olives.

I followed them from a short distance behind so I could hear them talking as they went. At one point Jesus stopped and turned to them and told them that they would all fall away, because it was written: 'I will strike the shepherd, and the sheep will be scattered.' He went on to say that after he had risen, he would go ahead of them into Galilee. I heard Simon Peter declare, "Even if all fall away, I will not."

Jesus then stopped and said to him, "Truly I tell you, today, yes, tonight, before the cock crows twice you yourself will disown me three times." Simon Peter insisted very emphatically that, even if he had to die with him, he would never disown him. All the others were saying the same.

They walked up the valley and arrived at a place where there was a garden called Gethsemane. I followed them, keeping a distance but I was still near enough to hear what was going on. When they got there Jesus asked his disciples to sit there while he went and prayed.

He took Peter, James and John along with him and went further into the garden. He was deeply distressed and troubled. I crawled on the ground between the shrubs and trees so I could see and hear him. He said to the three of them, "My soul is overwhelmed with sorrow to the point of death. Stay here and keep watch."

Going a little farther, he fell to the ground and prayed something about if possible the hour might pass from him. I was hidden among the bushes in the garden and knew that if I got caught by the disciples I would be in trouble, so I kept out of sight. I crept along the ground as close as I could until I could hear the actual words that Jesus was praying. He said, "Abba, Father, everything is possible for you. Take this cup from me. Yet not what I will, but what you will." He called God, Abba! That amazed me and it struck me that I had never heard anyone address God like that. It was the name I used to call my father when I was a little boy.

After a while he stood up and returned to his disciples and found them all sound asleep. "Simon," he said to Peter, "are you asleep? Couldn't you keep watch for one hour? Watch and pray so that you will not fall into temptation. The spirit is willing, but the flesh is weak."

Once more he went away and prayed the same thing. He addressed God as Abba again. When he came back, he again found them sleeping, because their eyes were heavy. They did not know what to say to him. Returning the third time, he said to them, "Are you still sleeping and resting? Enough! The hour has come. Look, the Son of Man is delivered into the hands of sinners. Rise! Let us go! Here comes my betrayer!"

Suddenly I was very afraid because I could see torches coming up the path into the garden. Just as Jesus was speaking, Judas, one of the Twelve, appeared. With him was a crowd armed with swords and clubs, who had been sent from the chief priests, the teachers of the law and the elders. It seemed that the betrayer had arranged a signal with them. The one he kissed would be the man to arrest and lead away under guard. Going at once to Jesus, Judas said, "Rabbi!" and kissed him. The men seized Jesus and arrested him. Then Peter who was standing near drew a sword that he had been carrying and struck the servant of the high priest, cutting off his ear. There was blood everywhere. You know how ears bleed! Jesus said, " Am I leading a rebellion, that you have come out with swords and clubs to capture me? Every day I was with you, teaching in the temple courts, and you did not arrest me. But the Scriptures must be fulfilled." Then all of his disciples scattered and ran, they deserted him and fled. I could not believe it. They just ran away.

One of the guards nearly fell on top of me in the dark and they tried to grab me too. I struggled and managed to break free and ran as fast as I could away from them. To my horror, I realised in my panic they had snatched my linen garment and I was running away naked. I kept running hoping no one would see me and I finally made it home.

It was a night I have remembered all my life. This was the only time I had seen Jesus. I was not one of his group in those days. My home in Jerusalem where my mother Mary lived became a centre of activity after that night. There was the terrible crucifixion and after the Sabbath, there was the amazing realisation that Jesus had risen from the dead. They met in our house on many occasions. In fact, Jesus himself came there at least twice. Well, really he just appeared there rather than came because no one heard him knock at the door. I had locked the doors myself because we were all rather afraid that the Temple guards might come and try to arrest us all. He just was there in the room with all of them. He even wanted something to eat which I took upstairs and gave to him. He was no ghost, he had quite a good appetite.

His friends and family came a lot to the house over the next few weeks. In fact, there were times when it was packed with people. It was a good job the room upstairs was large. I will never forget one morning, it was about ten days after Jesus had last been seen. That in itself was amazing because instead of just disappearing he seemed to rise up in the sky. Well, that morning there must have been well over a hundred or more people in the house. We were all praying and waiting as he told us to do. Then the house seemed to shake as a really strong gust of wind blew through the place. It was almost like an earthquake and then the wind seemed to fill the house. Except it wasn't like any wind I had ever felt before. It was like flames almost and seemed to individually separate out on to each one of us. This was what Jesus had promised, we were filled, overwhelmed and consumed with the Holy Spirit. I felt like I had been drinking too much. I just laughed and cried out in some strange language. I didn't have a clue what it meant. It was absolutely wonderful. We all seemed like drunkards. It caused such a noise that the neighbours started banging on the door to find out what had happened.

People just started falling out into the street. It was like the wildest party I had ever been to. Crowds of people started coming and asking what was going on. It was the beginning of a new adventure for me. You can read about it in Luke's second book.

Much later on, when my cousin Barnabas took me with him to Cyprus with Paul, or Saul as he was called in those days. I told them about that night when Jesus had been praying in the garden and the way Jesus called God Abba. Paul was very interested in that. He said it is the way we too can address God the Father. He is Abba to all of us because his Spirit is within us too.

Later on when I wrote down the things that Peter remembered I added the events of that evening into the story."

JOHN MARK THE GOSPEL WRITER

We know very little about John Mark, the writer of the second Gospel. He makes his first appearance in Acts 12. It is to his mother Mary's home that Peter goes after he is released from prison by an angel. The church had been gathering there to pray for his release,

> *"Peter went to the house of Mary the mother of John, also called Mark, where many people had gathered and were praying. Peter knocked at the outer entrance, and a servant named Rhoda came to answer the door."* Acts 12:12-14

This places John Mark as a resident of Jerusalem in the early period of the days of the church. Also potentially in Jerusalem in the final week of Jesus life. It is quite possible that in that last week Mark may have encountered Jesus and witnessed many of the events that he later records in his Gospel from Chapter 11 to the end which are very detailed and have the ring of an eyewitness to them.

Traditionally it was thought that John Mark was also a cousin to Barnabas the travelling companion of Paul. At the end of Acts 12 Saul, that is Paul, and Barnabas who had been in Jerusalem returned to Antioch *"taking with them John, also called Mark."*

In Acts 13 when Saul and Barnabas set off on the first missionary journey they take John Mark with them and he stays with them while on Cyprus. However, when crossing over the mainland again they came to *"Pamphylia, where John left them to return to Jerusalem."*

Luke records,

> *"Some time later Paul said to Barnabas, 'Let us go back and visit the believers in all the towns where we preached the word of the Lord and see how they are doing." Barnabas wanted to take John, also called Mark, with them, but Paul did not think it wise to take him, because he had deserted them in Pamphylia and had not continued with them in the work. They had such a sharp disagreement that they parted company Barnabas took Mark and sailed for Cyprus,"* Acts 15:36-39

We do not know what John Mark did after that except he is mentioned by Peter in his first letter I Peter 5:13 where he refers to him as "my son Mark". This is generally accepted to be the same Mark as mentioned in

Acts. At some point Mark and Paul are reconciled as he is mentioned by Paul in his second letter to Timothy he asks him to get Mark and bring him with him, because he is helpful to him in his ministry. 2 Timothy 4:11

Paul also mentioned Mark, the cousin of Barnabas, explicitly in Colossians when he says,

> *"Aristarchus, my fellow prisoner, sends you his greetings; and also Barnabas's cousin Mark, about whom you received instructions; if he comes to you, welcome him."* Colossians 4:10

Apparently Mark, the cousin of Barnabas was with Paul during his first imprisonment in Rome, during which he wrote the four Prison Epistles - Ephesians, Colossians, Philemon, and Philippians. Paul mentioned the same Mark in Philemon 24, which was written at the same time, and carried by the same letter carrier, Tychicus, Colossians 4:7, to the recipients in the city of Colosse.

There are no other specific references to him within the New Testament, except of course the Gospel that is credited to him as being the author. There is no point in the Gospel that specifically mentions him by name.

The Church however, very early on, accredited the second of the four Gospels to Mark. According to Papias, writing in the early second century, this gospel was by

> *"Mark, (who) having become the interpreter of Peter, wrote down accurately, though not in order, whatsoever he remembered of the things said or done by Christ."*

Other early writers such as Irenaeus of Lyon in Gaul (about 177AD,) agree with this who said. *"No early church tradition and no church father ascribes the Gospel to anyone other than Mark."*

On reading through Mark's Gospel it can be noted that Peter is often mentioned and not always in a very complimentary way. He is presented 'warts and all'. No attempt is made to sanitise Peter's failure. This is taken not as an attack on the character of Peter but more on his honesty in openness to his personal vulnerability if indeed he was the primary source of much of Mark's writings.

This brings us to the curious mention of the young man in Mark 14:51. This is the young man who flees naked from the Garden of Gethsemane. Many scholars have speculated that this is indeed a personal reference by the author to himself in his gospel. Some have even suggested it is like his signature albeit still anonymously. This literary device, whilst it may be used occasionally today, has never been identified in any other ancient literature. So this may be a romantic modern notion rather than a real reference by Mark to himself. The only other character who is possibly identified as this young man is Lazarus of John chapter 11. In my opinion that is a bit too speculative as he does not appear in Mark's Gospel at all.

In my story above I have taken that speculation one stage further and used dramatic license to place Mark not only in the garden but also in the vicinity of the upper room story also. Most of my reconstruction is taken straight from Mark's Gospel. Reading Mark chapter 14, we have some very specific information that has the feel of eyewitness testimony about it. Also it is generally accepted that Mark's Gospel was the earliest Gospel written and may have been used by Matthew and Luke as a source for some of their Gospel narratives. The chapter in question has many small details that seem to have come from someone close to the events described.

Perhaps the most significant is the description of what happened in the garden itself. Jesus is described as going alone to pray some way away from Peter, James and John. We are told that after Jesus has prayed and he returns to the disciples he finds them all asleep. It raises the issue of the description of Jesus' prayer that is recorded. If all the disciples, including Peter, are asleep, how would they know what he had prayed? Unless someone else was there in the garden who was listening and watching. It is my conclusion that this was John Mark and he was also the young man who flees naked from the garden.

JESUS CALLS HIS FATHER ABBA

What does Mark tell us about Jesus and how does this relate to the revelation of the Father that Jesus brings? The most obvious truth here is seen in the way Jesus prayed and how he addressed God in prayer.

Of the three Gospel writers who record Jesus praying in the garden only Mark says that he addresses his father as Abba. This is the most intimate expression that a small child uses to speak to his father. It is akin to papa or perhaps "daddy". It is the term still used all over the Middle East by little children when addressing their fathers.

It speaks of home, of love and affection, of closeness and belonging. It speaks of relationship and intimacy. When Jesus prayed, he enjoyed the very closest of connection with his Father. Mark says as he is "*deeply distressed and troubled*", overwhelmed with sorrow he falls to the ground.

It is in this moment of deep pain and anguish that Jesus cries out to his Abba. The very resonance in the word would have comforted his aching heart.

This is pure revelation that Mark hears and records for us. It becomes deeply ingrained into the DNA of the early church as they realised that they too were sons and daughters to the Father and that they could also address the Father in such terms of intimacy as Jesus did.

The apostle Paul, in the letter to the Galatians which is the first letter he wrote that is recorded in the New Testament, also uses this term.

> *"But when the time had fully come, God sent his Son, born of a woman, born under the law, to redeem those under the law, that we might receive the full rights of sons. Because you are sons, God sent the Spirit of his Son into our hearts, the Spirit who calls out, 'Abba, Father'."* Galatians 4:4

It is significant that this letter, written in response to the crisis that hit the early church recorded in Acts 15, is the first piece of Christian writing. It precedes any of the Gospels. It was probably written before the start of Paul's second missionary journey when Paul re visits Galatia. In this letter, Paul gives a very clear statement of the true gospel that he taught. He speaks about sonship and that it is by being in Christ that we become sons and daughters to the Father.

> *"But when the set time had fully come, God sent his Son, born of a woman, born under the law, to redeem those under the law, that we might receive the full rights of sonship. Because you are his sons, God sent the Spirit of his Son into*

our hearts, the Spirit who calls out, "Abba, Father." So you are no longer a slave, but God's child; and since you are his child, God has made you also an heir." Galatians 4:4-7

In this passage he explains how the Father places the spirit of sonship in our hearts through the Holy Spirit because of the redemption Jesus had bought for us by his death on the cross. Then he states that the very Spirit of his Son is in our hearts and welling up within us comes the cry of our hearts to the Father that says Abba!

This then places us in the position of sons. We receive the full rights of sonship. Redemption is the process that brings us into this position where we receive the spirit of sonship. The translation is often rendered 'adoption' but the context makes this an unhelpful idea. Adoption in modern thinking is a process whereby a child who is orphaned is taken on by new adoptive parents. It describes a whole long legal process. The Greek word Paul uses is 'uiothesia' which is a difficult word to translate. It literally means "son placed". The nearest word that early English translators used was adoption but this is not true to the context that Paul is describing. The process that brings us into sonship is redemption. God's lost and wayward offspring are redeemed by the death of Jesus and as a result are placed at the end of the process in the position of sons. We are Abba's sons and daughters in just the same way as Jesus is Abba's son. The same level of intimacy and closeness, of belonging and loving affection is ours too.

"And by him we cry, Abba, Father. The Spirit himself testifies with our spirit that we are God's children." Romans 8:15-16

The Spirit speaks to our spirit that we belong to Abba.

I have wondered how Paul received this revelation. Perhaps this was known widely in the early church. Or maybe he heard this from young John Mark who was with him on the first part of the journey that eventually took Paul to Galatia and the planting of those first churches. I can imagine that often they would have talked about what Mark had heard and seen in his brief encounters with the disciples and maybe even his observation of Jesus in the Garden of Gethsemane.

Whatever the way this was remembered it has become part of our glorious inheritance as sons and daughters. We too are Abba's children and we can relate to him in exactly the same way as Jesus did, with the same assurance and intimacy as him.

THE TWELFTH STORY TELLER

SALOME
JESUS' AUNT

"My husband Zebedee had been a fisherman since he was a boy, on Lake Gennesaret, or as we sometimes call it, the Sea of Galilee. His father before was a fisherman too. We owned our own boats and we had our own business. We were doing well, given that life in those days was hard. Galilee was always being overrun with foreign armies. Now it is the Romans. They are brutal with their taxes. There is hardly anything left after all those taxes.

We lived in Capernaum on the shore of the lake. I moved there from my home town Nazareth, when I married Zebedee. Most of my family lived in Nazareth including my sister Mary. She was a strange one as a young girl. It all began when she was engaged to Joseph Bar Heli. She had a very odd experience one day that she told me about. We shared a bed in our family home and you know how it is with sisters. We don't have many secrets from each other. Well Mary said she had been visited by an angel. Of course no one believed that! Then she went off to see a relative of ours who we had heard was pregnant down in Judea. My mother thought it would be good for this relative Elizabeth who was really quite old to have Mary there to help her for a while. When Mary came back a few months later it was obvious to everyone she was pregnant! It was shocking. The whole family was ashamed of her and everyone was talking about her in the village.

My parents sent for Joseph the local carpenter, who was betrothed to Mary, because they assumed that he was the father. The house was in uproar. You should have heard my father shouting when Joseph turned up. Joseph was very upset too. He denied it vehemently. There were tears and Mary was sobbing her heart out. She had some story about this angel coming to her and that the baby was a gift from God. She even said something about the baby being the Son of God. Father told her to be quiet in case any of the neighbours heard her say this and told the Rabbi as this was blasphemous. They said they might even stone her for being a harlot. It was a terrible evening. Eventually Joseph left after telling our father that he would divorce her quietly but he could not marry her as the baby was definitely not his.

When we went to bed that night Mary told me that the angel had told her the baby would be a boy and that she was to call him Jesus. That was ridiculous of course! No one knows what sex a baby will be until it is born. How could she know?

Next day Joseph came back to the house. He looked dreadful, as if he had been awake all night. He wanted to talk with our parents and he called Mary in too. I was in our bedroom and I could hear everything that they said and I was peeping through the curtain.

Joseph began by taking Mary's hand so tenderly and looking into her eyes with the most beautiful smile. He didn't look like a man about to disown her. Then he turned to my father and said that when he finally had fallen asleep he had a vivid dream. He said an angel came to him in the dream and said, "Joseph son of David, do not be afraid to take Mary home as your wife, because the baby that is conceived in her is from the Holy Spirit. She will give birth to a son, and you are to give him the name Jesus, because he will save his people from their sins." My parents were speechless. Mary was beaming but tears were running down her face. I burst in because I wanted to tell them what Mary had told me. She knew it would be a boy and to call him Jesus, but she had not told Joseph that!

My parents told me to mind my own business! But Joseph and Mary both said that it was true. They both had been told quite independently by the angel that the baby would be a boy and they would call him Jesus. My parents were amazed and finally my father began to calm down. Joseph said then that the angel had told him that all this had taken place to fulfil what the Lord had said through the prophet Isaiah, "*The virgin will conceive and give birth to a son, and they will call him Immanuel, which means God with us.*"

Then Joseph went on to say that he would not divorce Mary but that he would take her into his home as his betrothed wife. He then said he would not have a proper marriage until after the baby was born. He said he would not consummate their marriage until she gave birth to a son. I had no idea what he was talking about and started to ask him what he meant when suddenly my mother pinched my arm and told me to be quiet.

You know the rest of the story. The odd thing was that all sorts of rumours went around about her baby for years but in the family we knew the truth.

Many years later, Jesus began to start talking and teaching. There was only Mary and me who remembered those events, our parents had gone and so had Joseph. Mary and I, well we are getting on a bit now.

Our fishing business was doing well down in Capernaum. My own boys were growing up and had taken over the running of the family business as my Zebedee was not as fit as he used to be. We were doing well. We had hired servants who helped work the boats and my sons, John and James had even gone into partnership with two other brothers, Andrew and Simon Bar Jonah. I thought my boys would go a long way. They were hard working and with the right connections could take over most of the fishing fleet on Galilee. At least that is what I thought in those days.

My nephew, Jesus, started speaking regularly in our local synagogue and everyone was really impressed with him. My boys, well John, had been down to Judea to hear our relative Elizabeth's son, also called John, who was receiving a huge amount of interest and a fair amount of opposition. John the baptiser as they were calling him, had even got himself arrested by Herod Antipas. My John came back with stories about Jesus from down there. Not long after that we all went together to a family wedding in Cana. Mary was a widow by then and her family were there too. It was lovely to see them all. It turned into quite an event as Jesus did something very unusual with the wine. My John said he turned several very large jars of water into wine. I tasted the wine and it was not water it was definitely wine. Stories like this created a huge amount of interest.

One day as Jesus was walking along by the Lake of Gennesaret here in Capernaum, the people were crowding around him and listening to him speak. He saw two of our boats at the water's edge. The boys were there, along with the Bar Jonah boys who were washing their nets. He got into one of the boats, the one belonging to Simon, and asked him to put out a little from shore. Then he sat down and taught the people from the boat.

After he had finished speaking, Jesus apparently told Simon to put out into deep water, and let down the nets for a catch. When they had done so, they caught such a large number of fish that their nets began to break. So they signalled my boys in the other boat to come and help them, and they came and filled both boats so full that they began to sink. I think it was because of this that Simon started to be one of Jesus' followers.

When Jesus had gone a little farther, he saw my two boys with my husband Zebedee in one of our boats, preparing the nets for more fishing, as the fish were obviously easy to catch that day. He walked straight up to them and called them to follow him also, and they left my husband in the boat with our hired men and followed him! Just like that! That was the beginning of the end of my plans to take over the fishing fleet on Galilee. I had plans for my boys. I wanted the best for my boys. Going off with their cousin Jesus was not my idea of much of a future.

As time went by, Jesus' fame was becoming widespread all over the country. He kept talking about his kingdom and I began to think that maybe my boys were destined for greater things than being fishermen after all. Jesus' own brothers didn't follow him at that time so I thought as we were his nearest relatives it would make sense for my boys to be alongside him. I was thinking this could be a really big opportunity so one day I went to Jesus with my sons and, kneeling down, asked a favour of him.

He asked me what I wanted. I am very embarrassed about it now but back then I really didn't understand what he meant by his kingdom. I thought as he was the Messiah that he was going to get rid of the Romans and set up a new kingdom in Israel and I was sure this would be a wonderful opportunity for my boys. Anyway I asked him to grant that one of these two sons of mine might sit at his right and the other at his left in his kingdom.

"You don't know what you are asking," Jesus said to us. "Can you drink the cup I am going to drink?"

I nudged the boys and said, of course they could. I was thinking of that wine in Cana. So they said, "We can." Jesus said to them, "You will indeed drink from my cup, but to sit at my right or left is not for me to grant. These places belong to those for whom they have been prepared by my Father."

When the other ten of his closest disciples heard about this, they were very annoyed with my two boys. It caused quite a lot of ill feeling for a while. I didn't mean to do that. We just didn't understand things very well then. Jesus called them together and said, "You know that the rulers of the Gentiles lord it over them, and their high officials exercise authority over them. Not so with you. Instead, whoever wants to become great among you must be your servant, and whoever wants to be first must be your slave, just as the Son of Man did not come to be served, but to serve, and to give his life as a ransom for many."

We were all learning that Jesus was not like any other rabbi or leader.

Many months later when it all came to a dramatic head in Jerusalem at the Passover, I went up along with my sons and my sister Mary. Jesus was there and a whole group of us from Galilee.

Others have told you of that fateful week and the events that led up to the arrest of Jesus and his trial before the Roman Governor. As soon as I heard what was happening I went with John to find my sister. She was in great distress. We were desperate for news of what they were going to do to Jesus. We tried to get near the Roman Praetorium to find out but it was impossible. There were rumours spreading fast that he was going to be crucified. I was horrified. I had seen what happens when they crucify a person, it is a terrible, lingering death. We all remembered Sepphoris near Nazareth, a few years back. We were huddled together outside the governor's palace waiting for news. John who had pushed in to the courtyard came back in a while and looked ashen grey in the face. He told us that Jesus had been given the thirty-nine lashes by the Roman troops and that Pilate had agreed to have him crucified. I thought Mary was going to faint but we held her up and tried to comfort her.

Then there was a great shout from the crowd and we saw Jesus come through the gates of the palace yard being led out by soldiers. He was covered in terrible bloody welts all over his back and they had made a crude crown out of a thorn covered shrub which was rammed down on his head. A purple cloth draped across his shoulders. We all were weeping. He was also struggling to carry the wooden cross that they were going to nail him to. As the soldiers led him away, they seized some man who was on his way in from the country, and put the cross on him and made him carry it behind Jesus. A large number of people followed him, including us women who were mourning and weeping for him. Jesus turned and said to us, "Daughters of Jerusalem, do not weep for me; weep for yourselves and for your children. For the time will come when you will say, Blessed are the childless women, the wombs that never bore and the breasts that never nursed! Then they will say to the mountains, 'Fall on us and to the hills, cover us!' For if people do these things when the tree is green, what will happen when it is dry?"

Two other men, both criminals, were also led out with him to be executed. We followed along with a whole crowd of people, some we recognised. There was no sign of his other disciples. There was just John with me and Mary. We had been joined by a number of women who we knew by then. I had no idea where my James was either. When they arrived at the place called the Skull, they crucified him there, along with the criminals, one on his right, the other on his left.

I'm sorry it is hard to speak of those things.

As they were getting ready to lift up the cross I heard Jesus say, "Father, forgive them, for they do not know what they are doing." When the soldiers crucified Jesus, they took his clothes, dividing them into four shares, one for each of them, with the undergarment remaining. This garment was seamless, woven in one piece from top to bottom. I remember my sister making that robe for him.

They decided not to tear it up but instead they started to cast lots to see who would get it. So this is what the soldiers did. Then they divided up the rest of his clothes by casting lots.

His mother and I were standing near the cross where we had been joined by Mary the wife of Cleopas, and Mary Magdalene. When Jesus saw his mother there, and the disciple whom he loved, my John, standing nearby, he said to Mary, "Dear, woman, here is your son." Then he said to John, "Here is your mother." From that time on, John took her into our home to care for her. Jesus so loved his mother.

After this, Jesus said he was thirsty. There was a jar full of sour wine standing there; the soldiers had been given it, to get them drunk. It was to help them in their grisly task. So they put a sponge full of the sour wine upon a branch of hyssop and brought it up to his mouth.

Some people who were watching, and the Council members, even sneered at him. They were calling out , "He saved others; let him save himself if he is God's Messiah, the Chosen One." The soldiers also came up and mocked him too. They offered him wine vinegar and said, "If you are the king of the Jews, save yourself." It was so heartless of them.

There was a written notice above him, which read: This is the King of the Jews. Apparently Pontius Pilate, the Roman Governor had insisted that the sign be put up to show any other aspiring kings what would happen to them.

Even one of the criminals who hung there hurled insults at him. He said, "Aren't you the Messiah? Save yourself and us!" The other criminal disagreed with him. "Don't you fear God, since you are under the same sentence? We are punished justly, for we are getting what our deeds deserve. This man has done nothing wrong." Then he said, "Jesus, remember me when you come into your kingdom." Jesus said to him, "I tell you the truth, today you will be with me in paradise."

At noon, darkness came over the whole land. At about three in the afternoon, Jesus cried out in a loud voice, "Eloi, Eloi, lama sabachthani?"

in Aramaic. This means 'My God, my God, why have you forsaken me?' in our language.

When some of those standing near heard this, they said, "Listen, he's calling Elijah." Someone ran, filled a sponge with wine vinegar again and put it on a staff, and offered it to Jesus to drink. "Now leave him alone. Let's see if Elijah comes to take him down," he said. That was so cruel.

There was darkness over the whole land until about three in the afternoon, for the sun stopped shining. Then after a while Jesus called out with a loud voice, "Father, into your hands I commit my spirit."

When he had said this, he said, "It is finished." Then he took his last breath.

Later we were told at that exact moment the curtain of the temple was torn in two!

When all the people who had gathered to witness the crucifixion saw what took place, they beat their breasts and went away. But all those of us who knew him were watching from a distance.

A little while later one of the soldiers came up and thrust a spear into his side. Jesus was dead already. It was like one last indignity. By then it was beginning to get dark and we were wondering what to do as the Sabbath was only an hour or so away from beginning. We had unexpected help as it grew dark. Nicodemus who was one of the Ruling Council and another rich man, Joseph of Arimathea came with the news that Pilate had agreed that they could take Jesus' body down and get it buried nearby. It needed to be done quickly as it was almost the Sabbath. John and I took Mary away with us back to the city and two of the other women went with Nicodemus and his friend to get Jesus' body taken care of.

We spent the Sabbath in great sorrow and sadness. Mary was inconsolable. Towards the end of the day we made plans to go to the tomb at first light in order to finish off the burial procedures.

When the Sabbath was over, Mary Magdalene, Mary the mother of James and I bought spices so that we might go to anoint Jesus' body. It was very early on the first day of the week, just after sunrise, when we got up and went to the tomb. I remember we were concerned how we would get into the tomb and who would roll the stone away from the entrance of the tomb for us.

When we got there, we saw that the very large stone had been rolled away. As we entered the tomb, we saw a young man dressed in a white robe sitting on the right side, and we were terrified. "Don't be alarmed," he said, "you are looking for Jesus the Nazarene, who was crucified. He has risen! He is not here. See the place where they laid him. Now go and tell his disciples and Peter, 'He is going ahead of them into Galilee'. There they will see him, just as he told them. '

You can imagine how we felt. I was trembling all over and we were bewildered. We went out and ran from the tomb. We said nothing to anyone we met on the way, because we were so afraid yet filled with joy at the same time. Mary Magdalene stayed at the tomb but the other Mary, Cleopas' wife, Joanna and I ran to tell his disciples. I left them and went to look for my two sons. If I had stayed with the other women I would have met him, because later I learned that suddenly Jesus met them on the way.

However, I hurried back to where I knew many of his family and friends were meeting. I found my boys there and told them everything that I had seen and heard. Some of them didn't believe me and thought we were just being hysterical. That evening a whole group of us had gathered. We so much wanted to meet and find out what had happened, who had seen Jesus, or at least had though they had seen him. Some didn't believe it. Some said it was his ghost. Others just didn't know what to think. During the evening Cleopas and his friend arrived from Emmaus and told us what they had experienced. Then all of a sudden,

Jesus himself was in the room. My heart was racing, it was really him. It was no ghost. It was my sister's son! It was my nephew Jesus. He really was alive. More than that, he had risen from the dead! We knew that all he had said was true. It was the beginning of a completely new age for the whole world."

SALOME IN THE GOSPELS

In Mark15:40, Salome is named as one of the women present at the crucifixion. The parallel passage of Matthew 27:56 says: *"Among which was Mary Magdalene, and Mary the mother of James and Joses, and the mother of Zebedee's children."*

In John's gospel three or perhaps four women are mentioned at the crucifixion; this time they are named as "his mother, and his mother's sister, Mary the wife of Cleopas and Mary Magdalene." A common interpretation is to identify Salome as the sister of Jesus' mother, thus making her Jesus' aunt. Traditional interpretations associate Mary the wife of Cleopas, the third woman in the Gospel of John's list with Mary the mother of James, the son of Alphaeus, the third woman in the Gospel of Matthew. All the various streams of the church see Salome as Mary's sister.

It can at first be a bit confusing with all these other ladies being called Mary!

In the Gospel of Mark, Salome is among the women who went to Jesus' tomb to anoint his body with spices. They discovered that the stone had been rolled away and a figure in white then told them that Jesus had risen, and asked them to tell Jesus' disciples that he would meet them in Galilee. In Matthew, just two women are mentioned in the same story: Mary Magdalene and the "other Mary", Mary the mother of James, the son of Alphaeus.

The canonical gospels never go so far as to label Salome a disciple and so she is usually described as a "follower" of Jesus.

As Salome, wife of Zebedee, mother of James and John was Mary's sister, a number of other incidents and relationships fall into place.

At the cross, Jesus entrusted his mother to the care of his cousin John. John would have been her nephew. Mary also had the support of her sister Salome. John took Mary home afterwards. The three are missing from those named as present at the burial. Nor were Mary and John at the tomb on Easter morning, although Salome went there with the other women.

Looking back to the earlier occasion when the mother of James and John appears, it was she who came to Jesus with the request that her sons be given places of honour in his kingdom, seats on his right and his left. Matthew 20:20-28 and Mark 10:35-45.

As they were his cousins, this request suddenly appears in its true light. Jesus' own brothers had not, at that time, joined his following. John at one point tells us that they did not believe in Jesus during his public ministry. Among the disciples, his next nearest relatives were his cousins. Salome was not claiming that her sons were the best of his followers, merely the ones with the closest family connection.

Zebedee had a well-established fishing business and like carpenters, fishermen were respected as being highly skilled. Although not rich they were certainly not poor. The firm had two boats and five partners, Zebedee and his two sons and the brothers Peter and Andrew. Apparently, Zebedee had, or obtained, other workers when Jesus called both his sons and both his other partners to work with him full time.

Salome did not travel around with Jesus and his disciples but joined them on occasions such as Passover. We assume Zebedee stayed at home and continued the fishing business. Certainly the fishing boats were still available and were lent to Jesus on occasions, and were used by the disciples after the resurrection in John 21.

All of this leads to the conclusion that Salome, Jesus' aunt, was a significant eyewitness to a number of key events in the life of Jesus. Perhaps the most significant events of all were heard and seen by those who stood at the foot of the cross. Salome was there. She would have seen and heard what was said and how it happened. Undoubtedly others heard the words of Jesus from the cross. Each Gospel writer would have had a number of potential witnesses to draw from.

I have drawn them all together and into Salome's hearing and into her story. There are seven statements made by Jesus as he hangs on the cross. The four Gospel writers collectively record them. They are as follows:

> *"Father, forgive them, for they do not know what they are doing."* Luke 23:34

> *"Dear, woman, here is your son."* Then he said to John, *"Here is your mother."* John 19:26

"I am thirsty." John 19:28

"I tell you the truth, today you will be with me in paradise." Luke 23:43

"Eloi, Eloi, lama sabachthani?" in Aramaic. This means "My God, my God, why have you forsaken me?" Mark 15:34, Matthew 27:46

Father, into your hands I commit my spirit." Luke 23:46

"It is finished." John 19:30

THE FATHER DID NOT ABANDON HIS SON ON THE CROSS

The words of Jesus that are spoken from the cross each carry significance and are worthy of detailed thought and study. They reflect so many aspects of his life and destiny.

He addresses his Father at the outset as nails are hammered into his hand and feet. He asks the Father to forgive the men as they do this. They represent all humanity as we participate in the murder of Jesus. In this great redemptive moment he is able to pray that all of us will be forgiven because he knows that the purpose that the Father had given him was to bring forgiveness and reconciliation. Paul says of this in Colossians:

> *"And you, who were dead in your trespasses and the uncircumcision of your flesh, God the Father made alive together with Jesus, having forgiven us all our trespasses, by*

cancelling the record of debt that stood against us with its legal demands. This he set aside, nailing it to the cross. He disarmed the rulers and authorities and put them to open shame, by triumphing over them in him." Colossians 2:13-15

Through his death all mankind would be brought home. The soldiers did not know what they were doing but the incarnate Son of the Father knew exactly what was happening and he spoke forgiveness.

Jesus lovingly entrusted his mother into the caring hands of his beloved friend and cousin John. Amid his own agony he is concerned for the well being of the woman whose womb had hosted him and brought him into his humanity. It is touching and full of compassionate comfort. Jesus' Father of compassion and the God of all comfort was ministering his love to his faithful servant, the highly favoured and beloved daughter, Mary of Nazareth.

As his tongue became parched, Jesus the Son in his humanity experienced the full agony of crucifixion. He is thirsty. This is not some superhuman enduring the pain but an ordinary man who has fully embraced our humanity in his life and death. He is so thirsty.

As the two criminals on either side address him, one mocking the other pleading, Jesus speaks life and hope. That very day one would enter paradise because of Jesus. It is as if for the dying thief on the cross all the seven of the 'I Am' sayings of Jesus that John recorded were about to become his personal reality. The Good Shepherd was about to lay down his life for this sheep. Jesus' death on the cross would be the door to the Father's presence for this broken man. It would be the way to the Father bringing truth and life. He would experience that Jesus is the light of the world, the bread of life and the living water. All this healing and joy would become his as he steps into the resurrection life in Jesus. Paradise indeed!

Then comes the cry from the cross that is most shocking and challenging of all. "Eloi, Eloi, lama sabachthani?" in Aramaic. This means "My God, my God, why have you forsaken me?"

Has the Father forsaken Jesus? Is he abandoned to suffer alone? Are these words of dereliction, despair and failure?

Many have interpreted this to be how Jesus felt as the Father turned his back on his son who had taken on himself all the sins of the world. They are coming from an understanding of God, not as a loving Father, but a vengeful angry God who in his wrath and demands for absolute justice and holiness must have satisfaction for sin. All this sin is loaded onto Jesus on the cross and God must look away and abandon Jesus in his agony. This view of God has taken root in Western Christianity over many centuries. This whole issue has been addressed very thoroughly by C.Baxter Kruger in his writings. He points out that nothing could be further from the truth of the Bible.

Kruger says,

> *"There are those who want us to believe that on the day Adam fell, God the Father was filled with a bloodthirsty anger that demanded punishment before He would even consider forgiveness. And they want us to believe that when Jesus Christ hung on the cross, the Father's anger and wrath were poured out upon him, instead of us."*

He continues,

> *"Jesus Christ did not go to the cross to change God; he went to the cross to change us. He did not die to appease the Father's anger or to heal the Father's divided heart. Jesus Christ went to the cross to call a halt to the Fall and undo it, to convert fallen Adamic existence to his Father, to systematically eliminate our estrangement, so that he could accomplish his Father's dream for our adoption in his ascension."* Jesus and the Undoing of Adam. C Baxter Kruger 2003

So why is Jesus saying this? As a number of commentators have seen, these are the opening lines of Psalm 22. It is as if Jesus is being reminded by the Father of this amazing psalm. The psalm is one of the prophetic psalms of David. In particular this one describes the feelings of the Son as he hangs on the cross. There are so many verses in the psalm that resonate powerfully with what Jesus is going through.

It begins with the cry from the cross, *'My God, my God, why have you forsaken me? Why are you so far from saving me, so far from my cries of anguish?'* In quoting this there would have been those present who knew the psalm by heart. Perhaps Nicodemus, if he was there, may have heard these words and seen the full import of the incredible revelation contained within them. These words express what Jesus was feeling as he fully embraced our humanity because for us we have felt so afraid and alienated and far from God. In his death on the cross Jesus is totally uniting himself with our broken, rotten and fallen humanity. It is the ultimate incarnation of the beloved Son of the Father.

However Jesus, unlike us, has not lost hope or lost sight of God his Father. He knows his Father is the enthroned Holy One of Israel (verse 3) who is trustworthy, who has delivered Israel and saved them (verse 4). At the same time as he hangs on the cross,

> *"scorned by everyone, despised by the people. All who see me mock me; they hurl insults, shaking their heads. "He trusts in the Lord," they say, "let the Lord rescue him. Let him deliver him, since he delights in him."* Psalm 22:7-8

The mockers at the cross to which Jesus is nailed, use almost these same words:

> *"In the same way the chief priests, the teachers of the law and the elders mocked him. "He saved others," they said, "but he can't save himself! He's the king of Israel! Let him come down now from the cross, and we will believe in him. He trusts in God. Let God rescue him now if he wants him, for he said, 'I am the Son of God.'" In the same way the rebels who were crucified with him also heaped insults on him."* Matthew 27:41-44

In quoting this psalm Jesus is calling on his Father to comfort him.

> *"Do not be far from me, for trouble is near and there is no one to help. Many bulls surround me; strong bulls of Bashan encircle me. Roaring lions that tear their prey open their mouths wide against me."* Psalm 22:12-13

Jesus has entrusted his mother to John and in the psalm the psalmist reflects these thoughts:

> *"Yet you brought me out of the womb; you made me trust in you, even at my mother's breast. From birth I was cast on you; from my mother's womb you have been my God."* Psalm 22:9-10

The actions of the soldiers and the painful agony of crucifixion and exhaustion are described in the psalm.

> *"I am poured out like water, and all my bones are out of joint. My heart has turned to wax; it has melted within me. My mouth is dried up like a potsherd, and my tongue sticks to the roof of my mouth; you lay me in the dust of death. Dogs surround me, a pack of villains encircles me; they pierce my hands and my feet. All my bones are on display; people stare and gloat over me. They divide my clothes among them and cast lots for my garment."* Psalm 22:12-18

As Kruger says Psalm 22 moves from agony to God's victorious intervention and to a prophecy that the coming generations will look back upon this moment as the salvation of the Lord of Hosts.

> *"All the ends of the earth will remember and turn to the Lord, and all the families of the nations will bow down before him, for dominion belongs to the Lord and he rules over the nations. All the rich of the earth will feast and worship; all who go down to the dust will kneel before him those who cannot keep themselves alive."* Psalm 22:27-29

Baxter Kruger continues,

In the greatest of ironies, the cry of Jesus, "My God, My God, why have You forsaken me?" actually sets in motion a line of thought that completely reinterprets what is happening on the cross. Far from being a perverse moment when the angry God pours His wrath out upon the Son and utterly rejects him, the cross is the moment when the Father absolutely refuses to forsake His Son, the moment of moments when He does not hide His face, or turn His back upon him in disgust. Here, according to the Psalm and its interpretation of the event, there is no forsaking at all. In fact, the Psalm tells us that the coming generations will see this event not as divine rejection, but precisely as divine presence and rescue and salvation." pp 37 Jesus and the undoing of Adam

"For he has not despised or scorned the suffering of the afflicted one; he has not hidden his face from him but has listened to his cry for help." Psalm 22:24

The Father has NOT despised or turned his back on the suffering of the Son nor hidden his face from him, quite the contrary. The triune God, Father, Son and Holy Spirit were all intimately involved in this great consummation of their plan to enter fallen humanity and bring us back home to them.

Psalm 22 continues,

"Future generations will be told about the Lord. They will proclaim his righteousness, declaring to a people yet unborn: He has done it!" Psalm 22:30-31

In the amazing climax of the psalm there is the prophetic declaration that the finished work of Christ on the cross will be proclaimed to all future generations since Jesus has died for all. Paul declared this amazing truth,

"For the love of Christ controls us, having concluded this, that one died for all, therefore all died; and He died for all, so that they who live might no longer live for themselves, but for Him who died and rose again on their behalf." 2 Corinthians 5:12-14

Peter also picks up this refrain,

"For Christ also died for sins once for all, the just for the unjust, so that He might bring us to God, having been put to death in the flesh, but made alive in the spirit." 1 Peter 3:18

As Jesus endures the agony of the cross, the words of the psalm resonate within his Spirit. As it reaches its terrible and dramatic climax, Jesus says,

"Father, into your hands I commit my spirit."

The final sentence of the psalm is magnificent. The words are "He has done it."(verse 31). The Hebrew verb used here carries a very strong emphasis on completion, accomplishment and finishing. Not abandoned, nor forsaken, but received and welcomed by his Father. Then the great and earth shattering cry, not of dereliction, failure and despair but of triumph, glorious exaltation and joy.

"tetealestai!" IT IS ACCOMPLISHED! It is finished.

"And Jesus cried with a loud voice, and yielded up his spirit. And at that very moment the veil of the temple was torn in two from the top to the bottom; and the earth did quake; and the rocks were split." Matthew 27:50-51

The first major part of the revelation of the amazing love of the Father has been completed. There remains one final great revelation that Mary Magdalene will receive.

THE THIRTEENTH STORYTELLER

MARY
FROM MAGDALA

"Exhaustion had virtually overwhelmed me to the point of complete collapse. My eyes were puffy with incessant crying. I woke up in the early hours of the day following the Sabbath, the first day of the week.

The last three days had been the most terrible of my whole life. My world had crashed about me and I was devastated at the events that had unfolded. My dearest friend Jesus had been maliciously betrayed by one of his own disciples and had been arrested and tried on trumped up charges before the hated Roman governor. The shocking events had unfolded dramatically on Thursday evening and into Friday morning. In disbelief I followed crowds of people to the place of execution outside the city wall of Jerusalem. Over the heads of the shouting and angry crowd I caught a glimpse of a large wooden crossbeam being dragged through the streets of the city by the condemned. This was the man who I had followed and supported for the best part of the last two years since that amazing day when I first met him.

The day I first met him was a day when the sense of torment and inner pain that I had been wracked with for years finally came to an end. All my life I had struggled with these inner voices that accused me and tormented me. They mocked my every attempt to get free. They made me feel so worthless. I tried to ignore them, to keep telling myself it was just my imagination but they were constantly there. Everyone said I was demonised, whatever that meant. What was going on left me feeling isolated and lonely. The demons that had lied to me and afflicted me since my earliest days finally fled from me when I met this man Jesus. He had been so kind, so loving and so compassionate. I would never forget the look in his eyes that day. There was no accusation, no condemnation, no ridicule, no fear. He looked into my eyes and I felt that he was seeing deep into my heart. For the first time in my whole life I felt instantly loved, accepted, treasured and respected. A simple word from him and the pain, the anguish, the guilt and shame, the loneliness and above all the fear left me. Finally I felt whole again, as complete and free as the sacred Hebrew number seven.

Ever since that day I had followed him, along with a number of others who had been through similar experiences. I loved this man. I adored him, not with a motive that sought my own gratification but out of sheer thankfulness. I had often heard him talk and had listened intently to his teaching and his stories. Oh how I loved his stories! He had such a wonderful way with words and the sound of his voice was amazing.

Just listening to him filled me with joy and light. He seemed to really understand me. He spoke words that resonated deep within my heart and soul. Sometimes he would look at me and just say my name, 'Mary'. It melted my heart. I felt so clean, so whole, so loved, just by the way he said my name. No one has ever said it to me in the way he did. After all the years of believing I was such a failure, so unworthy, so crippled emotionally by the incessant voices that lied to me, I was finally beginning to hear life and truth being spoken to me by Jesus.

He was continually reassuring me that I was unique and deeply loved by God whom he described as his Father. The way he talked about God as being his Father was so different from anything I had ever heard before. Initially I thought he was talking about his father Joseph when he talked about his Father. Soon it became clear that he meant that God was his Father. No one had ever spoken like this about Almighty God before. It was shocking! No wonder some of the Pharisees didn't like him and kept attacking him. I remember the day he called the Pharisees white-washed tombs, all clean and sparkling on the outside with all their religious good behaviour but inside full of rotting bones and stinking dead corpses. How everyone had laughed and hooted, except the Pharisees of course. They were not amused. I knew what it felt like being rotten on the inside. I had been set free from that and if they could only open their eyes to the truth they could be set free too.

Just being with him was so comforting and life giving. I told my friend Joanna one day that I would follow him anywhere. To my surprise she said she would too. After a few months we did. We packed up and followed him to Jerusalem. It wasn't what we had expected or had hoped for. Up in Jerusalem there were loads more Pharisees and they were nasty, vicious types. They set out to trap him at every turn. After all the fuss when we arrived in the city and all the palm waving that made a real mess of the gardens on the way into the city we thought that any minute he would be proclaimed King of the city. However, as the week went on it became clear that there was real opposition mounting. At times it turned really nasty.

On the final evening he celebrated Passover with the boys, the Twelve. We had helped prepare and left them to it. Halfway through the evening that shifty one, Judas left in a hurry looking all suspicious and clutching his money belt. I was still downstairs at the house helping clear up with Joanna and Mary, who owned the house. Her son, John Mark was being a great help upstairs in the upper room, keeping things tidy up there.

Joanna thought that Judas had gone off to pay a bill or something but it seemed a strange time of the day to be doing that. He headed off up the hill in the direction of the Priest's quarter of the city. I was sure he was up to no good. I just wish I had got Simon the Zealot to follow him, it might have changed the course of history. Simon was always very handy with his knife.

Mary offered us a room to spend the night as it was quite late and they were still all upstairs. In the early hours Joanna and I were woken by furious banging on the door. It was John Mark who burst in when we opened the door. Poor boy he was stark naked! He told us what had happened and we both immediately headed off to the Governor's Palace to see what we could find out.

By first light there was a large crowd of really rough types who seemed to be under the control of the priests who were very much in evidence. We tried to press through the crowds and get to the front to hear better. It was impossible. Finally, an hour or two later, Pilate came out and called for silence and shouted out to the crowd gathered there that he was bringing Jesus out to let everyone know that he found no basis for a charge against him. When Jesus came out my heart nearly failed me. He had obviously been very seriously beaten or whipped. His face was bloodied and bruised. He was wearing a crown made of thorns that was forced down on his head and also a torn purple robe. It was a terrible sight. He had been so badly attacked and treated. Pilate shouted out to the crowd, "Here is the man!"

As soon as the chief priests and their officials saw him, they shouted out that he be crucified. Then they chanted like hooligans, "Crucify! Crucify!"

Pilate called for silence and shouted back, "You take him and crucify him. As for me, I find no basis for a charge against him." The Council leaders insisted that they had a law, and according to that law he must die, because he claimed to be the Son of God. When Pilate heard this, he looked very afraid, and he went back inside the palace.

The council leaders and the priests kept shouting, "If you let this man go, you are no friend of Caesar. Anyone who claims to be a king opposes Caesar." When Pilate heard this, he brought Jesus out and sat down on the judge's seat at the Stone Pavement . It was about noon. Then he said "Here is your king."

But they shouted all the louder, "Take him away! Take him away! Crucify him!"

Pilate asked them if they wanted him to crucify their king, at which they replied that they had no king but Caesar.

I started to call out to let him go as did a few others at the back. The moment I started to call out two of the thugs turned on me and started pushing me and they punched me in the mouth so hard that I fell to the ground. I am so glad that Joanna was there to help me up or I could have been trampled by the crowd.

Finally Pilate called for silence and then handed Jesus over to them to be crucified.

Then the whirlwind swept me up and Joanna and I were carried along in the mass of people until we were outside the city and huddled against a wall. I found John bar Zebedee with Mary, Jesus' mother. She was strained and in agony of heart but she was not hysterical. We held onto each other as the terrible scene unfolded. We covered our faces and wept together. After quite some time John came and said that Jesus was asking for her. The two moved slowly towards the brow of the hill. I held back and was joined by a number of the other women who had come from Galilee. There was no sign of any of the other men in our group.

John brought Mary back to us and we watched. Finally around mid afternoon the sky darkened and clouds gathered. It was unnaturally dark. I heard a voice cry from the cross, "Father into your hands I commend my spirit." Then a final shout from Jesus. He seemed to take his last breath and he gave up his spirit. Suddenly the earth began to violently shake and there was an earthquake that threw us to the ground. It was as if God himself was crying in agony.

The evening was approaching and there was much to do. We wanted to get his body down and at least get him in a grave or tomb before the Sabbath began at dusk. It all happened so fast. Surprisingly, two of the Council came and helped us, Nicodemus and Joseph. There was no time to bathe him or anoint him for burial. He was wrapped in a simple linen cloth and we planned to go to the tomb at first light after the Sabbath to complete the burial rights. I agreed to go with some of the other women to the tomb.

The next day was agonising. I wept and tried to sleep but it alluded me. I could not believe the speed of the events that had overtaken us. We met some of the men who one by one were reappearing. They were afraid and were expecting a dawn raid from the temple guards, and perhaps more arrests. Peter, who had been very much the leader, was a broken man. I had heard rumours that he had told a servant girl that he was not one of Jesus' followers. Some of the others were refusing to speak to him. He looked as if he had aged overnight. All his bravado and brashness had disappeared.

I had a second night of weeping and a little restless and fitful sleep. Long before dawn I could bear it no longer. I got up and headed out into the darkness to go to the tomb. I saw that the stone had been removed from the entrance. So I went running back to Simon Peter and John and told them that they had taken the Lord out of the tomb, and we didn't know where they had put him. So Peter and John started for the tomb. Both were running, but John outran Peter and reached the tomb first. He bent over and looked in and saw the strips of linen lying there but did not go in. Then Simon Peter came along behind him and went straight into the tomb. He saw the strips of linen lying there, as well as the cloth that had been wrapped around Jesus head. The cloth was still lying in its place, separate from the linen. Finally, John who had reached the tomb first, also went inside. He said later at that moment he believed. We still did not understand from Scripture that Jesus had to rise from the dead, I don't think any of us did before this. Then the disciples went back to where they were staying.

I stood outside the tomb crying. As I wept, I bent over to look into the tomb and saw two people inside the tomb clothed in dazzling white. They were seated where Jesus body had been, one at the head and the other at the foot. It gave me such a shock. It was not what I was expecting to see. I wondered if they were angels!

Then they asked me why I was crying! I felt like saying, "Why do you think?" Instead I said, "They have taken my Lord away and I don't know where they have put him." At this, I turned around and saw someone standing in the early morning mist. It was Jesus standing there, but I did not realise that it was him to start with. I thought it must have been the gardener or someone.

He asked me, "Woman, why are you crying? Who is it you are looking for?" I answered that if he had taken him away, tell me where he had put him, and I would get him.

Then he simply said my name, Mary.

I turned toward him and cried out in Aramaic, "Rabboni!" which means Teacher in our language, it's the name I always gave him. Then Jesus said to me, "Do not hold on to me, for I have not yet ascended to the Father. Go instead to my brothers and tell them, I am ascending to my Father and your Father, to my God and your God." I ran as fast as I could back to where the disciples were staying with the news. All I said was "I have seen the Lord!" Then I gave them the message.

After that, well, others can tell you the rest of the story. He certainly was alive. Yet somehow he was changed. Maybe that is why some of us struggled to recognise him to start with. He was no ghost, that's for sure. He had flesh and blood just like you and me. He ate food too, but also he would come and go as he pleased. The last time I saw him was the day he led us all out of the city of Jerusalem in the direction of the Mount of Olives, out towards Bethany. I wondered if we were going to Lazarus' house, but he and his sisters were with us. I asked them if this was the case and Martha gave me a look as she was already thinking how on earth could they feed this many people. There were quite a crowd of us that day. In the end it was only about a Sabbath day's journey, you know, about a thousand paces. He stopped and we all gathered around him. He lifted up his hands and blessed us. While he was doing this, he left us and was taken up into heaven. I realised he was ascending to his Father. That's what he had told me he was going to do that morning in the garden. He just went up in the air that day when we were all looking at him. He looked so happy and, well I don't know, triumphant. It was as if he was taking us with him. We were so much part of him. I felt like he was bringing many sons and daughters to glory with him. I knew that I would be where he was one day too.

We were gazing up into the sky as he got smaller and smaller and faded from our sight. Then suddenly we noticed that two men dressed in white were standing beside us. They looked very familiar to me. Then I remembered where I had seen them before. They were the two men, or maybe indeed they were angels, who had been in the tomb when I looked inside it that first day. They asked us why we were all standing there looking into the sky because Jesus, who had just been taken up into heaven, would come back in the same way we had seen him go into heaven. We did not feel sad at all, in fact, we were full of joy and expectation about what would happen next!

We stayed in the city for about another ten days after that. We all joined together constantly in prayer. There were the remaining eleven disciples and Matthias, who made the number up to twelve again, along with a number of the women and Mary the mother of Jesus, and also a bit of a surprise, his brothers from Nazareth. I never did understand why Peter was so sure that they needed a replacement for Judas. They cast lots to choose between Matthias and Joseph Barsabbas. It was a typical man thing to cast lots. Never mind. It all changed on the day of Pentecost as you know."

MARY MAGDALENE IN THE GOSPELS

The gospels introduce us to this woman in the last days of Jesus' life. She is there at the cross and in the garden on the resurrection morning. We only know her as Mary Magdalene.

However, there is a vast amount of speculative information about her. An apocryphal gospel has her name attached to it. There are legends and myths about this woman that have captured the popular imagination. A web search will produce pages about her. The vast majority of this is not founded in any real historical fact though some would claim it to be so. Most is shrouded in mystery.

Perhaps most notoriously, some have suggested her as being the mother of a child by Jesus who carries the divine bloodline. This has been associated with the holy grail of legend and most recently popularised by Dan Brown in the fiction novel, The Da Vinci Code.

For some reason Mary has a huge pull on people's minds. She is described as a prostitute by some. She is often confused with being the woman who washed Jesus' feet with her tears. She is portrayed by others as the archetypal immoral woman who is redeemed. Though Mary Magdalene is named in each of the four gospels in the New Testament, not once does it say that she was a prostitute or a sinner. Nothing in the New Testament even hints of her as a prostitute or a morally loose woman. This idea grew in the sixth century when Pope Gregory delivered a series of sermons about Mary in which he equated each of the seven demons cast out of her with the seven deadly sins of Catholic thought. This became cemented into early and mediaeval imagination and she came to be viewed as a redeemed prostitute. This somewhat tarnished her previously acclaimed position as the "Apostle to the Apostles". This honorific title was first bestowed on her by Hippolytus Bishop of Rome 170 - 235AD.

Today however, contemporary scholarship is said to have restored the understanding of Mary Magdalene as an important early Christian leader.

Whatever the source of their information most people have heard of Mary Magdalene.

In reality we know very little about her except a few references to her in all four of the canonical gospels. She is mentioned at least twelve times which is more than most of the apostles. She has been described by some as the second most important woman in the New Testament. The first being Mary, the mother of Jesus.

The first mention of Mary Magdalene is found in Luke 8 verse 2. In this passage which Luke sets in Galilee, he lists a number of people who were the travelling companions of Jesus. He groups the male disciples together as "the twelve". Then in a way typical of Luke, gives some tantalising detail about a group of women followers who were with Jesus.

> *"The twelve were with him, and also some women who had been cured of evil spirits and diseases: Mary (called Magdalene) from whom seven demons had come out; Joanna the wife of Chuza, the manager of Herod's household; Susanna; and many others. These women were helping to support them out of their own means."* Luke 8:1-3

Glimpses like these invite all manner of speculation. We are only left wondering who these women were and how they had become part of Jesus' inner circle. Like so much of these gospel accounts we are hearing the testimony of eyewitnesses and memories of people who took part in the events. For Luke to have mentioned these women by name indicates they were probably known to the early church. I can only assume he met some of these people personally and collected information, stories and most important of all, testimonies of what Jesus had said and done.

Significantly, in Luke there was the mention of Jesus casting out or freeing Mary Magdalene of seven demons. Mark's gospel also refers to this in 16:9, though it has to be said this in the final eleven verses of Mark's gospel. This section does not appear in the oldest existing manuscripts of the gospel. Some scholars have hypothesised and suggested that these last verses were added some time after the original Gospel of Mark began to circulate in order to finish off the gospel after its somewhat abrupt end in verse 8. This may then indicate a reference to Luke's mention of Mary being released from seven demons rather than the original intent of Mark. Clearly there was a widespread understanding that Mary had received a significant healing and deliverance from Jesus that connected her to him and his followers.

The fact that she is known as Mary Magdalene or Mary of Magdala may indicate that she came from the Galilean village of Magdala, which lies on the shore of the lake. If she was a native of that area as is suggested by her first mention in Luke 8, it may indicate that she had seen and experienced much of the ministry of Jesus in Galilee first hand. Certainly her healing and deliverance took place sometime early on in Jesus' ministry.

Her subsequent appearances in the Gospel stories and the prominence of her presence in his last days would have no doubt been partly out of the gratitude she would have felt following her release and new found freedom and almost certainly an adherence to his teaching and message. When Jesus was crucified by the Romans, Mary Magdalene was there supporting him in those final traumatic moments and mourning his death. She remained with him at the cross after all the other male disciples had fled, with the exception of, 'the one whom Jesus loved', John, the writer of the fourth Gospel, who was also personally deeply involved in these final hours and resurrection morning appearances.

Perhaps the prominent part that she plays in these events as recorded in his Gospel indicates John's knowledge of Mary's role and her recounting to him of the information that she alone was party to and received directly from Jesus. She was at his burial, and she is the only person to be listed in all four Gospels as first to realise that Jesus had risen. John and Mark both specifically name her as the first person to see Jesus after his resurrection in John 20:11 - 18 and Mark 16:9.

MARY MAGDALENE AT THE TOMB

When the four accounts of what happened on the morning of the first day of the week are placed alongside each other there are some significant differences, also some common ground between each account, which at first glance may appear confusing. Much has been written by commentators and bible scholars seeking to explain these variations. My intention in this is not to seek to ingeniously harmonise the accounts or indeed to present a critical analysis. I would simply point out that there are a number of differences between each account which may indicate the different points of view of each woman and from whom the gospel writers may have got their information. As in any significant and traumatic event each person's perspective is often markedly different from the others. The common denominator in each account is Mary Magdalene and her reactions.

All four gospel writers record Mary Magdalene going to the tomb at first light on the first day of the week. According to John she had gone initially on her own. In all the other accounts she is accompanied by at least another two women, one of whom is known as the other Mary, the mother of James and another called Salome (Mk 16:1). Luke also mentions a woman called Joanna (Lk 24:10) who he had previously referred to as among the women who followed Jesus. Mark records their discussions on the way to the tomb. They bought spices so that they might go to anoint Jesus' body. They were on their way to the tomb and they asked each other, "*Who will roll the stone away from the entrance of the tomb?*" But when they looked up, they saw that the stone, which was very large, had been rolled away.

What is clear in all the stories is that there was an angelic presence in the tomb that shone brilliantly and seemed like lightning flashes.

Whether it was one or two angels may reflect the fear and alarm that the women felt. The guards were so shaken they looked like dead men according to Matthew's account. Clearly there was great confusion and fear. The descriptions of the fear included trembling, falling on the floor and fleeing. It would explain very well the variations in the accounts.

All four gospel writers are clear that the resurrection was real and the physical body of Jesus had been raised from the dead. The whole event is supernatural and powerfully dynamic. The angelic visitors all bring exactly the same message to the traumatised and terrified women.

> *"Why do you look for the living among the dead? He is not here; he has risen."* Luke 24:5-6

> *"Do not be afraid, for I know that you are looking for Jesus, who was crucified. He is not here; he has risen, just as he said."* Matthew 28:5-6

> *"You are looking for Jesus the Nazarene, who was crucified. He has risen! He is not here. See the place where they laid him."* Mark 16:6

There is a very specific and consistent message that has resounded down the centuries and is at the heart of the Christian gospel. He is risen!

Each gospel writer is not only writing a history of the life of Jesus, they each have their own interests and reasons for writing. Mark with his source, most likely the memories and teaching of Peter, naturally includes a reference to him.

> *"But go, tell his disciples and Peter, He is going ahead of you into Galilee. There you will see him, just as he told you."* Mark 16:7

Luke's intention was to write an orderly account to his reader Theophilus, *"so that you may know the certainty of the things you have been taught"* Luke 1:4

Therefore not surprisingly, he adds the following words from the angels,

> *"Remember how he told you, while he was still with you in Galilee: The Son of Man must be delivered over to the hands of sinners, be crucified and on the third day be raised again."* Luke 24:7

The message is carried by the women to the disciples who respond with varying degrees of belief and disbelief. There follows a lot of running back and forward to the tomb by Peter and John but for these two men there are no angelic encounters nor meetings with Jesus. That is reserved for the women and most significantly for Mary Magdalene.

John records in great detail Mary's experience that morning. This adds weight to the high probability that much of John's account came directly from Mary Magdalene as so much of it would have been known only by her and blended with his own memories and experiences.

Matthew has knowledge of this conversation and abbreviates it in his account,

The angel said to the women, "Do not be afraid, for I know that you are looking for Jesus, who was crucified. He is not here; he has risen, just as he said. Come and see the place where he lay. Then go quickly and tell his disciples, he has risen from the dead and is going ahead of you into Galilee. There you will see him. Now I have told you."

So the women hurried away from the tomb, afraid yet filled with joy, and ran to tell his disciples. Suddenly Jesus met them. "Greetings," he said. They came to him, clasped his feet and worshiped him. Then Jesus said to them, "Do not be afraid. Go and tell my brothers to go to Galilee; there they will see me." Matthew 28:6-10

WE ARE JESUS' BROTHERS AND GOD IS OUR FATHER TOO

This is the first day of the new age of God's amazing grace. It is resurrection day. Jesus has risen from the grave. Death is conquered. Life has come. The curse is broken. Satan had tried to strike at his heel but the offspring of the woman has crushed his head. Man is no longer bound by the old covenant of law. This is the new age of grace. We have been rescued from the dominion of darkness and brought into the kingdom of the Son. The first Adam went back to the dust from which he came and we all lived with the consequences of his fall. The last Adam has stepped out of the grave and has some really good news to share with all of the first Adam's descendants.

Satan had set a trap for the first Adam and his wife and they lost their assurance and were filled with fear and shame. They hid from God behind their makeshift fig leaf clothes, unable to look into the eyes of their Father, their creator.

The scene in the first garden was one of utter loss and fear. Adam's word's said it all when questioned by the Lord God, "Where are you?",

> *"I heard you in the garden and I was afraid because I was naked so I hid."* Genesis 3:10

All of humanity had suffered as a result and were separated from God, afraid of him, hiding from him.

Here in another garden, the garden of the empty tomb stands another woman. She is afraid, weeping, confused. She has seen death do its worst to the one she loved, her master, her Rabbouni. She felt hopeless, abandoned and alone. She was covered in the clothes of mourning, of loss and grief.

This woman, Mary Magdalene, also has an angelic encounter like the first woman did in Eden. She stoops to look into the empty tomb just in case in her grief she had somehow missed the body the first time she had looked or perhaps Simon Peter and John had not made a thorough enough search. This time there is a presence in the tomb. There are two angels seated either end of the empty grave space. This time they ask her why she is crying. These angelic messengers are not there to set a trap for her but to reassure her, to take away her fear, to comfort, to bring hope and good news.

Her reply is a statement that all mankind has been making in different ways, *"They have taken my Lord away and I don't know where they have put him."*

It is as if she is saying in her fear and dressed in her clothes of grief, "*I am looking for the Lord who has been hidden from us.*" We have hidden from God for so long that we believe in our brokenness and fallenness that he is hidden from us, cannot be found, shrouded in mystery. Here in this garden the age old lie is about to be broken.

She turns around and sees a figure in the shadowy mists of the early morning. It is Jesus but like so many millions throughout the coming ages she doesn't recognise him at first. It is not what she is expecting or who she is expecting. Through her tear blurred eyes she assumes it is a gardener. He asks her two very significant questions. Why is she crying and who is she looking for. At first glance these would seem to be the most insensitive and inappropriate questions to ask. But Mary is locked in her grief of the last few days. She is about to discover that joy has come in the morning.

She asks the gardener for the whereabouts of the body, still unable to recognise him, still thinking that her Lord is dead and his body discarded perhaps into the Valley of Hinnon outside the city, the traditional dumping ground of unclaimed corpses. This valley was also known as Gehenna. Indeed, Jesus had been to Gehenna but not as a corpse but as the saviour of the world. Now he was risen and was standing in the garden and about to proclaim a message that has changed the history of the world.

His reply is just one word. Her name. "Mary."

He knew her. He had said it so many times before. The familiar tone, the intimacy, the heart connection. It was all in that one word. Instantly she knew it was him. All her fears evaporated. All her sorrow vanished, turning to joy. Disbelief turned to faith. She seemed to have run to him and was held by him in a comforting embrace. Jesus then says to her, *"Do not hold on to me, for I have not yet ascended to the Father."* He is not forbidding her or correcting her. Her natural inclination was to hang on to him to try to contain him and retain him with her. He is telling her that when he ascends to the Father she would be eternally in his embrace as are all who are in Christ.

C Baxter Kruger explores this fully in his book, 'Jesus and the Undoing of Adam." He says.

> *"The gospel is the astonishing news that something has happened to the Son of God, and the equally astonishing news that in him something has happened to the human race. If the whole human race fell into ruin in Adam, a creature, a mere man, what happened to the human race in the death of Jesus Christ, the incarnate Son of God? Paul tells us. When Jesus Christ died, we died. But that is only the beginning. When he rose, we rose. He ascended and sits at the right hand of God the Father almighty, the place of honour and love and delight and complete and utter acceptance, and Paul tells us that in his ascension we too were lifted up and seated with him at the Father's right hand, and there and then welcomed, accepted, embraced forever."*

Jesus is telling Mary that she can know his embrace for ever when he ascends to the Father and she along with all those who confess him as Lord will share in that eternal reality. This is a revelation that would only be fully understood a little later. The Apostle Paul would be the one who fully explored the revelation that the sons and daughters of God are in Christ. In the meantime Jesus has a job for Mary that precedes the revelation that we are in Christ. She is about to become the "Apostle to the apostles" as she is going to be the one who will bring the next vital part of the revealing of God the Father to us through the words and life of Jesus.

Jesus commissions Mary with an important task and an astonishing message for his friends, his disciples.

> *"Go instead to my brothers and tell them, I am ascending to my Father and your Father, to my God and your God."*
> John 20:17

Before the crucifixion, at the meal in the upper room Jesus had said his disciples were no longer servants but friends. (John 15: 15). In the Garden of Gethsemane the friends had fallen asleep when their friend needed them the most. The friends had fled when the guards arrested Jesus. Peter had denied that he was a follower of Jesus or even knew him. Judas had betrayed him and taken his own life. Only John, the beloved, had been at the cross. Now here in the resurrection garden Jesus tells Mary to go to "my brothers." A significant and startling new day has dawned. We are now brothers to Jesus, not just friends or mere followers. We are relationally connected to him in a more intimate way. We are now family, joined to him in filial love and affection. We are his brothers! This has an immediate effect on our connection with the Father. The disciples knew that God was Jesus' Father, that he related to him as his only begotten son. He even invited them to address him in prayer as Father. They knew that Jesus had an intimate relationship with his Father, so intimate that he called his Father Abba.

Now however, a deep and profound relational change had occurred for the disciples and indeed all who enter into the new resurrection life that has become ours through Jesus' death and resurrection. We have become brothers to Jesus and therefore not just the offspring of God but sons of God, who has always been our Father.

Jesus tells Mary to convey the amazing news to his brothers, that he is ascending to "my Father and your Father, to my God and to your God." A great transaction had taken place as a result of his atoning death on the cross and his resurrection from the dead. His defeat of death, breaking of the curse of the tree of the knowledge of good and evil and his releasing of life to the world has brought redemption to the world.

Redemption is the word Paul uses to describe the events of the last few hours.

The eternal son of God had bought back that which had been lost, the life of mankind. The offspring of God whom God had predestined before creation to be his sons and daughters had been redeemed. He cancelled our indebtedness, by his very life blood shed on the cross, and the Father has bought back his sons and daughters out of the dominion and control of darkness and brought them into the kingdom of his Son.

> *"For he has rescued us from the dominion of darkness and brought us into the kingdom of the Son he loves, in whom we have redemption, the forgiveness of sins."* Colossians 1:13-14

Paul says we have redemption, the forgiveness of sins, the cancelling of the debt. All this had been achieved by the sacrificial death of Jesus on the cross. The deal is done. The sons are redeemed and bought by his death. Henceforth and forever we are now brothers to Jesus and sons and daughters to God the Father. He is now truly our Father and our God.

This is the message that Mary is to carry to the disciples, that they are now his brothers and like him they have the same Father. God the Almighty is their Father also. They are therefore his sons. They have a new identity as sons and they have a new position, they have been established in sonship.

THE FINAL STORY TELLER

JOHN
THE ONE JESUS LOVED

Unlike all the previous sections of this book, where I have begun with the story of the main character, in this case I have decided to give the last word to John the apostle, the one whom Jesus loved. His story is so fully entwined in the gospel he wrote, it is almost superfluous to recount it here. His is perhaps the richest of all the eyewitness accounts and memories. His is the deepest of all the revelations inspired by the Holy Spirit.

Nearly all bible scholars agree, 'the disciple whom Jesus loved', whilst he is not named in the fourth Gospel, is none other than John bar Zebedee. John the disciple and gospel writer was the son of Zebedee and the younger brother of James. According to the Gospels, their mother was Salome, a sister of Mary. James and John were therefore the cousins of Jesus. Zebedee and his sons fished in the Sea of Galilee. John had been a disciple of John the Baptist. Jesus then called these two sons of Zebedee to follow him. James and John did so and thus rank highly among the disciples of Jesus. They both held prominent positions for not only being the first of the disciples to be called but also because of their relationship to Jesus among the Apostles. Jesus referred to the pair collectively as "Boanerges" which is translated as "sons of thunder" in Mark 3:17. This may have been given to them because although their nature may have been of a calm and gentle manner, when their patience was pushed to its limits their anger became wild, fierce and thunderous causing them to speak out like an untamed storm. At one point, John and his brother James wanted to call down fire on a Samaritan town, but Jesus rebuked them. John survived longer than James, by more than half a century, after James became the first Apostle to die a martyr's death according to Acts 12:2.

James and John, along with Peter were the only witnesses of the raising of Jairus' daughter. All three also witnessed the transfiguration of Jesus and the agony in the garden before going to sleep.

Jesus sent only John and Peter into the city to make the preparation for the last meal. At this meal the "*disciple whom Jesus loved*" reclined next to Jesus and leaned on his chest. Tradition identifies this disciple as John. John, alone among the disciples, remained at the foot of the cross alongside some other women. As instructed by Jesus from the cross, John took Mary, who would have been his aunt, into his care. After Jesus returned to his Father and the outpouring of the Spirit, John, together with Peter, took a prominent part in the leading of the church. He is with Peter at the healing of the lame man in the temple. With Peter he is also thrown into prison. He is also with Peter visiting the newly converted in Samaria.

There is no information in the Bible concerning the length of time of this activity in Judea. According to tradition, John and the other Apostles remained some twelve years, until the persecution of Herod Agrippa led to the scattering of the Apostles throughout the Roman Empire and beyond.

Paul meets John in Jerusalem according to his letter to the Galatians. Paul, in his opposition of the Judaisers in Galatia, recalls that John explicitly, along with Peter and James, the Lord's brother, were referred to as "pillars of the church". He says they recognised his Apostolic preaching of a gospel free from Jewish law and released him to take that Gospel to the gentile world.

Of the other New Testament writings, it is only from the three Letters of John and the Book of Revelation that anything further might be learned about John. From this we may suppose that John belonged to the multitude of personal eyewitnesses of the life and work of Jesus. Also that he had lived for a long time in Asia Minor and was thoroughly acquainted with the conditions existing in the various communities there. He had a position of authority recognised by all these churches as the leader of this part of the church. Moreover, the Book of Revelation says that its author was on the Island of Patmos '*for the word of God and for the testimony of Jesus*', when he received the visions contained in Revelation.

It is an issue of great debate among bible scholars when the Gospel was written. Some scholars agree in placing the Gospel of John somewhere between 65 AD and 70 AD. There is also a strongly held view amongst contemporary scholars that the Gospel was not written until the latter third of the first century AD as late as 80 - 90AD.

Catholic tradition states that after the 'assumption' of Mary in 54AD, John went to Ephesus and from there wrote the three epistles traditionally attributed to him. John was allegedly banished by the Roman authorities to Patmos. According to Tertullian (in Adversus Heresies), John was banished after being plunged into boiling oil in Rome and suffering nothing from it. This event would have occurred during the reign of

Domitian in the late first century.

When John was very old, he trained Polycarp who later became Bishop of Smyrna. This was important because Polycarp was able to carry John's message to future generations. Polycarp taught Irenaeus and passed on to him stories about John. In one of Irenaeus' works against various heresies he relates how Polycarp told a story about John and the gnostic teacher Cerinthus.

> *"John, the disciple of the Lord, going to bathe at Ephesus, and perceiving Cerinthus within, rushed out of the bath house without bathing, exclaiming, "Let us fly, lest even the bath-house fall down, because Cerinthus the enemy of the truth, is within."* Irenaeus, Adversus Heresies

It is traditionally believed that John lived to an extreme old age, dying naturally at Ephesus in about AD 100. An alternative account of John's death, ascribed by later Christian writers to the early second century bishop Papias, claims that he was slain by the Jews. John's traditional tomb is thought to be located at Selcuk, a small town near Ephesus.

THE FATHER REVEALS THE SON AND THE SON REVEALS THE FATHER

John saw clearly that the knowledge of God the Father was shown to us, offered to us and revealed to us through the coming of the Son who was the Word made flesh. He explains this at the beginning of his Gospel in John 1: 1 - 18. Jesus comes into our world and lives among us, makes his home among us, pitches his tent among us. The rest of the Gospel is an explanation of how that happened and what it looked like, and what the dwelling among us meant. Jesus lived a life of total connection with us at every level. He shares fully with us in the full range of human experiences, joys and sorrows and emotions. He shares a life of intimate fellowship and relationship with us. John saw this and understood it, wrote about it, passed it on to us through his writings in the New Testament.

Of all the Gospel writers John gives us the fullest picture of the way Jesus reveals the Father in his life and teaching. John had a personal revelation for himself. Not only did Jesus know the love of the Father but John knew that God was his Father also. John knew that the Father loved him in exactly the same way as he loved Jesus. The message that Jesus gives Mary Magdalene in the resurrection garden is the final piece of the revelation. Its inclusiveness that God is our Father also and we are his brothers is the clearest expression of this truth. The whole Gospel builds, chapter by chapter, on this revelation. It is John who, led by the Holy Spirit, carefully selects the material that we have today from the vast amount available to him to choose from, in order to present Jesus as the Messiah, the Son of God and who is the one uniquely able to reveal God as the Father of all. At the end of Chapter 20 he says,

> *"Jesus performed many other signs in the presence of his disciples, which are not recorded in this book. But these are written that you may believe that Jesus is the Messiah, the Son of God, and that by believing you may have life in his name."* John 20:30-31

Then again at the end of his gospel,

> *"Jesus did many other things as well. If every one of them were written down, I suppose that even the whole world*

would not have room for the books that would be written."
John 21:25

In John's Gospel we see Jesus completely dependent on the Father. John relates how Jesus said that he only does the things that he sees his Father doing. In himself he is incompetent.

> *"I tell you, the Son can do nothing by himself; he can do only what he sees his Father doing, because whatever the Father does the Son also does. For the Father loves the Son and shows him all he does. Yes, and he will show him even greater works than these, so that you will be amazed."*
> John 5:19-20

In addition, John tells us Jesus says that he can only speak the words that he hears his Father speaking.

> *"For I did not speak on my own, but the Father who sent me commanded me to say all that I have spoken. I know that his command leads to eternal life. So whatever I say is just what the Father has told me to say."* John 12:49-50

In response to Philip's question in the upper room, *"Lord, show us the Father and that will be enough for us,"* Jesus makes very clear the nature of the relationship between the Father and the Son.

> *"Jesus answers him by saying, "Don't you know me, Philip, even after I have been among you such a long time? Anyone who has seen me has seen the Father. How can you say, 'Show us the Father'? Don't you believe that I am in the Father,*

> *and that the Father is in me? The words I say to you I do not speak on my own authority. Rather, it is the Father, living in me, who is doing his work. Believe me when I say that I am in the Father and the Father is in me; or at least believe on the evidence of the works themselves."* John 14:9-11

The stunning message that Jesus comes to bring is put into one sentence by John. It is this,

> *"On that day you will realise that I am in my Father, and you are in me, and I am in you."* John 14:20

John realises that the unity which Jesus has with the Father and that the Father has with the Son is inclusive also of us. We are included in their relationship of love.

> *"As the Father has loved me, so have I loved you. Now remain in my love. If you keep my commands, you will remain in my love, just as I have kept my Father's commands and remain in his love. I have told you this so that my joy may be in you and that your joy may be complete."* John 15:9-11

John remembers all these statements made by Jesus and carefully weaves them into his Gospel. Undoubtedly he is being reminded by the Holy Spirit to record these thing just as the Spirit said he would do.

Did John have a revelation of God as Father? Without a doubt!

And so to John's story. It is he who will have the last word.

JOHN'S STORY

"I am not sure what more I can add to what has been said already. I know all the people who have told their stories so far. They are my friends and family. Jesus was my cousin, as you know. My mother and his mother were sisters and they have told you many things from their own perspectives. I grew up knowing Jesus. We shared together as children and young boys and then young men in many things. I grew up in Bethesda which is not far from Nazareth so we often saw each other at family gatherings. I have known Jesus all my life which is why I like to call myself the one Jesus loved. I know some think that this is a bit selfish, but it isn't at all! I just know who I am, that is all and I don't mean it arrogantly. Of course I know he loved all of us, yet for me there was always that special friendship and connection. I was younger than him, which is maybe why I looked up to him so much and really loved him.

I have known this from the beginning, I heard him speak, I saw things with my own eyes, I watched him do things and I touched him with my own hands. He was real, a real man, a real human being, as well as being the Word of life. I have spent all my life since then proclaiming this amazing fact. The life appeared. I have seen it and testify to it, and I proclaim to anyone who will give me a hearing that this life that Jesus brings is the eternal life, which was with the Father and has appeared to us. I want to tell everyone what I have seen and heard, so that everyone also may share in this fellowship with us. You see our fellowship, our sense of being deeply connected together, is with the Father and with his Son, Jesus Christ. I say all these things because this really makes me happy. It makes my joy complete!

There I go, preaching again. I just can't help it.

Knowing Jesus has changed everything for me. What has really changed me perhaps most of all is that Jesus has shown me not only who he really is but ultimately and perhaps most importantly who God himself is. He is the Father of Jesus and he loves Jesus and in exactly the same way that the Father loved him, Jesus has loved us. He has opened the door so we can go through it to the Father. Jesus is the way to the Father, he is the truth about the Father, he shares the very life of the Father and he brings us into that life also. For me Jesus has shared everything that the Father has given him with us. It is incredible. I have discovered through Jesus that I can know God as my Father in just the same way that Jesus does. I have found that God is love itself. It is his very nature and he has shared that with us. He is a Father to me too and he is loving me all the time in spite of my sin and failure. I have found that he is always ready to forgive me. You see, in him there is no darkness at all and walking in him and walking as he walked, enables us to live in the light that he lives in. This brings us into fellowship with each other and with the Father himself. It's amazing. That fact is the blood that was shed on the cross, his blood, cleanses us and purifies us from all our sin and wrong thinking and ways of living. However, I have discovered that if anybody does sin, we have an advocate with the Father, that is Jesus Christ himself, the Righteous One. He is the atoning sacrifice for our sins, and not only for ours but also for the sins of the whole world. The whole world!

I've written a lot of this down for others to read, so that they can know him too. I've written a few letters but I wrote down the story of his life first and included specifically the stories that others have spoken about. I listened very carefully to them and also to the Holy Spirit. I think the thing that has impressed me more than anything is what Jesus revealed to us about his Father. We didn't understand it initially. However, over time, little by little we began to see it. Even that last evening together, when he washed our feet and then he gave us the bread and wine to eat and drink to always remember that he really was with us, we still did not fully understand that God was the Father to all of us. That night we kept asking questions, Thomas, Philip, Judas, not the one who betrayed him, the other one. We all knew that he was about to go away and we so wanted to ask him things. He answered us and taught us and was so patient with us.

The wonderful thing was that he made it really clear that he did not intend to leave us like orphans, comfortless and alone. He said he would give us another comforter who would be with us forever. This is the Holy Spirit, who would continue to reveal the Father to us and teach us truth just in the same way as Jesus had been doing. I really understood that as I was so conscious of him prompting me about which stories to include in my account of his life.

Sometime after Jesus' resurrection, about ten days after he went back to his Father in heaven, we were all together in Jerusalem. There were loads of us, probably about one hundred and twenty all together. Even my aunt Mary was there and many of the women who were his followers too. It was in the morning when it happened. He had told us all to wait in Jerusalem, until the Holy Spirit was given to us. We didn't really know what to expect. Then it happened. It was the day of Pentecost. Suddenly a sound like the blowing of a violent wind came from heaven and filled the whole house where we were sitting. We saw what seemed to be tongues of fire that separated and came to rest on each of us. All of us were filled with the Holy Spirit and began to speak in other languages as the Spirit put the words into our mouths. You should have seen it or rather heard it! We were laughing and so excited. The joy was indescribable and the noise! Well, we were like drunkards, yet it was only nine o'clock in the morning. It was the beginning of a whole new day. Individually, we were filled with the very presence of Jesus, we were in him and he was in us. From that day, we started to experience the Father speaking to us and show us what to do, just like Jesus said he would.

I began to see how great the love the Father has lavished on us really is. He loves us and calls us the children of God! And that is really who we are!

Well, most of what I saw and heard and remembered you can read in my book. As I said, Jesus did many other things as well. If every one of them were written down, I suppose that even the whole world would not have room for the books that would be written. I hope you will go back and read my book, the one they call a Gospel, as it will explain things very much more clearly.

So dear friends, let us love one another, for love comes from God. Everyone who loves has been born of God and knows God. Whoever does not love does not know God, because God is love. This is how God showed his love among us, he sent his one and only Son into the world that we might live through him. This is love, not that we loved God, but that he loved us and sent his Son as an atoning sacrifice for our sins. Dear friends, since God so loved us, we also ought to love one another. No one has ever seen God; but if we love one another, God lives in us and his love is made complete in us.

This is how we know that we live in him and he in us, he has given us of his Spirit. And we have seen and testify that the Father has sent his Son to be the Saviour of the world. If anyone acknowledges that Jesus is the Son of God, God lives in them and they in God. And so we know and rely on the love God has for us. There is only one way of saying it, God is love. I will say it to my dying day. So little children let us love one another."

For more information and resources by Trevor and Linda visit:

www.trevorlindafhm.com

Additional resources from Fatherheart Media are available at:

www.fatherheart.net/shop - New Zealand
www.fatherheartmedia.com - Europe
www.amazon.com - Paperback & Kindle versions

FATHERHEART MEDIA
PO BOX 1039
Taupo 3330, New Zealand

Visit us at www.fatherheart.net

www.ingramcontent.com/pod-product-compliance
Lightning Source LLC
Chambersburg PA
CBHW050121020526
44112CB00035B/2239